S

Nelson

# Contents

# Chapter 1
# Rural and urban settlement

Most of us live in settlements, and most of us take them for granted; yet there is a huge variety of settlements, and they are changing rapidly. For example, some settlements in rural areas (Figure 1.1) differ greatly from those in urban areas (Figure 1.2), although the distinction between urban and rural is becoming less clear. In developing countries, large cities are growing at the expense of rural areas, despite recent movements out of some very large cities ('supercities'). Population change, technological developments, and changing lifestyles are having a tremendous impact on settlement geography.

This chapter gives an overview of rural and urban settlements. We begin with rural settlements and examine their pattern, site and situation, function, and hierarchy. We then assess a number of geographic models relating to settlements, and run through a worked example showing how one of the models could be tested statistically. We consider in detail the differences between rural and urban, and examine the nature of the rural-urban fringe, where rural meets urban. We then look at the main features of urbanisation and urban growth, and compare the trends in EMDCs and NICs. Finally, the main models relating to urban structure are discussed.

## DEFINITION OF TERMS

Urbanisation – the increase in the proportion of a country's population that is classified as urban

Urban growth – an increase in the absolute number of people living in an urban area

Urban sprawl – an increase in the area covered by urban activities

Counter-urbanisation – the movement from larger cities to smaller cities and towns; it is a movement down the settlement hierarchy. Counter-urbanisation does not, however, suggest that urban characteristics are being discarded and replaced by rural ones

Ruralisation – an increase in the proportion of people classified as rural

Deconcentration, decentralisation and deurbanisation – all these terms are used to describe the counter-urbanisation process and its effect on the distribution of population generally

Re-urbanisation – 'urban renewal', rehabilitation of city areas which have fallen into decline and suffered urban decay

Urban – having specific characteristics such as a large population, with a high percentage employed in manufacturing and services; a large built-up area with specific administrative functions, defined as urban by the government

Rural – areas characterised by low population densities, primary industries, small settlements

Site – the area upon which a settlement is built

Situation – the relative location of a settlement to other settlements

Form – the shape of a settlement

***Figure 1.1*** *Rural settlement urin Mgwali, South Africa*

***Figure 1.2***
*Shinjuku, Tokyo –
an urban settlement*

## RURAL SETTLEMENTS

A settlement can be defined as a place in which people live and where they may be involved in various activities, such as trade, agriculture or manufacturing. Most rural settlements are hamlets and villages. The study of rural settlement includes:

- pattern
- form (or shape)
- site and situation
- function and hierarchy
- change.

### Settlement pattern

A **dispersed** settlement pattern is one in which individual houses and farms are widely scattered throughout the countryside (Figure 1.3). It occurs when farms or houses are set among their fields or spread along roads, rather than concentrated at one point. They are common in sparsely populated areas (Figure 1.4), and in recently settled areas, such as the East Anglian Fens, which were settled after the drainage of the land in the seventeenth century. The enclosure of large areas of common grazing land in the eighteenth century, into smaller fields separated by hedges, led to a dispersed settlement pattern, because it became more convenient to build farmhouses out in the fields of the newly established farms. Similarly, the break-up of large estates (such as after the Reformation in the sixteenth century) also led to a dispersed settlement pattern.

A **nucleated** settlement pattern is one in which houses and buildings are tightly clustered around a central feature such as a church, village green or crossroads, with very few houses in the surrounding fields. Such nucleated settlements are usually termed hamlets or villages according to their size and/or function. They are the traditional form of settlement in the British Isles. A number of factors favour nucleation:

- joint and co-operative working of the land (the open field system before enclosure)
- good defensive positions (hilltop locations, sites within a meander)
- presence of water at specific locations (spring line settlements)
- swampy conditions on low lying ground
- a lack of suitable building materials in certain areas.

### Village form

Village form refers to the shape of a village (Figure 1.3). In a **linear** settlement, houses are spread out along a road. This suggests the importance of trade and transport during the growth of the village. Linear villages are also found where poor drainage prevents growth in a certain direction. The villages on Otmoor, near Oxford, are an excellent example of villages stretched out along high ground, above the level of flooding.

**Cruciform** settlements occur at intersections of roads, and usually consist of lines of buildings radiating from the crossroads, along the roads. The exact shape depends on the position of the roads and the amount of infilling that has taken place. A **green** village consists of dwellings and other buildings, such as a church, clustered around a small village green or common, or other open space.

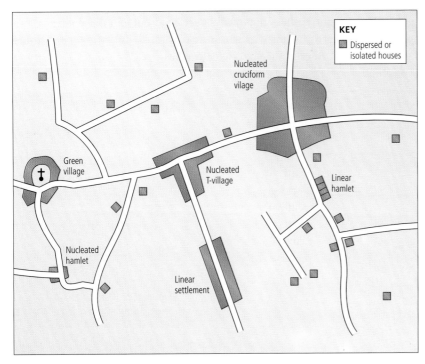

*Figure 1.3* Rural settlement shapes and patterns

*Figure 1.4* Dispersed settlements on the west coast of Ireland

## Site and situation

The **site** of a settlement is the actual land on which a settlement is built, whereas the **situation**, or position, of a settlement is the relationship between a particular settlement and its surrounding area. Before the 1970s, geographers emphasised the importance of the physical conditions affecting the pattern of settlement, land tenure and type of agriculture practised (Figure 1.5). The importance of social and economic factors is increasingly recognised, especially in explaining recent changes in rural settlements.

Early settlers took into account the relative advantages and disadvantages of alternative sites for agriculture and housing. These included:

- freedom from flooding (a **dry point**)
- availability of clean water (a **wet point**)
- level sites to build on (although these were less easy to defend than hilltop sites)
- availability of local timber for construction and fuel
- sunny, south facing slopes for crop cultivation
- proximity to rich soils for cultivation and lush pasture for grazing
- the potential for trade and commerce, determined by factors such as proximity to a bridging point, confluence site, the head of an estuary, limit of navigation (point above which most boats cannot pass), upland gap (often the only way through a highland region).

The presence, or lack, of water is a major influence on settlement site and situation.

A **dry point** is an elevated site in an area of otherwise poor natural drainage. It includes small hills (knolls) and islands. Gravel terraces along major rivers, such as the Wolvercote and Summertown terraces along the River Thames in Oxford, are well favoured. Water supply and fertile alluvial soils, as well as the use of the valley as a line of communication, are all positive advantages. The position of some **hilltop** villages, such as Islip on Otmoor, near Oxford, suggests that the site was chosen to avoid flooding in marshy areas, as well as for defence.

A **wet point** is a site with a reliable supply of water from springs or wells in an otherwise dry area. Spring line villages, such as Cheddar, Wells, and Westbury sub Mendip, at the foot of the chalk and limestone ridges are good examples. **Spring line settlements** occur when there is a line of sites where water is available, for example along the foot of the North Downs.

Settlements where major rivers meet can become excellent centres of transport links. Oxford is a good example, being located at the confluence of the Cherwell and the Thames, and at a ford.

## Settlement hierarchy

Dispersed, individual households are at the base of the rural settlement hierarchy. At the next level are hamlets. A hamlet is a small collection of farms and houses, which generally lacks all but the most basic services and facilities. The trade generated by the population, which is often less than a hundred people, may support **low order services** such as a general store, a sub post office or a pub. By contrast, a village is much larger in population and may support a wider range of services, such as primary school, church or chapel, community centre and a small range of shops (Figure 1.6).

Only basic or **low order functions** are found in hamlets; the same functions and services are found in larger settlements (villages and market towns) together with more specialised **high order functions**. The market towns draw custom from the surrounding villages and hamlets as well as serving their own population. The definition of hamlet, village and town is not always very clear cut and these terms represent features which are part of a sliding-scale (**continuum**) rather than separate categories.

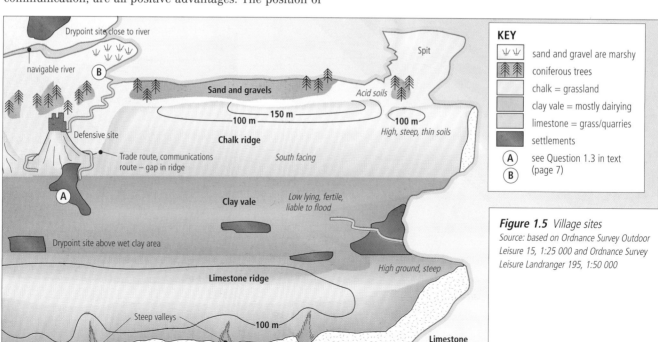

KEY

| | |
|---|---|
| ⍦ ⍦ | sand and gravel are marshy |
| 𐑭𐑭 | coniferous trees |
| | chalk = grassland |
| | clay vale = mostly dairying |
| | limestone = grass/quarries |
| | settlements |
| Ⓐ Ⓑ | see Question 1.3 in text (page 7) |

Labels within diagram: Drypoint site close to river; navigable river; B; Spit; Sand and gravels; Acid soils; 150 m; 100 m; 100 m; High, steep, thin soils; Defensive site; Chalk ridge; South facing; Trade route, communications route – gap in ridge; A; Clay vale; Low lying, fertile, liable to flood; Drypoint site above wet clay area; Limestone ridge; High ground, steep; Steep valleys; 100 m; Limestone cliffs

**Figure 1.5** *Village sites*
*Source: based on Ordnance Survey Outdoor Leisure 15, 1:25 000 and Ordnance Survey Leisure Landranger 195, 1:50 000*

| Hamlet | Village | Small market town |
|---|---|---|
| general store | general store | general store |
| sub-post office | sub-post office | post office |
| pub | pub | pub |
| | butcher | butcher |
| | garage | garage |
| | grocer | grocer |
| | hardware | hardware |
| | primary school | primary school |
| | | baker, bike shop, chemist, confectionery, dry cleaner, electrical shop, TV/radio shop, furniture shop, hairdresser, laundrette, local government offices, off licence, photo shop, restaurant, shoe shop, solicitor, supermarket, undertaker |

*Figure 1.6* A simple rural hierarchy

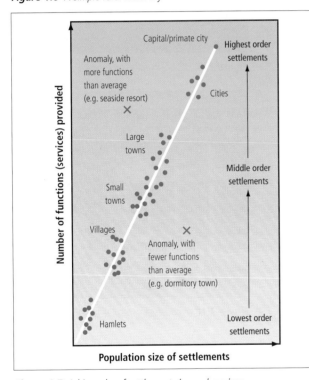

*Figure 1.7* A hierarchy of settlement size and services
Source: Nagle, G. and Spencer, K., Advanced geography revision handbook, 1997, OUP

## QUESTIONS

1 What is the difference between site and situation; wet point and dry point settlements; linear and cruciform villages? Give examples to support your answer.

2 Under what conditions would you expect rural settlements to be:
(i) dispersed and (ii) nucleated?

3 Study Figure 1.5 which shows settlement sites. Compare sites **A** and **B** in terms of their advantages and disadvantages for settlement location.

## EXPLAINING SETTLEMENT PATTERNS AND SETTLEMENT EVOLUTION

Every geographic model is a simplification. This is because geographic features and patterns are very complex and need to be simplified to be understood. The following models all examine aspects of settlement patterns and evolution. They vary, however, in their assumptions and the particular aspect of settlement geography that they examine. Some of the most widely used models in geography relate to settlements, including **central place theory** and the **evolution of settlement patterns**.

### Central place theory

Central place theory attempts to explain the **relative** size and spacing of settlements. It was developed by Walter Christaller in 1933, based on his observations in southern Germany. He uses a number of key terms:

- **range** – the maximum distance that people are prepared to travel goods or services
- **threshold** – the minimum number of customers required for a goods or services provider to stay in business
- **low order goods and services** – necessity goods or convenience goods, bought or used frequently, such as bread, papers and hairdressers
- **high order goods and services** – luxury or shopping goods or services, bought or used infrequently, for example, cookers and solicitors
- **sphere of influence** – the area served by a settlement, also referred to as a **hinterland**.

Central place theory makes two assumptions: that settlement occurs on an isotropic plain, and that people exhibit rational behaviour.

1 An **isotropic plain** is an area in which there is no variation in relief, climate or population density. It is the geographical equivalent of a snooker table without any holes.

2 **Rational behaviour** means that people visit their nearest central place to obtain whatever goods or services they require. According to central place theory, people minimise the distance in which they travel in order to obtain goods or services.

In central place theory, Christaller predicted that people who lived in a hamlet would obtain low order goods or services from that hamlet. They would visit their nearest village or town to buy goods and services which were not available in their hamlet. Hence a hierarchy occurs (Figures 1.6 and 1.7), with:

- hamlets providing the most basic low order goods (Figure 1.9, see page 8) to their own inhabitants
- villages providing a greater range and number of goods to a wider range of people, living in the village and surrounding hamlets (sphere of influence)
- towns providing a wider range of high order and low order goods (Figure 1.10, see page 8) to a larger population drawn from the town, surrounding villages and hamlets.

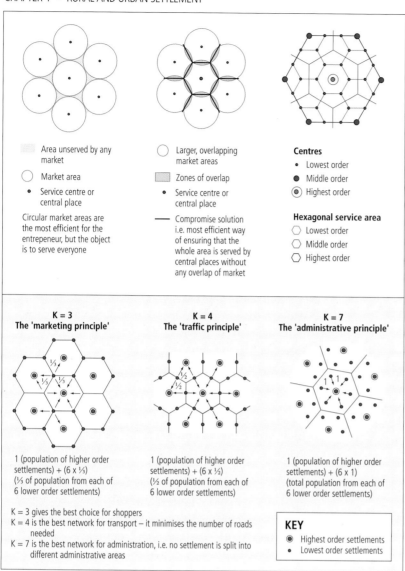

Area unserved by any market

◯ Market area

• Service centre or central place

Circular market areas are the most efficient for the entrepeneur, but the object is to serve everyone

◯ Larger, overlapping market areas

▨ Zones of overlap

• Service centre or central place

— Compromise solution i.e. most efficient way of ensuring that the whole area is served by central places without any overlap of market

**Centres**
• Lowest order
● Middle order
◉ Highest order

**Hexagonal service area**
◯ Lowest order
◯ Middle order
◯ Highest order

**K = 3**
**The 'marketing principle'**

1 (population of higher order settlements) + (6 x ⅓)
(⅓ of population from each of 6 lower order settlements)

**K = 4**
**The 'traffic principle'**

1 (population of higher order settlements) + (6 x ½)
(½ of population from each of 6 lower order settlements)

**K = 7**
**The 'administrative principle'**

1 (population of higher order settlements) + (6 x 1)
(total population from each of 6 lower order settlements)

K = 3 gives the best choice for shoppers
K = 4 is the best network for transport – it minimises the number of roads needed
K = 7 is the best network for administration, i.e. no settlement is split into different administrative areas

**KEY**
◉ Highest order settlements
• Lowest order settlements

**Figure 1.8** *Central place networks*
Source: based on Bradford, M. and Kent, A., 1977, Human geography: theories and their applications, OUP

**Figure 1.9** *Islip – a hamlet in Oxfordshire*

**Figure 1.10** *Woodstock – a small town in Oxfordshire*

The different order centres can be distinguished by their **(i)** type and **(ii)** number of functions, **(iii)** market area, **(iv)** employment and **(v)** population size.

Christaller developed three main models, K=3, K=4, and K=7 (Figure 1.8). In all of these a hexagonal market area was developed as the most efficient way of serving the whole population.

### Criticisms of central place theory

Central place theory has a number of advantages:
- Like any model, it acts as a frame of reference and allows comparison, showing how and why settlements differ from each other, and how and why settlements differ from the model.
- In very flat areas and in primitive societies, central place theory has been found to approximate reality.
- It has been used extensively in rural planning, especially in the key settlements plans (see page 88).

It also has its disadvantages:
- Isotropic plains do not exist.
- People are not completely rational. Even using the limited assumptions of the model, there is preference in terms of shopping, and increasingly there is bulk shopping. Time or cost may be a more useful measure than distance.
- The model deals only with goods and services: most settlements have other functions as well, for example providing social activities.
- It is static, and there is no explanation of how patterns change.
- It does not take into account speciality towns, such as tourist towns.
- In many cases, chance has played a part in determining settlement pattern. The model does not allow for this.

# Inset 1.1
# Determining spheres of influence

Central place theory is one of the most widely used theories in geography. In particular, the relative importance of settlements is studied, judged by the number and range of services offered by a settlement, and also its pulling power. This is known as their sphere of influence.

There are a number of ways of determining spheres of influence and the relative importance of settlements. Spheres of influence are sometimes called catchments or urban fields. Measures which can be used include the catchment areas of hospitals, clinics, primary and secondary schools, delivery areas of major stores, bus routes and the distribution of local newspapers. The spheres of influence of a number of Cornish settlements are shown in Figure 1.11.

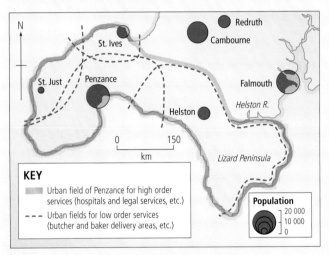

**Figure 1.11** *Spheres of influence for Cornish villages*
*Source: Knowles, R. and Waring, J., Economic and social geography, 1981, Made Simple Books*

The margins of the sphere of influence can be calculated theoretically using the **breaking point theory**. The breaking point divides the residents who will travel to one town from those who will travel to another. By calculating breaking points around a town (between it and its neighbouring settlements) it is possible to predict the sphere of influence. To work out the breaking point, the following formula is used:

$$d_{jx} = \dfrac{d_{ij}}{1 + \sqrt{\dfrac{P_i}{P_j}}}$$

where
$d_{jx}$ is the distance of the breaking point from the smaller town, j
$d_{ij}$ is the distance between the two towns, i and j
and $p_i$ and $p_j$ are the populations of the two towns.

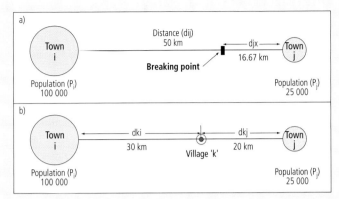

**Figure 1.12** *Spheres of influence according to a) breaking point theory and b) law of retail gravitation*

As shown in Figure 1.12, if there are two towns with populations of 100 000 and 25 000 that are 50 kilometres apart, the breaking point should be 16.67 kilometres from the smaller settlement. There are, however, a number of weaknesses with this theory. Population size is not the only factor which determines the attraction of a settlement, and distance is not the only factor which reduces levels of use. We could, for example, use time instead of distance and the number of shops, rather than population size.

Another way of examining spheres of influence is by using the law of **retail gravitation**. This attempts to discover the percentage of retail trade that two towns will derive from a settlement lying between them. It is found by using the formula:

$$\frac{M_{ki}}{M_{kj}} = \left( \frac{p_i}{p_j} \times \frac{d_{kj}}{d_{ki}} \right)^2$$

where
$M_{ki}$ is the proportion of trade going to town i from settlement k
$M_{kj}$ is the proportion of trade going to town j from settlement k
$P_i$ is the population of town i
$P_j$ is the population of town j
$d_{kj}$ is the distance from k to j
$d_{ki}$ is the distance from k to i

In Figure 1.12, a settlement, k, is located 30 kilometres from the larger town, i, and 20 kilometres from the smaller town, j. Using the above formula, we would predict that 1.7 times as many people from settlement k would visit town i as would visit town j. That means that for every ten people who visit town j, seventeen visit town i, or about 62% of settlement k's population would visit town i. The law of retail gravitation is open to the same criticism as the breaking point theory. It is useful, however, in allowing us to compare theory with reality and is useful for project work.

## Lösch's model of central places

According to Lösch (1954):

- the size of central places varies with distance from the main city, namely they get larger away from the main centre (Figure 1.13)
- a sectoral pattern emerges, with a distinctive city-rich, city-poor pattern (Figure 1.14).

Moreover, Losch claimed that settlements of the same size do not necessarily have the same function, and that large settlements do not necessarily have all the functions that smaller ones have. Although it is more complex, Losch's model produces a pattern which fits with observed distributions, such as the pattern around London, which shows city-rich sectors around the M4, M1 and M2 with intervening city-poor sectors (Figure 1.14).

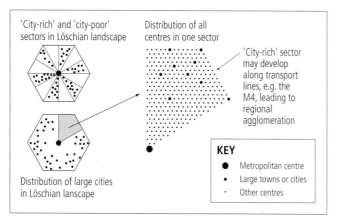

*'City-rich' and 'city-poor' sectors in Löschian landscape*

*Distribution of large cities in Löschian lanscape*

*Distribution of all centres in one sector*

*'City-rich' sector may develop along transport lines, e.g. the M4, leading to regional agglomeration*

**KEY**
- ● Metropolitan centre
- • Large towns or cities
- · Other centres

***Figure 1.13*** *Lösch's distribution of central places*
Source: Nagle, G. and Spencer, K., Advanced geography revision handbook, 1997, OUP

## Vance's mercantile model

Vance's mercantile model shows the development of central places over time due to colonial mercantile (trade) interaction between a colonial power and a colony (Figure 1.15). It is based on a case study of the north east USA and adds a historical-geographical dimension to the study and emergence of central places. In this case the colony was centred around Boston (Massachusetts) and the colonial power was Britain.

Christaller's model shows the settlement pattern of areas that are uniform in character, and economically isolated. By contrast, Vance's model stresses the importance of external influences. The hierarchy evolves from the top down, with large seaboard cities acting as centres of innovation for external commercial forces. According to Vance, Boston was the focal point for change in the north east USA. The model can also be applied to Australia, although the nature of the Australian landscape has not allowed the same pattern of infilling to develop.

In the case of the USA, initial settlements in the colony were linked with a search for raw materials and mineral resources. As trade developed, new settlements developed in the colony, linked with exploration of the interior for new resources. The increasing volume of trade reinforced port towns in the mother country, and an emerging trade corridor began to develop. In later stages, the settlement pattern became infilled – in the case of the USA, many settlements were arranged on a grid-like pattern – whereas in the mother country there was a more clustered pattern.

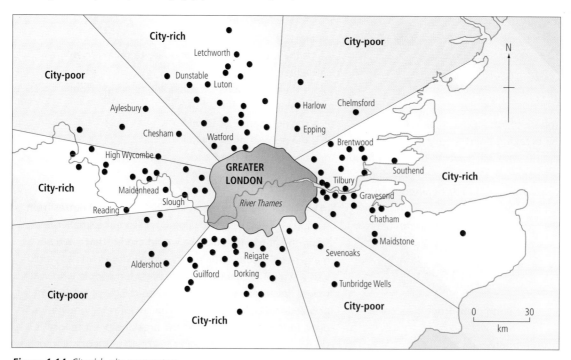

***Figure 1.14*** *City-rich, city-poor sectors*
Source: Whynne-Hammond, Elements of human geography, 1979, Unwin Hyman

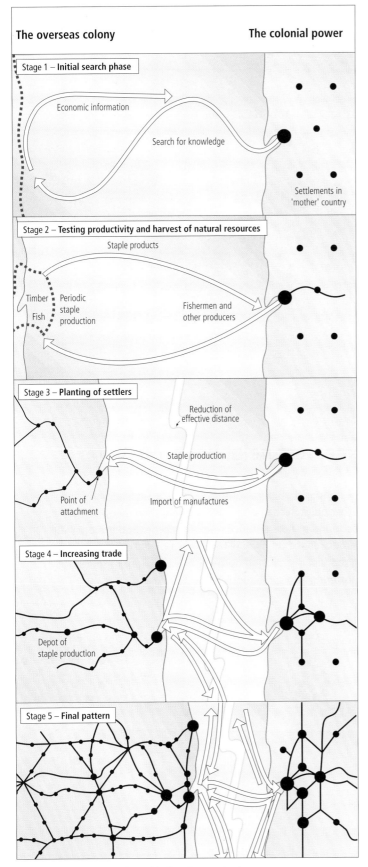

## Taaffe, Morrill and Gould (1970)

Although their model is basically concerned with the development of transport networks in the developing world, Taaffe, Morrill and Gould also show how settlement patterns may emerge (Figure 1.16). There are a number of similarities with Vance's model. First, their model is based on external forces. In this case it is the exploitation of an ELDC country. Second, it is dynamic and functional. Third, it is explanatory. It was developed to explain the transport pattern in West Africa, although it has been applied to south east Brazil. It is a useful contrast to Christaller and offers an example from ELDCs.

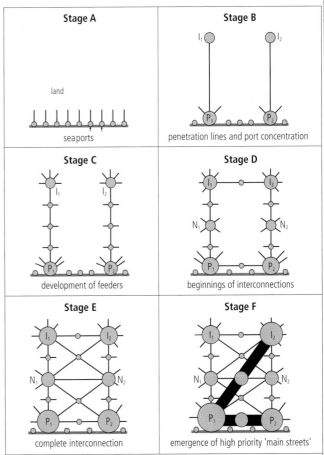

Stage A shows a scatter of small ports and trading posts along the sea coast. Only small indigenous fishing craft and irregularly scheduled trading vessels provide lateral inter-communications. Each port has an extremely limited hinterland.

Stage B shows that market areas have expanded for two ports ($P_1$ and $P_2$). Transport costs into the hinterland are reduced for these two ports. Port concentration begins ($P_1$ and $P_2$). Feeder routes begin to focus on the major ports and interior centres ($I_1$ and $I_2$).

Stage C The major ports begin to enlarge their hinterlands at the expense of the smaller ports. Feeder development continues and small nodes develop along the main lines of penetration.

Stage D Certain of the nodes ($N_1$ and $N_2$) capture the hinterlands of the smaller nodes on each side. Feeder lines continue to develop and some of the large feeders begin to link up.

Stage E Lateral links occur until all the ports, interior centres, and main nodes are linked. There are the beginnings of the development of national trunk routes or 'main streets', again increasing the connectivity of the network.

Stage F The main streets have reached their full development, an urban heirachy has emerged.

**Figure 1.16** *Taaffe, Morrill and Gould's model of transport (and settlement) evolution*
*Source: Bradford, M. and Kent, A., Human geography, 1977, OUP*

**Figure 1.15** *Vance's model of settlement development*
*Source: Potter, R. Urbanisation in the Third World, 1992, OUP*

## QUESTIONS

1 Explain what is meant by these terms: high order goods, low order goods, range, threshold and sphere of influence.

2 Explain how high order goods and low order goods compare in terms of their range and threshold. Give examples to support your answer.

3 Describe how the transport network has affected the evolution of central places in the models of Lösch and Vance.

4 Study Figure 1.17 which shows settlements on the Isle of Purbeck, in the south of England. Classify the settlements into hamlets, villages and towns. Justify your classification. What evidence is there to support a settlement hierarchy on the Isle of Purbeck? How useful is Christaller's theory in explaining the relative size and spacing of settlements on the Isle of Purbeck?

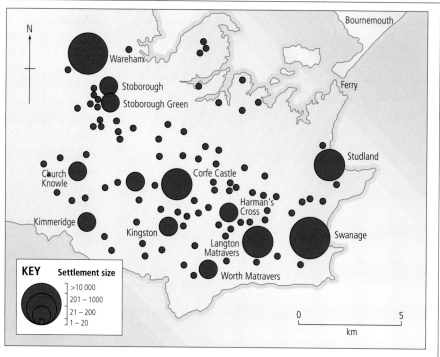

***Figure 1.17***
*Settlement distribution on the Isle of Purbeck*
*Source: Oxford and Cambridge Examinations Board*

## Inset 1.2
# Testing central place theory with the nearest neighbour index

There are a number of ways by which we can test elements of central place theory. One is to investigate the settlement hierarchy. We can compare the population size of a settlement with the number and range of services it provides, and use Spearman's rank correlation coefficient to test whether the two are related. (See *Development and Underdevelopment* in this series for the method and a worked example.) Another aspect we can test is the spacing of settlements. According to Christaller's model, there is a regular pattern of settlements.

The **spatial distribution** of settlements in an area can be described by looking at a map. This may lead us to conclude that the settlements are scattered, dispersed or concentrated. However, the main weakness with the visual method is that it is **subjective** and individuals differ in their interpretation of the pattern. Some **objective** measure is required and this is provided by the nearest neighbour index.

There are three main types of pattern which can be distinguished: **uniform or regular; clustered or aggregated,** and **random**. These are shown on Figure 1.18. If the pattern is regular, the distance between any one point and its nearest

neighbour should be approximately the same as from any other point. If the pattern is clustered, then many points will be found a short distance from each other and there will be large areas of the map without any points.

A random distribution normally has a mixture of some clustering and some regularity.

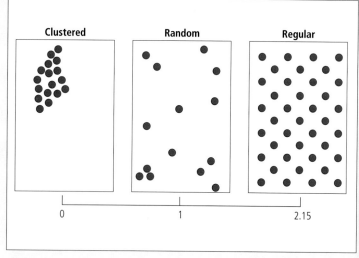

***Figure 1.18*** *Nearest neighbour patterns*

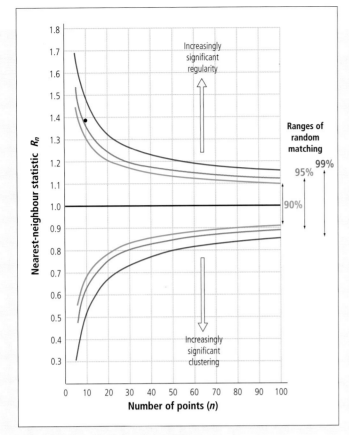

**Figure 1.19** *Levels of statistical significance*
Source: Pindar, D.A., The elimination of under-estimation in nearest-neighbour analysis, 1978, University of Southampton

The nearest neighbour index (NNI) is a measure of the spatial distribution of points, and is derived from the average distance between each point and its nearest neighbour. This figure is then compared with computed values which state whether the pattern is regular (NNI = 2.15), clustered (NNI = 0) or random (NNI = 1.0). A value below 1.0 shows a tendency towards clustering, a value above 1.0 a tendency towards uniformity. Figure 1.19 shows whether the result is statistically significant.

The formula is NNI or $Rn = 2\bar{D}\sqrt{\left(\dfrac{N}{A}\right)}$ where

$\bar{D}$ is the average distance between each point and its nearest neighbour and is calculated by finding $\dfrac{\Sigma d}{N}$
(d refers to each individual distance)
N is the number of points under study
A is the size of the area under study.
(N.B. It is necessary to use the same units for distance and area; for example, metres or kilometres, but not a mixture of both.)

## Worked example

| Settlement | Nearest neighbour | Distance (km) |
|---|---|---|
| Swanage | Langton Matravers | 3 |
| Studland | Swanage | 3.5 |
| Corfe Castle | Harman's Cross | 3 |
| Worth Matravers | Langton Matravers | 3 |
| Langton Matravers | Harmans Cross | 2 |
| Stoborough | Wareham | 2 |
| Wareham | Stoborough | 2 |
| Harman's Cross | Langton Matravers | 2 |
| Kingston | Corfe Castle | 2.5 |
| Kimmeridge | Kingston | 4 |
| | $\Sigma d = 27$ | |

Formula NNI or $Rn = 2\bar{D}\sqrt{\left(\dfrac{N}{A}\right)}$

$\bar{D} = \dfrac{\Sigma d}{N} = \dfrac{27}{10} = 2.7$

$Rn = 2 \times 2.7 \times \sqrt{\dfrac{10}{150}}$

$Rn = 1.39$

The results vary between 0 and 2.15 (Figure 1.18). There is a continuum of values and each distribution must lie between the two extremes. The answer of 1.39 (with ten points) shows that there is a regular pattern of settlements on the Isle of Purbeck. It is above the 95% level of statistical significance, meaning that it is more than 95% certain that there is a significantly regular pattern of settlements in the study area.

There are important points to bear in mind when using NNI:
- What is the definition of a settlement? Should all settlements be included – even individual houses – or just those above a certain size?
- Where do you measure from – the centre or the edge of a settlement?
- Do you measure in a straight line or by road?
- The choice of the area, and the size of the area studied, can alter the result and make a clustered pattern appear regular and vice-versa (see Figure 1.20).
- Although the NNI may suggest a random pattern, it may be that a controlling factor, such as soil type or altitude, is randomly distributed, and that the settlements are not located in a random fashion at all.
- What is the effect of paired distributions (see Figure 1.20)?
- One overall index may obliterate important sub-patterns (see Figure 1.20).

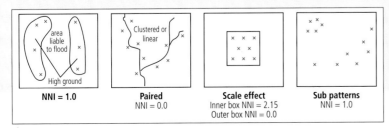

**Figure 1.20** *Some problems with nearest neighbour patterns*
Source: Nagle, G. and Spencer, K., 1997, Geographical enquiries, Stanley Thornes

## QUESTIONS

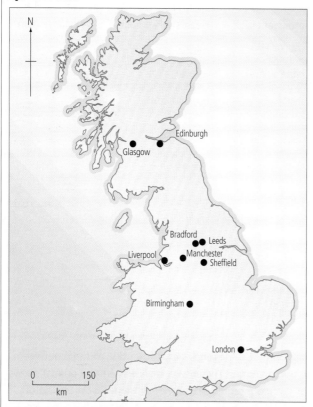

**Figure 1.21** *Distribution of large cities (population over 400 000) in the UK*

**1** Figure 1.21 shows the distribution of cities with a population over 400 000 in the UK. Work out the NNI for the cities shown on the map.

**a)** Measure the distance from each point to its nearest neighbour, to the nearest 50 km.

Set out your answer as in the worked example.

**b)** Add the values of d and divide by N to find D. Put this value into the formula NNI or

$$Rn = 2\bar{D}\sqrt{\left(\frac{N}{A}\right)}$$

(N.B. N = 9, A = 250 000 )

**c)** What does the answer tell you about the distribution of cities with a population over 400 000 in the UK? Are they spread evenly throughout the country, or are they clustered in a particular area? What does this suggest about the locational characteristics of large cities? Use an atlas to explain your answer.

## RURAL DIVERSITY

Not all rural settlements are the same. As early as 1950, Mitchell classified rural settlements as being open or closed, and integrated or disintegrated (Figure 1.22). **Open** settlements are those receptive to change and able to adapt. **Closed** settlements do not change easily. **Integrated** villages are socially successful whereas **disintegrated** settlements contain much social conflict. He identified a fourfold classification.

### Urban populations

Urban populations are classified as those people living in areas which are defined as urban for the census. The criteria used to specify what is an urban area vary widely from country to country and it is not possible to give a single definition. (See Definition of terms at the beginning of this chapter.) However, there are a number of underlying principles:

- population size
- specific urban characteristics, such as a central business district and residential zones
- predominant economic activities, such as manufacturing and services
- an administrative function.

Most censuses combine these four aspects. Even with elaborate definitions, however, a three-way distinction of rural, urban, and semi-urban/suburban is often necessary to reflect the range of settlement patterns. Although the density of population is implicitly involved in most definitions, it is rarely mentioned explicitly.

### Contrasting rural and urban

So rapid is the change affecting rural communities in the late twentieth century, that some geographers, for example Pahl, 1966, have claimed that there are no significant differences between rural and urban populations in the life they lead, in their hopes and aspirations, and in their attitudes. The cause of this change has been the decline of traditional rural economic activities, combined with the growth of material

**Figure 1.22** *Mitchell's classification of rural settlements*
*Source: based on Carr, M., 1997, New patterns: process and change in human geography, Nelson*

| **Open integrated** | **Closed integrated** | **Open disintegrating** | **Closed disintegrating** |
|---|---|---|---|
| • quite large settlements | • isolated | • rapidly growing | • small |
| • a diversity of occupations | • stable population | • high population turnover | • population decline |
| • social and economic centre for surrounding villages | • inward looking | • outward looking | • closure of village services |
| • self sufficient | • self-contained and traditional | • social tensions | common in older mining areas |
| • active local organisations | • unwelcoming to newcomers | commonly found where new housing is grafted onto an old village | |
| often found in rural areas, away from major cities | sometimes found in traditional rural areas, distant from the seat of government | | |

| Social characteristics | Rural – gemeinschaft | Urban – gesellschaft |
|---|---|---|
| 1 Dominant social relationships based on | 1 Kinship, locality and neighbourliness; fellowship – a sharing of responsibilities and fates, a common purpose | 1 Commerce, specified functions, formal and limited responsibilities |
| 2 Ordering of social institutions | 2 Family life, rural village life | 2 City life, national life, cosmopolitan life |
| 3 Characteristic forms of wealth | 3 Land | 3 Money |
| 4 Central institutions and forms of social control | 4 Family law, extended family groups, customs, religion | 4 The state, convention, political legislation, public opinion |
| 5 Status role | 5 Everyone's role is fully integrated in the system | 5 Roles based on specific relationships, status based on personal achievement |

**Figure 1.23** *Major characteristics of gemeinschaft and gesellschaft*
Source: adapted from Jones, G. 1973, Rural life, Paul Chapman

and personal mobility and mass communications, for example, television. To an extent this claim is true, although areas such as Western Ireland still retain many features of a traditional rural lifestyle. According to one sociologist, Wirth (1938), urban lifestyles are 'impersonal, superficial, transitory and segmented'.

One of the earliest and best known classifications of urban and rural is that of the German geographer, Ferdinand Tonnies. The urban extreme was called the **gesellschaft** and the rural extreme **gemeinschaft**. He described the rural ideal as an unchanging peasant society, organised in small inward-looking, idyllic communities, based on kinship and supported by subsistence agriculture. By contrast, the urban gesellschaft is the ever-changing life of the large cosmopolitan, commercial city (Figure 1.23). It is clear that Tonnies' classification is over-simplified, and it is arguable whether any settlements could ever match the strict criteria for the rural gemeinschaft. But his model is a useful starting point for comparative studies.

Tonnies' model has been adapted by a number of rural sociologists, including Worth and Pahl, to show the main characteristics of rural communities. Unlike urban settlements, in traditional rural communities there is:
- much interaction between individuals
- a distinct nucleus centred on the village
- involvement in village-based activities
- a heightened local awareness and a sense of belonging
- a shared set of attitudes.

Cloke's **index of rurality** (Figure 1.24) combines a number of measures which vary from extreme urbanism at one end to extreme ruralism at the other.

| Indicator | Characteristic of rural areas | Characteristic of urban areas |
|---|---|---|
| Population density | Low | … |
| % change in population 1951-61, 1961-71 | Decrease | … |
| % total population over 65 years | High | … |
| % total population males 15-45 years | Low | … |
| % total population females 15-45 years | Low | … |
| Occupancy rate: % population at 1.5 people per room | Low | … |
| Households per dwelling | Low | … |
| % households with exclusive use of a) hot water b) fixed bath c) inside WC | High | … |
| % farmers | High | … |
| % farm workers | High | … |
| % residents in employment outside the rural district | Low | … |
| % population resident for less than 5 years | Low | … |
| % population moved out in last year | Low | … |
| % in-/out-migrants | Low | … |
| Distance from nearest urban centre of 50 000 | High | … |
| Distance from nearest urban centre of 100 000 | High | … |
| Distance from nearest urban centre of 200 000 | High | … |

**Figure 1.24** *Cloke's index of rurality*

**QUESTIONS**

1 Describe the characteristics of populations in rural areas as suggested by Cloke's model.

2 Explain what is meant by (i) households per dwelling and (ii) occupancy rate.

3 Fill in column 3 in Figure 1.24 to show the characteristics of urban areas.

4 In what ways have rural areas changed since the period 1951-71?

5 Which of the indicators is no longer a characteristic of rural settlements?

## The urban fringe

The urban fringe, or the rural-urban fringe, is the zone at the edge of the city into which urban growth is extending. Over time, the characteristics of the area change from largely rural to largely urban. Suburbanisation takes place at the rural-urban fringe. Generally there is a mixed land use, forming a transitional zone between urban and rural areas. It is characterised by:

- limited access to housing
- changes in the local community
- reductions in services
- rising land prices.

The rural-urban fringe in the UK faces a number of pressures. These include industrial, residential, commercial and recreational pressures. Some of these are discussed in Chapter 4, Green Belts. One of the main forms of development on the urban fringe has been the retailing industry. Increasingly, retail outlets have located there because of the availability of large amounts of land more cheaply than in urban centres, and the increase in car ownership.

The nature of the rural-urban fringe is influenced by four main factors: agricultural policy, regional planning, the urban economy and the agricultural economy (Figure 1.25). Baker *et al* have identified four types of rural-urban fringe resulting from these influences:

- disturbed landscapes
- neglected landscapes
- simplified landscapes
- valued landscapes.

This model is useful as it shows that the rural-urban fringe varies from place to place.

## The rural-urban continuum

According to Pahl (1966) 'the terms rural and urban are more remarkable for their ability to confuse than their power to illuminate'. He used the term 'metropolitan village' to describe villages which had become suburbanised. An increasing number of middle class commuters moved into rural settlements, and changed their characteristics. Pahl felt that urban and rural were no longer defined by place or location, but by lifestyle and behaviour. It was therefore increasingly difficult to distinguish between urban and rural. Although two extreme forms could be identified, it was better to think of an urban-rural continuum.

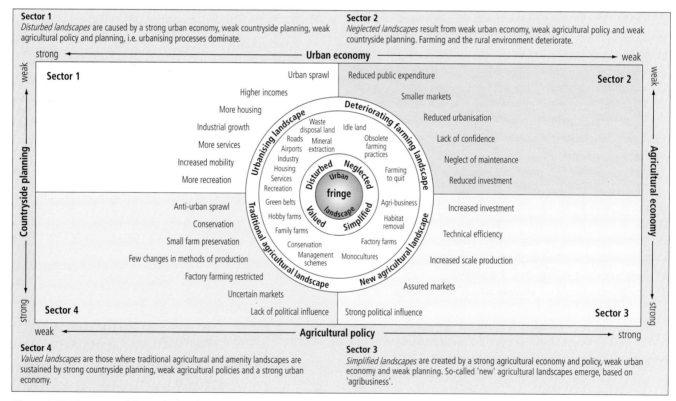

**Figure 1.25** *The nature of the rural-urban fringe*
Source: Baker et al, Pathways in senior geography, 1996, Nelson

## QUESTIONS

1 Compare urban and rural lifestyles as described by Tonnies.

2 How useful is his model as a means of describing differences in urban and rural settlements in the developed world? Use examples to support your answer.

## MODELS OF URBAN FORM

In this final section we look at models of urban land use. There are a number of urban models which describe the layout of a city, and they are all very simplified. We must not, therefore, expect that any city will conform entirely to the pattern they suggest. However, they are useful in that they focus our attention on one or two key factors. Here we look at the main models that are relevant to cities in the developed world.

Underlying many of these models is the idea of **bid rent** (Figure 1.26). This is the value of land when used for different purposes, such as commercial, manufacturing and residential. Land at the centre of a city is most expensive for two main reasons: it is (or was) the land most accessible to public transport, and only a small amount is available. Land prices generally decrease away from the most central area, although there are secondary peaks at the intersections of main roads and ring roads (Figure 1.27). It is the change in levels of accessibility, caused by the overuse of private transport rather than public transport, which explains why areas on the edge of town are often now more accessible than inner areas. This phenomenon is examined in detail in Chapter 6, Changing cities, when we consider the growth of out of town retailing and the decline of high street retailing.

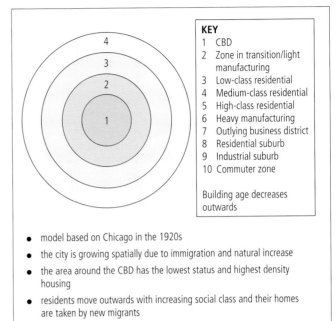

- model based on Chicago in the 1920s
- the city is growing spatially due to immigration and natural increase
- the area around the CBD has the lowest status and highest density housing
- residents move outwards with increasing social class and their homes are taken by new migrants

**Figure 1.28** *Burgess's concentric model of land use, 1925*
*Source: Nagle, G. and Spencer, K., Advanced geography revision handbook, 1997, OUP*

### Burgess

The simplest model is that developed by Burgess (1925) (Figure 1.28). In his model he assumes that new migrants will move into poorer, inner city areas and that over time residents will move out of the inner city area as they become wealthier. Housing quality improves and social class rises with distance from the city centre. Land in the centre is dominated by commercial activity which is most able to afford the high land prices of the city centre. Beyond the central business district is a manufacturing zone, complete with high density, low quality housing to accommodate the workers. The paradox of the poorest people being located on expensive land is due to their need to be close to sources of employment because they cannot afford the relatively high price of transport.

### Housing density curve

Landlords achieve their profits by cramming as many tenants as they can into the housing in these zones. By contrast, wealthier people are often located in the outer areas, in lower density housing (Figure 1.29, on page 18), from where they can afford to commute to work. In some areas, subur-

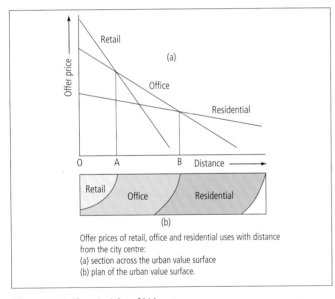

Offer prices of retail, office and residential uses with distance from the city centre:
(a) section across the urban value surface
(b) plan of the urban value surface.

**Figure 1.26** *The principles of bid rent*

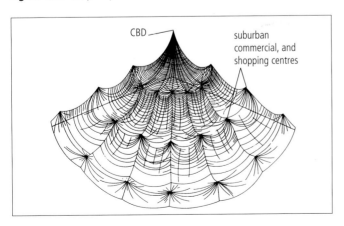

**Figure 1.27** *Variations in bid rent with levels of accessibility*
*Source: Bradford, M. and Kent, A., 1977, Human geography: theories and their application, OUP*

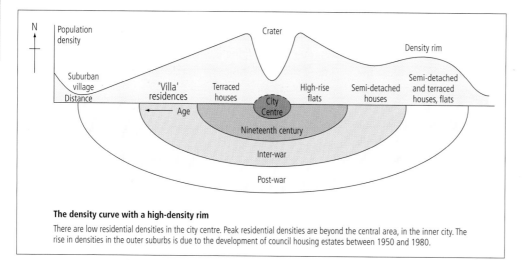

**Figure 1.29**
*The housing density curve*
Source: Nagle, G. and Spencer, K., *Advanced geography revision handbook, 1997, OUP*

**The density curve with a high-density rim**
There are low residential densities in the city centre. Peak residential densities are beyond the central area, in the inner city. The rise in densities in the outer suburbs is due to the development of council housing estates between 1950 and 1980.

ban villages develop as centres of commuting. These are places which offer urban functions in small centres, which possess a 'rural feel'.

The density rim, shown in Figure 1.29, is the population density at a distance from the city centre. Eastern sides of towns often developed as the industrial side of town. This was partly as a result of prevailing wind conditions. Early industrialists located their factories in areas of cheap land. By contrast, wealthy people gravitated towards cleaner areas in the west of the town. Once started, these basic east-west divides were difficult to change.

**Figure 1.30** *Hoyt's sector model of urban land use, 1939*
Source: Nagle, G. and Spencer, K., *Advanced geography revision handbook, 1997, OUP*

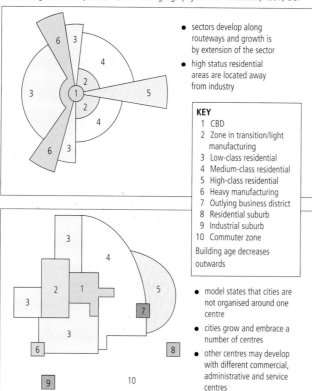

- sectors develop along routeways and growth is by extension of the sector
- high status residential areas are located away from industry

**KEY**
1 CBD
2 Zone in transition/light manufacturing
3 Low-class residential
4 Medium-class residential
5 High-class residential
6 Heavy manufacturing
7 Outlying business district
8 Residential suburb
9 Industrial suburb
10 Commuter zone
Building age decreases outwards

- model states that cities are not organised around one centre
- cities grow and embrace a number of centres
- other centres may develop with different commercial, administrative and service centres

## Hoyt

Hoyt (1939) emphasised the importance of transport routes (Figure 1.30). Sectors develop along important routeways. In addition, certain land uses, for example high class residential and manufacturing industry deter other land uses. A much later model is the multiple nuclei model of Harris and Ullman (1945) (Figure 1.31). They show that cities do not have a single centre, but consist of many pre-existing centres; as cities grow, they incorporate some of these centres. In addition, new centres may be planned for commercial, industrial and residential purposes.

## Mann

One model which was designed specifically for UK cities is Mann's (1960s). His model includes concentric circles and sectors (Figure 1.32). He found that there was an east-west split in most UK towns. Most industry and working class populations were located in the east, especially if prevailing

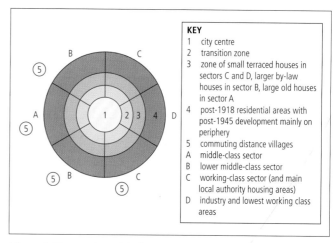

**KEY**
1 city centre
2 transition zone
3 zone of small terraced houses in sectors C and D, larger by-law houses in sector B, large old houses in sector A
4 post-1918 residential areas with post-1945 development mainly on periphery
5 commuting distance villages
A middle-class sector
B lower middle-class sector
C working-class sector (and main local authority housing areas)
D industry and lowest working class areas

**Figure 1.32** *Mann's model of urban land use for a UK city*
Source: Nagle, G. and Spencer, K., *Advanced geography revision handbook, 1997, OUP*

**Figure 1.31** *Harris and Ullman's multiple nuclei model, 1945*
Source: Nagle, G. and Spencer, K., *Advanced geography revision handbook, 1997, OUP*

winds carried pollution eastwards. The wealthier people located in the cleaner, west end of town.

All of these models are gross oversimplifications. They do not, and cannot, take into account the unique characteristics of each city. Cities are complex, dynamic structures with a diverse mix of economic, social, ethnic, and physical characteristics. One model, however, Murdie's model of urban ecological structure (1969), attempts to bring these together (Figure 1.33). The result shows us that cities are indeed complex.

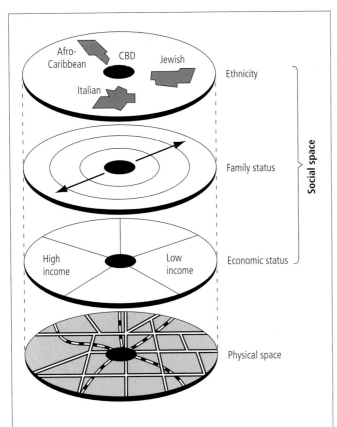

- identifies social, economic and ethnic areas
- the 'residential mosaic' is superimposed on the physical space
- economic status has a sector pattern, family status has a concentric pattern, ethnic groups occur in clusters

**Figure 1.33** Murdie's model of urban land use, 1969
Source: Nagle, G. and Spencer, K., Advanced geography revision handbook, 1997, OUP

## QUESTIONS

1  Briefly explain the high value of land in (i) central areas of cities and (ii) on the edges of cities.

2  For any **two** models of urban land use explain **two** strengths and **two** weaknesses of each model.

3  Study Figure 1.33 which shows Murdie's model of ecological areas. Describe the pattern of land use as shown in the diagram. Explain how such a pattern might come about.

4  Compare the advantages of large cities with their disadvantages.

## SUMMARY

In this introduction to settlement geography we have seen that there are substantial differences between urban and rural settlements, and between the main processes operating in EMDCs and ELDCs and NICs. All settlements are characterised by change. However, it is difficult to make detailed comparisons as the definitions of rural and urban differ between countries. We now look in detail, in a more or less chronological sequence, at the development of urban areas in the UK (with comparisons made to other countries where most relevant), changing rural settlements, and urban issues in ELDCs and NICs.

## QUESTIONS

1  For any **two** models of settlement geography:
(i)  describe the models
(ii) explain how they are useful to geographers
(iii) briefly describe the weaknesses of the model
(iv) state which one you think is best, and explain why.

2  What evidence is there to suggest that population is becoming more concentrated in large cities?

3  Distinguish between urbanisation and counter-urbanisation. Why is counter-urbanisation occurring in many countries with large cities?

## Suggestions for extended (project) work

1  Describe the variations in social and economic conditions for a city of your choice. Why do these variations occur? How useful are the models of urban land use in explaining the pattern you have shown?

2  For a small area that you have studied, describe and explain the settlement hierarchy that can be observed. Work out the spheres of influence for the most important centres and compare this with their breaking point.

## BIBLIOGRAPHY AND RECOMMENDED READING

Bradford, M. & Kent, A., 1977, *Human geography: theories and their applications*, OUP

Carr, M., 1997, *New patterns: process and change in human geography*, Nelson

Carter, H., 1972, *The study of urban geography*, Arnold

Daniel, P. & Hopkinson, M., 1981, *The geography of settlement*, Oliver and Boyd

Drakakis-Smith, D., 1987, *The Third World city*, Routledge

Knox, P. & Taylor, P., 1995, *World cities in a world system*, CUP

## WEB SITES

**CTI Centre for Geography –**
http://www.geog.le.ac.uk/cti/index.html
**Millennium Institute: State of the World Indicators**
– http://www.igc.apc.org/millennium/inds/
**UK Government Index –**
http://www.open.gov.uk/index/findex.html

# Chapter 2
# Urbanisation in the UK

We have seen in Chapter 1 how urbanisation has had a profound impact on many parts of the world. In this chapter we focus upon urbanisation in the UK and trace its development from the eighteenth century until the late nineteenth century. Urban planning was in its infancy at the start of the eighteenth century, and took off in the mid-nineteenth century. Planning was partly a response to the poor living conditions in which people lived, and partly to the need to have a healthy and reliable workforce.

## URBANISATION IN THE EARLY INDUSTRIAL PERIOD

The eighteenth century saw the beginning of an urban-industrial society in Britain. Important developments occurred such as:

- changes in the agricultural landscape
- the introduction of steam
- concentration of industry on the coalfields
- migration of the workforce to urban-industrial areas.

These changes intensified during the nineteenth century.

At the start of the eighteenth century, Britain was largely rural and agricultural. Notable changes were about to take place in agricultural practices and the agricultural landscape. **Intensification** of agriculture and **increased food production** was brought about by:

- three-year crop **rotation** replacing the traditional four-year Norfolk rotation (in which land was left fallow for one year out of four), allowing more intensive farming to take place
- land **enclosure**, whereby communal open land was converted into individually-owned, small fields
- moorland and fen **drainage**, creating new agricultural land
- **mechanisation** to increase crop harvests.

Even in the eighteenth century, parts of Britain were densely populated. These included a large number of important market towns and regional centres (Figure 2.1). London was the largest, followed by Bristol and Norwich. By the end of the century, Liverpool had become the second largest city. Most towns were quite small, however, and were closely spaced. Their size was limited by local food availability and transport networks; food had to be brought in for the residents.

The speed of industrialisation increased after 1750 as machinery and factory systems began to develop, but still remained mostly small-scale, supplying a domestic market and powered by water. Industry was diverse (Figure 2.2). This was all set to change in the nineteenth century.

***Figure 2.2*** *Distribution of industry in the UK, 1750*
*Source: Howe, G., 1972, Man, environment and disease in Britain, Pelican*

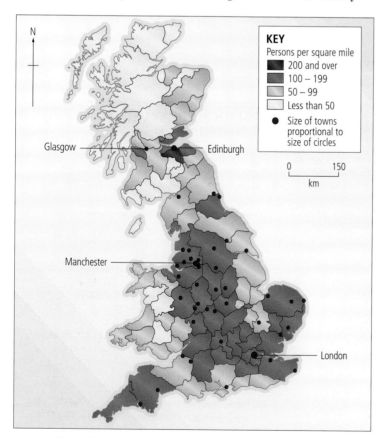

***Figure 2.1*** *Distribution of population in the UK in the eighteenth century*
*Source: Howe, G., 1972, Man, environment and disease in Britain, Pelican*

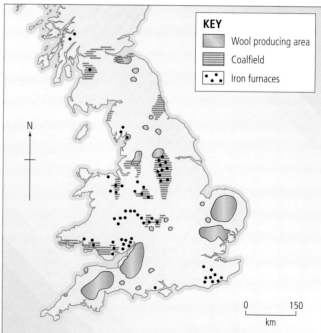

## URBANISATION IN THE NINETEENTH CENTURY

The nineteenth century was a period characterised by:

- rapid industrialisation
- rapid rural to urban migration
- high birth rates, declining death rates
- social reform
- increases in wages.

These changes were neither steady nor uniform throughout the country. The growth in population responded to the development of the cotton industry in Lancashire, the woollen industries in Yorkshire and the textile, mining and metal industries in the Midlands. Coalfields in Durham, Yorkshire, Nottinghamshire and Derbyshire, the Black Country and the Welsh borders also grew in population. The main axis of growth was from London to Liverpool. This became the urban and industrial belt of the UK.

Outside this main axis, other areas developed less intensely. South Wales developed because of its coal mining and metal industries. In central Scotland, there was a gradual shift in economic activity from east to west associated with the rapid expansion of Glasgow.

The lack of employment opportunities in rural areas and the high demand for employment in urban areas, led to rural-urban **migration**. Migration was **age-selective** – young adults without ties, more innovative, energetic age groups moved into the expanding cities, changing the **age-structure** of the population. The high rates of migration to the cities led to high rates of **natural increase** (excess of birth rates over death rates).

Nineteenth-century urbanisation was extremely rapid. In 1851 50% of the country's population was classified as urban. By 1871, this had increased to 61%, and by 1911 to 77%. Industries grew around the steam-driven machines. Towns developed around the industries to house the workers, and developments in transport, notably the canals and railways, allowed urban expansion to occur on a massive scale.

## Inset 2.1
# Plotting a semi-logarithmic graph

*Figure 2.3 Using a semi-logarithmic graph to show urbanisation in the nineteenth century*

| Town | 1801 | 1831 | 1851 | 1901 |
|---|---|---|---|---|
| Birmingham | 71 000 | 144 000 | 233 000 | 760 000 |
| Bradford | 13 000 | 44 000 | 104 000 | 228 000 |
| Keighley | 6000 | 11 000 | 15 000 | 42 000 |
| Liverpool | 82 000 | 202 000 | 376 000 | 685 000 |
| Manchester | 75 000 | 182 000 | 303 000 | 654 000 |
| Sheffield | 53 000 | 123 000 | 172 000 | 385 000 |

Semi-log graphs can be daunting at first. But with care they can be quite easy to draw. And they allow geographers to compare small-scale features with large-scale ones. This would not be possible with an ordinary graph.

The logarithmic scale compresses the range of values. It gives more space to smaller values, as in the case of Keighley and Bradford in this example. It compresses the larger values. Hence it shows relative growth very well.

Each of the cycles is logarithmic. This means it increases by the power of ten. The first cycle (a) increases by 1 eg 1, 2, 3, 4, 5 etc. The second (b) by 10, eg 10, 20, 30, and the third (c) by 100 eg 100, 200, 300 etc.

The vertical axis on a semi-log graph begins at 1.

The horizontal axis can begin at any number. The horizontal axis in 'normal'. This means the scale is regular, each unit is the same value.

On this graph each unit is ten years.

**Exam hints**
- use different colours for each town
- label the axes clearly
- make sure you label the lines clearly – in this example Birmingham, Manchester and Liverpool could cause some confusion

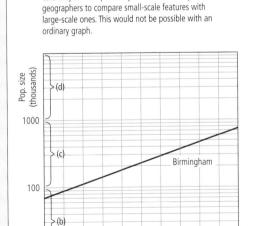

## QUESTIONS

**1** Study Figure 2.3 and read the information on how to plot a semi-logarithmic graph.

**a)** Plot the data from the table in Figure 2.3 on semi-logarithmic graph paper. (Birmingham has already been drawn on the example here.)

**b)** Which settlement grew the most (i) overall and (ii) between 1801 and 1851? Are the results the same for absolute increases as well as relative increases?

**c)** How useful are semi-logarithmic graphs in showing geographic data? (You should think about the weaknesses as well as the strengths.)

**Large towns** became increasingly common. In 1801, about 20% of the population lived in towns of over 5000. This increased to 55% by 1851 and 77% by 1911. In 1801, only London had a population greater than 100 000, with about 10% of the nation's population. By 1851 there were ten towns with over 100 000 people, accounting for about 25% of the country's population. By 1911, however, there were nearly forty such towns, accounting for nearly 50% of the population; the age of conurbations had started.

The five main conurbations were:

| | |
|---|---|
| Greater London | 6 600 000 |
| South East Lancashire | 2 100 000 |
| West Midlands | 1 500 000 |
| Merseyside | 1 000 000 |
| Tyneside | 680 000 |

The urban demographic revolution led to increased pressures on **natural resources**. In urban areas, the high density of people made health conditions hazardous. Water, fresh air, soil and space were in short supply. Common practices, such as throwing out of night-soil (excrement) became dangerous to health in urban areas; in low density rural areas this practice did not cause such a problem. Increasingly, as overcrowding took place, the poorer, more densely populated, more industrialised areas of towns were the worst affected. For example, the causes of ill health were:

*'traceable to the density of population, to the want of ventilation, and consequent impurity of the air; to the defective state of the paving, drainage, and sewage; to the filthy state of the dwellings of the poor and their immediate neighbourhood; to the concentration of unhealthy and putrescent emanations from narrow streets, courts and alleys; to the crowded and unhealthy state of workshops, and to the injurious occupations which are carried on in them'.*

Source: Gavin, H., 1847, The unhealthiness of London and the necessity of remedial measures quoted in Wohl p.5.

### THE EARLY GROWTH OF URBAN AREAS

The typical industrial town developed from a small core. Bradford, for example, had little more than two streets in the mid-eighteenth century (Figure 2.4). In the early 1800s it was:

*'a miserable looking place, ... destitute of almost any public convenience or accommodation, its streets narrow and irregular, its buildings jumbled together without a design, or if they had been dropped together by accident'.*

Source: Gavin, H., 1847, The unhealthiness of London and the necessity of remedial measures quoted in Wohl p.5.

Early population growth was contained within the original nucleus of the town. Single and double rows of cottages were erected in the long gardens of existing houses. These could only be reached by long passageways. These early developments were to become the 'old slums'. Early industrial

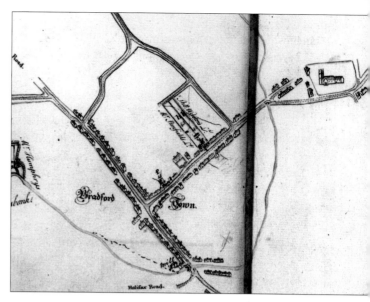

**Figure 2.4** *Bradford in 1750*

development occurred on the edge of this residential core.

By the 1830s, developments on a larger scale took place. Two-storey working class back to back houses became a typically British type of housing. A block of houses generally occupied an area of about 70 metres by 35 metres. In the centre was an airless court, which could be reached only by tunnels (see Figure 2.9 on page 24). These houses were to become the 'new slums'.

Much of the housing was poorly built. Many houses were mud walled, poorly ventilated, damp, and lacking in running water and toilet facilities. Some houses had pig sties attached to them, while others kept their animals indoors! The streets were narrow, unpaved, muddy and worn into deep ruts; most of the districts occupied by the labouring classes lacked any sewerage system, so the streets became the dumping ground for refuse and all forms of human and animal waste; open slaughterhouses were nearby.

Conditions in the small towns, such as Bradford, were probably worse than in London. This was because they lacked any effective local authority capable of providing even the most basic hygiene. An observer of the mid-nineteenth century, Keighley, commented on:

*'two privies [toilets] adjoining these premises in a state not fit to use, being very dirty, and one of them being so badly ventilated that the stench was suffocating, and above in the room [and] one privy is shared by 29 houses, three privies shared by 69 houses and six privies to 90 houses ... some houses have no access to privies at all.'*

Glasgow was possibly the filthiest and unhealthiest of all the towns in Britain. The scale of in-migration was unprecedented and the accommodation and facilities to meet this were totally inadequate. The lack of transport meant that workers had to live close to their place of employment. This led to extremely high densities of buildings per site and very high rates of overcrowding.

Manchester was described as an active volcano (Figure 2.5). This was due to the large amounts of soot and ash given off by the factories. In addition, the River Irwell was so heavily polluted that it was at risk of catching fire! The plight of the urban poor was hazardous. They were surrounded 'on every side by some of the largest factories, whose chimneys vomit forth dense clouds of smoke, which hang heavily over this insalubrious region'.

*Source: Howe, G., 1972, Man, environment and disease in Britain, Pelican*

**Figure 2.5** *Air and water pollution in Manchester in the 1870s*

| District | Professional | Farmers and tradesmen | Labourers and artisans |
|---|---|---|---|
| Rutland | 52 | 41 | 38 |
| Bath | 55 | 37 | 25 |
| Leeds | 44 | 27 | 19 |
| Bethnal Green | 45 | 26 | 16 |
| Manchester | 38 | 20 | 17 |
| Liverpool | 35 | 22 | 15 |

**Figure 2.6** *Life expectancy (years) by occupation and geographic location*
*Source: Wohl, A., 1983, Endangered lives, Methuen*

Life expectancy in Victorian times was low, especially for labourers (Figure 2.6). The working classes were also affected by a new variety of diseases, such as tuberculosis (TB) and pneumonia. The infant mortality rate (IMR) in Victorian times was extremely high. In the slums of industrial towns the IMR was as high as 200 per thousand. A further 20% of children died before the age of fifteen years. Children suffered from pneumonia, bronchitis, diarrhoea and vomiting, and rickets. Diarrhoea was associated with the general level of uncleanliness and lack of hygiene (Figure 2.7); the respiratory disorders were associated with overcrowding, air pollution, and the lack of resistance, due to poor diet, lack of vitamins and fresh fruit and vegetables. There was a seasonal pattern to disease (Figure 2.8).

---

## QUESTIONS

**1** Why was Manchester described as an 'active volcano'?

**2** Describe the urban and industrial environment of Manchester, as shown in Figure 2.5.

**3** Explain fully **two** contrasting health hazards that developed in urban-industrial environments such as those shown in Figure 2.5.

---

*... a maze of close, narrow and muddy streets ... tottering housefronts, projecting over the pavement, dismantled walls that seem to totter as he passes, chimneys half crushed half hesitating to fall ... Crazy wooden galleries common to the backs of half-a-dozen houses, with holes from which to look upon the slime beneath; windows broken and patched, with poles thrust out, on which to dry the linen that is never there; rooms so small, so filthy and squalor which they shelter; wooden chambers thrusting themselves out above the mud, and threatening to fall in – as some have done; dirt-besmeared walls and decaying foundations; every repulsive lineament of poverty, every loathsome indication of filth, rot and garbage.*

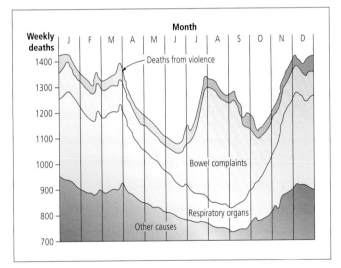

**Figure 2.8** *Seasonal variations in deaths in London, 1845-74*
*Source: Howe, G., 1972, Man, environment and disease in Britain, Pelican*

**Figure 2.7** *Description of Dockhead in the Borough of Southwark, London, from Oliver Twist*
*Source: Charles Dickens, Oliver Twist*

---

## QUESTIONS

**1** Describe the seasonal pattern of disease as shown in Figure 2.8.

**2** Explain why **(i)** respiratory diseases, such as TB and pneumonia, and **(ii)** gastro-enteritis (diarrhoea and vomiting) should vary seasonally.

## URBAN GROWTH IN LATE VICTORIAN TIMES

The late Victorian period contrasted strongly with the earlier period. For example:

- economic growth had slowed
- Germany and the USA had developed as economic powers, and rivalled the UK
- cheap North American and Russian wheat was being imported
- up to 70% of the population lived in urban areas
- sanitary and hygiene reforms were established.

Following a Public Health Act in 1875, most cities banned the development of cheap, back to back houses, and bylaws (local legislation) which set minimum requirements for housing were passed. 'By-law' houses were built on a grid-iron pattern, with characteristic narrow fronted houses (Figure 2.9). The houses were built at densities of about 92 houses per hectare: given the large size of households, this created population densities of up to 900 per hectare, even up to the 1940s. The houses lacked baths and had outside toilets. By-law housing developed on a large-scale in the 1870s and 1880s, as cities grew rapidly. Figure 2.10 shows the growth of Bradford between 1800 and 1873. Today, by-law housing is easily recognised, consisting of rows of two-storey housing and roads of a uniform minimum width, forming large rings around the earlier slums.

Similarly, there were improvements in health, albeit slight. In 1842, the *Report on the sanitary conditions of the Labouring population of Great Britain* by Edwin Chadwick, called for national action to improve hygiene and sanitation. Living conditions gradually improved. Better housing, cleanliness, ventilation, disinfection, improved water supplies and sewage disposal developed during the second half of the nineteenth century. This led to a reduction in some **infectious** diseases, such as cholera and typhus, which were mostly related to overcrowding and poor sanitary conditions. By 1871, mortality rates were declining. However, **degenerative** diseases, related to unhealthy lifestyles and stress, were increasing. These included heart diseases, cancers and strokes.

Unhealthy lifestyles and stress were brought about by many factors, including inadequate diet, alcoholism, smoking, long working days, and overcrowding. Even by 1901, the proportion of the population living in overcrowded conditions was still very high:

| | | | | |
|---|---|---|---|---|
| Gateshead | 34% | | Plymouth | 20% |
| South Shields | 32% | | Devonport | 17% |
| Tynemouth | 31% | | Dudley | 17% |
| Newcastle upon Tyne | 30% | | London | 16% |
| Sunderland | 30% | | | |

At the end of the nineteenth century there were still wide-scale health defects. About 40% of recruits for the Boer War (1898-1902) were rejected on the grounds of physique, health and efficiency; in some places the rejection rate was as high as 60%. The appalling health conditions struck the public conscience. It appeared that the economic progress of the nineteenth century had been bought at the cost of public health.

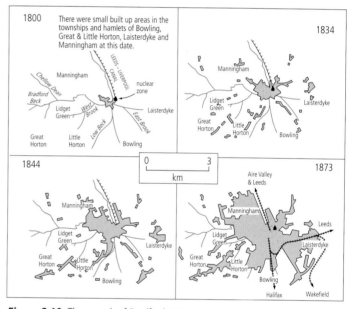

**Figure 2.10** *The growth of Bradford 1800-1873*
Source: Richardson, C., 1976, A geography of Bradford, Univ. of Bradford

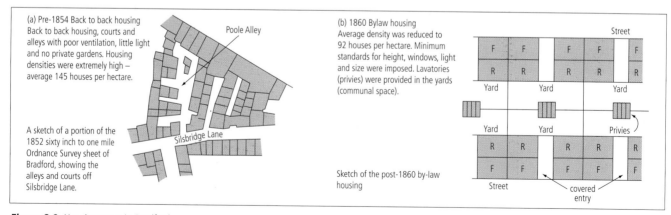

(a) Pre-1854 Back to back housing
Back to back housing, courts and alleys with poor ventilation, little light and no private gardens. Housing densities were extremely high – average 145 houses per hectare.

A sketch of a portion of the 1852 sixty inch to one mile Ordnance Survey sheet of Bradford, showing the alleys and courts off Silsbridge Lane.

(b) 1860 Bylaw housing
Average density was reduced to 92 houses per hectare. Minimum standards for height, windows, light and size were imposed. Lavatories (privies) were provided in the yards (communal space).

Sketch of the post-1860 by-law housing

**Figure 2.9** *Housing types in Bradford*
Source: Richardson, C., 1976, A geography of Bradford, Univ. of Bradford

# Case study: **The growth of London up to the twentieth century**

| Year | The City of London | Rest of London | Total London | England and Wales | London as a % of England and Wales |
|---|---|---|---|---|---|
| c. 200 | 20 | | 20 | 1000 | 2 |
| c.1100 | 15 | | 15 | 1500 | 1 |
| c.1400 | 45 | | 45 | 2250 | 2 |
| c.1500 | 75 | | 75 | 3000 | 2.5 |
| c.1600 | 186 | 34 | 220 | 4500 | 5 |
| c.1700 | 208 | 367 | 575 | 6000 | 9.6 |
| 1801 | 128 | 831 | 959* 1117** | 8890 | 10.8 12.6 |
| 1851 | 128 | 2235 | 2363* 2685** | 17 983 | 13.1 14.9 |
| 1901 | 27 | 4398 | 4425* 6586** | 32 612 | 13.6 20.2 |
| 1951 | 5 | 8188 | 8193** | 43 758 | 18.7 |

\* Total London defined as The City plus the rest of the London County Council Area

\*\* Total London defined as The City plus the rest of the Greater London Council Area

*Figure 2.11* The growth of London's population (000s)
Source: Clout, H., and Wood, P., 1986, London, problems of change, Longman

## Early London

London has been an important settlement since Roman times (Figure 2.11). During the Anglo-Saxon period, seventh to ninth century, it was an established manufacturing, trading and religious centre, as well as a royal residence. These functions attracted people and industries to London, and the settlement prospered. It expanded rapidly during mediaeval times. The preindustrial town was characterised by a number of features:

- a concentration of population
- specialist economic functions, such as craftspeople, textiles, food and wine
- an organised political system
- a sphere of influence which reached beyond the city walls.

The land use zones in mediaeval towns were different from those of modern industrial towns – religious, administrative, political and social functions were important in determining mediaeval urban land use patterns.

The result was that:

- a small, elite group occupied central areas
- the poorer majority lived further away, but within the city walls
- distinct 'quarters' developed, for example, trading areas, craft and industrial districts, and monastic houses.

In addition, by 1400 London was already an important port, located towards the east of the city, for example, around the mouths of the Rivers Fleet and Warbrook, an area close to St. Paul's Cathedral.

Some functions, including slaughterhouses, livestock markets and the leather industry, were kept outside London's city walls. Many of these established themselves east of the city walls, downstream from the port. Many migrants and refugees were attracted to this area by the work, and by 1500 cheap, poorly constructed housing was erected to meet their needs. This was the start of the East End of London.

## London's rapid growth

London's population had risen to 75 000 people by 1500. However, mortality rates were high: population growth occurred due to massive in-migration. By 1801, London's population had risen to 1 117 000. The area of the city had also increased.

The main changes between 1500 and 1800 were:

1 the City was devastated by the Great Plague (1665) and the Great Fire (1666) causing many richer residents to move out westwards
2 'planned' settlements were developed in the West End, on lands formerly owned by the church, but sold after the dissolution of the monasteries (1536-38)
3 expansion in the east – largely unplanned, fuelled by the growth of the port and the large number of migrants
4 new bridges were constructed from 1750 onwards, allowing development south of the River Thames
5 London's rapid growth led it to rely increasingly on surrounding areas for food supply, recreation land, and raw materials.

The Great Plague resulted in the death of about 100 000 people and the Great Fire destroyed over 11 000 dwellings in an area of two square kilometres. The fire allowed for some planning and rebuilding and the rebuilt area had:

- brick houses with tiled roofs
- wider streets
- larger public buildings.

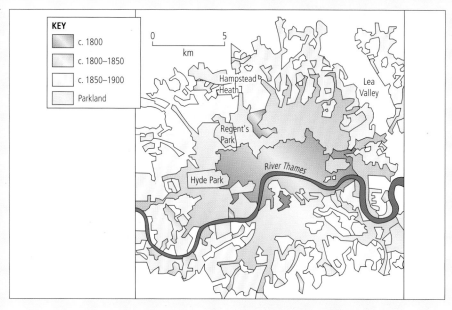

***Figure 2.12*** *The growth of London during the nineteenth century*
*Source: Clout, H. and Wood, P., 1986, London, problems of change, Longman*

**KEY**
- c. 1800
- c. 1800–1850
- c. 1850–1900
- Parkland

## London in the nineteenth century

In the nineteenth century, London was the world's leading financial, political, commercial, industrial and trading centre. It was not just the capital of Britain, it ruled the Empire. It was one of the world's most important cities – if not *the* most important. London's commercial functions expanded rapidly. As a result, services such as schools, churches, stations, theatres and museums developed all over the West End of London.

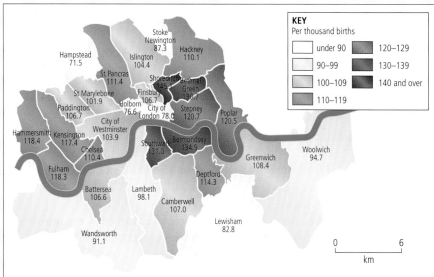

**KEY**
**Per thousand births**
- under 90
- 90–99
- 100–109
- 110–119
- 120–129
- 130–139
- 140 and over

***Figure 2.13*** *Infant mortality rate in London, at the start of the twentieth century*
*Source: Wohl, A., 1983, Endangered lives, Methuen*

Increasingly, the City took on a commercial role and its residential function declined. Its night-time population (residents, as opposed to its day-time population consisting mainly of workers) fell from 128 000 in the early Victorian period, to under 30 000 in 1901.

In the East End conditions were harsh (Figure 2.13). Little of the wealth generated in London made its way to the area. The East End became associated with poverty, overcrowding and slum conditions (Figure 2.14). Employment was irregular and low-paid. One commentator recorded that:

*'the East End of London is the hell of poverty. Like an enormous black, motionless, giant kraken (a type of sea monster), the poverty of London lies there in lurking silence and encircles with its mighty tentacles the life and wealth of the City and the West End.'*

Advances in economic growth during the nineteenth century concealed the poor quality of life experienced by many Londoners. The Metropolitan Police force was set up in 1829 to deal with rising crime rates. Epidemics killed thousands of people; for example, over 5000 people were killed in a cholera epidemic in 1832, and 14 000 in 1849. Poor water and sanitation were largely to blame.

***Figure 2.14*** *London's East End in the nineteenth century*

Ironically, early attempts at improving sanitation led to a decline in water quality. Flushing lavatories were in use from 1810 but their waste discharged directly into the River Thames. By 1856 it was against the law to use water from the Thames downstream of Teddington. (Teddington is the upper limit of the tidal Thames, so polluted water could be carried up this far, from London.) However, by the mid 1860s there was a crude sewer system in operation which carried waste to beyond the eastern edge of London.

During the nineteenth century, London's population increased to over 2 685 000 people, nearly 15% of the nation's total. During the 1840s and 1850s the East End attracted large numbers of Irish migrants, fleeing the horrors of the potato famine. In addition, up to 25% of the nation's natural increase took place in London. By the end of the century, London accounted for 20% of the population of England and Wales.

The East End remained a favoured location for ethnic migrants; for example, Jewish people congregated in Whitechapel and the French Huguenots in Spitalfields and Soho. However, it was for its port that the East End became most famous. The port's trade had doubled during the eighteenth century, attracting many more migrants as the demand increased for labourers in shipbuilding and repair, and cargo handling and distribution. The need for new, expanded docks was clear:

- the average size of ships doubled in the eighteenth century
- increased congestion caused some ships to have to wait three months before being unloaded
- in periods of war, ships arrived in convoys, requiring large amounts of space
- it was not uncommon for there to be over 1200 ships waiting to unload at any time.

The City authorities eventually approved a series of new docks. To function, the docks required a large amount of casual labour for unloading, loading and transportation. Dock employment was low paid, insecure, and variable. This caused a great deal of poverty among dock workers and their families.

### Housing developments and transport in the nineteenth century

Housing developments in the late nineteenth century were associated with improvements in transport links. Railways, trams, buses, and the underground network enabled London to expand. What is unique about London is that these changes occurred there first and more rapidly than anywhere else in the world.

Initially, the purpose of the railways was to link London with other industrial regions and ports, not specifically to serve commuters. There were few stations on the urban fringe, hence suburbanisation was limited. However, by 1870 there had been important changes to London's rail network:

- local stations were built
- new suburban lines were developed
- lines across the River Thames were completed.

The underground railway network began operating in 1863, from Paddington to the City. The overground network was more developed south of the river, whereas the underground network was more developed north of the river. Urban tramways began

operating in the 1870s and these were followed by buses in 1905.

Space was needed for the rapidly expanding rail network and up to 100 000 people were forcibly displaced by the building of the railways and their stations. There was very little attempt at rehousing and the displaced people moved into surrounding areas, making conditions there worse.

Towards the end of the century, suburbanisation increased dramatically. Cheap transport and rising wages allowed some workers to move further away from their workplace. The Cheap Trains Act of 1883 forced railway companies to charge low fares on their suburban lines. This allowed the suburbs to stretch out towards such places as Tottenham, Leyton and Walthamstow.

Early in the twentieth century attempts were made to house people from inner city slums in suburban 'cottage estates', council estates with lower density and higher quality housing, such as Norbury and Tooting in south London.

### QUESTIONS

1 Explain how, and why, the urban problems in London have been different in type and intensity from other parts of the country.

2 Study Figures 2.11 on page 25 and 2.12 on page 26. Describe how urban growth and urban sprawl took place in London in the nineteenth century.

3 Give at least three contrasting reasons why the East End of London became the poorer end rather than the richer end. How does this compare with other cities?

# Case study: **The growth of Manchester up to the twentieth century**

In the eighteenth century, south-east Lancashire was predominantly an agricultural area, with Manchester, a market town, as its centre. As the demand for cotton increased in the late eighteenth century, Manchester became the centre of the cotton industry. It had the right natural conditions – cotton and flax grew well in the area, there was soft water for processing cotton and good access to British markets via the canals. Manchester concentrated on cotton and used it to improve its economic base. Dramatic increases in mill building occurred, and during the Industrial Revolution (1800-1850) the population of Manchester grew from 76 000 in 1801 to 316 000 in 1851. Transport developments during this period reinforced the economic position of Manchester – the canals gave the town good links with the rest of the UK, encouraging trade and industrial activity and creating jobs. Manchester became the largest and most highly concentrated centre of cotton manufacture and distribution in the world. Moreover, its chemical industry developed from demands for bleaches and dyes for cotton goods, and its engineering industry developed from the need to build and repair cotton manufacturing machinery.

The growth of Manchester's financial sector stemmed directly from its industrial growth. The road layout, architectural form of buildings and the main streets and spaces were all determined in the Victorian and Edwardian periods and, today, Manchester is still dominated by the physical forms of that time.

During the Industrial Revolution, the population in Manchester had increased at a very rapid rate, and before 1868 there were no construction bylaws. Speculative builders could build as many houses as possible onto a site, with no restrictions as to light, fresh air or space (Figure 2.15). This led to the creation of slum areas with high densities of housing and people.

Manchester City Council came into being in 1853, after the incorporation of several surrounding townships in 1838. Around the same time:
- the mills began to decline, with increasing competition from Germany and the United States
- the price of land in and around the city was becoming very high
- competition for space from housing developers, speculative developers and industrialists was increasing.

There was a desperate need to deal with the economic and social problems. To address the economic problem, Manchester embarked upon a radical solution – to join Manchester directly to the open sea by a huge canal, decreasing transport costs and time, and thus boosting exports.

Less attention was devoted to housing. Until the end of the nineteenth century, the provision of housing of all kinds was the sole responsibility of private enterprise. A few enlightened social reformers provided cheap and reasonable quality housing for their workers, but most of the housing was designed and built to minimum standards.

Municipal housing in Manchester dates back to 1891, with the first municipal housing schemes on Oldham Road, Pollard Street and Rochdale Road. New housing and public health laws in the 1880s and 1890s led to the demolition of sub-standard dwellings, but Manchester's population was still increasing, causing the lack of affordable, reasonable quality housing to continue.

***Figure 2.15*** *Nineteenth-century Victorian housing in Manchester*

## QUESTIONS

1  **How has the development of Manchester differed from that of London?**

2  **Compare and contrast the urban problems of Manchester with those of London. Explain any differences that you have noted. Explain also why they have similar problems.**

## THE DEVELOPMENT OF URBAN PLANNING

Urban planning is the art of planning and building towns. It is as old as towns themselves. For example, there is abundant evidence of urban planning in Greek and Roman cities, such as Athens and Rome. This is often based on a grid pattern and was of religious significance. Evidence of residential segregation in terms of class is available from the earliest times. In the UK, modern urban planning can be traced from **planned settlements** in the eighteenth century.

The first planned industrial settlement was at New Lanark in Scotland. Others included the textiles towns of Yorkshire and Lancashire. However, these settlements were mostly small-scale.

During the nineteenth century there were more ambitious attempts – a greater number, at a larger scale – at planned settlements (Figure 2.16). Again, these were largely carried out by industrialists, with the best-known 'company towns' dating from the late nineteenth century – Cadbury built Bournville, near Birmingham, and Lever was responsible for Port Sunlight, on Merseyside. Similarly, in Germany, the engineering and armaments firm, Krupp, built company towns in the Ruhr region at Essen.

Bournville, for example, was developed at a density of 20 houses per hectare. This compared with 50 houses per hectare in adjoining areas. Cottage-style housing in semi-detached and short terraces was provided for the workers, for rent. Open space and recreational amenities were considered vital for health and welfare. In addition, moral and cultural development was aided by a range of churches, chapels, libraries, art galleries and theatres. In all of these towns, industry was decentralised from the inner city to the outskirts. A new town was built around the new factory to house the workers in healthy conditions. Some of this housing has now been sold off to people outside the company, but they still provide a residential function.

Among nineteenth century reformers and **philanthropists**, a great deal of importance was placed on nature and scenery, and village life was highly romanticised. The interest in picturesque qualities led to the Victorian villa estates on the fringes of rich industrial towns. Victorian villa estates for the middle and upper classes became common from the 1850s. Detached and semi-detached houses with big gardens were designed, with trees and winding roads producing a village effect. However, they had a social function as well as a scenic one. They were developed in order to help some people

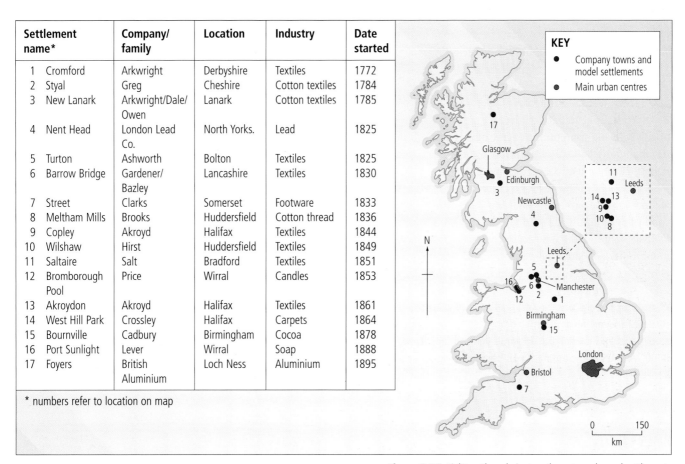

| Settlement name* | Company/ family | Location | Industry | Date started |
|---|---|---|---|---|
| 1  Cromford | Arkwright | Derbyshire | Textiles | 1772 |
| 2  Styal | Greg | Cheshire | Cotton textiles | 1784 |
| 3  New Lanark | Arkwright/Dale/ Owen | Lanark | Cotton textiles | 1785 |
| 4  Nent Head | London Lead Co. | North Yorks. | Lead | 1825 |
| 5  Turton | Ashworth | Bolton | Textiles | 1825 |
| 6  Barrow Bridge | Gardener/ Bazley | Lancashire | Textiles | 1830 |
| 7  Street | Clarks | Somerset | Footware | 1833 |
| 8  Meltham Mills | Brooks | Huddersfield | Cotton thread | 1836 |
| 9  Copley | Akroyd | Halifax | Textiles | 1844 |
| 10  Wilshaw | Hirst | Huddersfield | Textiles | 1849 |
| 11  Saltaire | Salt | Bradford | Textiles | 1851 |
| 12  Bromborough Pool | Price | Wirral | Candles | 1853 |
| 13  Akroydon | Akroyd | Halifax | Textiles | 1861 |
| 14  West Hill Park | Crossley | Halifax | Carpets | 1864 |
| 15  Bournville | Cadbury | Birmingham | Cocoa | 1878 |
| 16  Port Sunlight | Lever | Wirral | Soap | 1888 |
| 17  Foyers | British Aluminium | Loch Ness | Aluminium | 1895 |

\* numbers refer to location on map

***Figure 2.16*** *Eighteenth and nineteenth century planned settlements*

escape from the overcrowded, unhealthy inner cities.

Company towns and planned settlements were both attempts to create a better living environment and a more just society. There were a number of other reasons for creating planned settlements:

- to enhance the view for the landowner
- to provide a healthy, stable and loyal workforce for the industrialist
- as acts of philanthropy (a genuine desire to help the poor for their own sake).

The creation of a hard working, loyal workforce was made easier by providing them with good housing and living conditions. It was not that different from the situation for agricultural workers who had often been provided with housing and a small parcel of land in return for their labour. In the urban areas, rapid growth had led to poor quality housing and low life expectancy. High rates of illness and absenteeism lowered productivity. The company owners needed a healthy, and, ideally, happy workforce.

# Inset 2.2
# Saltaire

Saltaire, built by the industrialist, Titus Salt, is one example of a planned settlement. It shows that Victorian philanthropy was not as simple as it seemed. Salt did not just provide good housing and social facilities for the sake of it: he attracted and maintained a healthy, loyal and hard-working workforce.

Titus Salt lived in Bradford between the 1820s and the 1870s and was associated with the woollen trade. During the 1840s there was serious unrest in Bradford, caused, in part, by the appalling living conditions of many of its inhabitants. Salt was Bradford's richest citizen and also a very religious man. Throughout the 1840s he became increasingly concerned by the living conditions of Bradford's working class. In 1850, he decided to replace his mills in Bradford by a large mill five kilometres west of the town (Figure 2.17). The new factory was within reach of the commercial and financial core of Bradford but also had the room to expand and modernise. It employed 3000 workers and occupied a 13 hectare site.

**Figure 2.17** *Saltaire – a new type of development – notice the very neat, regular layout of the houses, their location close to the factory, and the way in which the factory dominates the local environment*

At the beginning, workers were transported daily to the new factory from inner Bradford, until the village of Saltaire was built, between 1851 and 1872. By 1863, over 4000 people were living in Saltaire, in over 800 newly constructed houses. The quality of housing was far superior to that in Bradford, although decreasing seniority within the factory was reflected by decreasing size of house. Each house had its own bedrooms, lavatory, kitchen, parlour, coal shed and backyard. Nevertheless, housing density was quite high, with as many as 91 houses per hectare.

Saltaire was provided with a number of public buildings, including a church, hospital, school, chapel, public baths, a library, and almshouses (houses for those too old or ill to work).

---

**QUESTIONS**

1 Describe the distribution of planned settlements as shown on Figure 2.16.

2 How do you account for this distribution?

## THE GARDEN CITY MOVEMENT

In 1898, Ebenezer Howard wrote *Tomorrow: a peaceful path to real reform*. This was reprinted in 1902 as *Garden cities of tomorrow*. Howard tried to bring together town and country and was far more interested in social and political reform than architecture. His famous diagram, *The Three Magnets*, contrasts the two magnets of urban and rural life and their advantages, with the third magnet the Garden City, portrayed as having the best of both worlds (Figure 2.18).

Howard was interested in land ownership, finance and housing rents. He wanted to ensure low rents for working people by reducing private ownership of land. In addition, he wanted to create a sense of community in his settlement, a 'feeling of belonging'. Two model settlements were created in the early twentieth century, Letchworth in 1903, and Welwyn Garden City in 1920. Both cities became famous for their layout and design. In particular they became associated with:

- cul-de-sacs
- houses clustered around greens
- neighbourhoods
- varied architectural styles
- trees and open spaces.

However, the underlying concerns for Garden Cities drifted away from the social and political to the architectural. Garden suburbs, such as Mitcham Garden village, had a largely residential funtion, whereas Howard had envisaged larger, self-contained settlements which employed, educated and housed people.

Raymond Unwin, who wrote *Town planning in practice – an introduction to the art of designing cities and suburbs (1909)*, brought wider social and political ideals to his writing than Howard's original ideas. Unwin and Parker (Unwin's brother-in-law) built New Earswick outside York. New Earswick was based on the idea of having just 26 houses per hectare, angled to catch the sun, and using cul-de-sacs to maintain privacy.

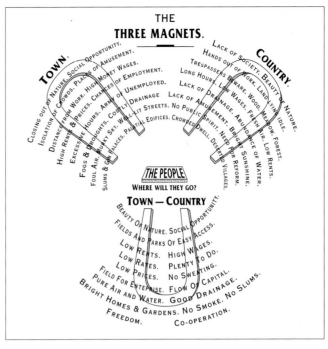

**Figure 2.18** *Howard's 'three magnets' diagram, by which he represented the new attractive force of the garden city, overriding the two traditional forces of town and country*
Source: Howard, E., 1902, Garden cities of tomorrow

Unwin and Parker were employed as architects by Howard to design Letchworth (1903), with a target population of 30 000. This was designed on a greenfield site, with wide roads or boulevards, trees and grass verges, and also with houses angled to catch the sun yet maintain their own privacy. It was village green type housing with a low density, just six to twelve houses per hectare. Unwin and Parker went on to design Hampstead Garden Suburb in 1907. They drew up minimum standards for housing densities of 26 houses per hectare. This was adopted in the Housing Act of 1919 and subsequently adopted for private and municipal estates.

## SUMMARY

Urbanisation in the UK in the eighteenth and nineteenth centuries has many parallels with modern urbanisation in ELDCs. We have seen how death rates were high, disease rife and living conditions appalling. Life in the slums was 'nasty, brutish and short'.

In the UK, attempts to improve living conditions evolved over time. These attempts were initially small-scale, but became more widespread and effective during the nineteenth century. They included the provision of water and sanitation, as well as the development of planned settlements, which were the foundation for modern urban planning. However, conditions were still poor at the beginning of the twentieth century, especially in inner city areas.

## QUESTIONS

1 Describe and explain the patterns of urbanisation and industrialisation in the UK up to the end of the nineteenth century.
2 What are the social, economic and environmental problems associated with urbanisation in the UK in the nineteenth century?
3 How do the problems of rapid urbanisation in ELDCs today compare with the problems experienced in Britain in the nineteenth century? Give examples to support your answer.

## BIBLIOGRAPHY AND RECOMMENDED READING

Clout, H. & Wood, P., 1986, *London: problems of change*, Longman

HMSO, 1995, *Manchester: 50 years of change*, HMSO

Howard, E., 1898, *Tomorrow: a peaceful path to real reform*, Sonnenschein (later published as Garden cities of tomorrow, 1902 and 1946)

Howe, G., 1972, *Man, environment and disease in Britain*, Pelican

Ogden, P., 1992, *London Docklands*, CUP

Reynolds, J., 1985, *Saltaire*, Bradford Art Galleries and Museums

Richardson, C., 1976, *A geography of Bradford*, University of Bradford

Roberts, R., 1971, *The classic slum, Salford life in the first quarter of the century*, Pelican

Trend, R., 1995, *Precursors to Britain's New Towns*, Geography Review, 9, 2, 18-23

Wohl, A., 1983, *Endangered lives: public health in Victorian Britain*, Methuen

# Chapter 3
# Suburbanisation in the UK

We saw in Chapter 2 the importance of urban growth in the nineteenth century. Suburbanisation began later, in the late 1800s and early 1900s, and towns and cities in England and Wales began to spread out after 1860. In this chapter we examine the changes in cities in the early twentieth century. The chapter follows developments in London and Manchester, continuing the case studies from Chapter 2. Finally, we look at changes in urban planning.

## THE EARLY UK SUBURBS

By the end of the nineteenth century, social conditions had improved considerably over the previous fifty years:

- average incomes were higher
- medical standards had improved
- new housing regulations were coming into effect.
  On the other hand:
- up to a quarter of London's East End were living below the poverty line
- over 3 million people lived in densities of over two per room
- rural areas were economically threatened by cheap imports from North America
- life expectancy in Manchester was only 29 years.

In the early twentieth century there were significant changes to British towns and cities. Improvements in transport systems allowed cities to expand, and by the early twentieth century railways, electric tramways and buses were crucial to the growth of middle-class, residential suburbs. Some towns had unplanned suburban growth along the routes of trams and trains. Between 1897 and 1906, 2200 miles of tramways were laid in England and Wales. Transport was very cheap. In addition, the price of farmland had declined dramatically and there was scope for urban expansion on a great scale.

It was a period of optimism for many. Rising wages and living standards were matched by rising expectations. Housing was now available, affordable and of a quality unimaginable only a few decades earlier. The lives of many working class people were being transformed. Instead of overcrowded slum conditions there were new low density, well equipped houses in pleasant locations. Suburban locations offered security and respectability. Moreover, most of the

**Figure 3.1** *Slum conditions in inner London, c. 1900*

**Figure 3.2** *Suburban development at Mitcham Garden Village*

housing in the suburbs was privately owned. People were willing to accept the new and better housing, and did not question whether there were hidden costs – such as a decline in the extended family and less social interaction.

## QUESTIONS

1 Make a table to contrast living conditions in inner city areas, such as London's East End, with suburban locations. Use the two photographs, Figures 3.1 and 3.2 to help you.

2 'Home ownership generally promotes conservatism.' What are the effects of this upon suburban development? Use examples to support your answer.

The need for urban redevelopment in the UK was influenced indirectly by World War I. Most suburbanisation before World War I had been of the wealthy, who could afford to move out to larger, more costly housing. In addition, the wealthy could afford the costs of travel to work. In some cases, local authorities provided housing – such as at Totterdown, Tooting. This housing was cheaper, and affordable to working class people. Nevertheless, they had to pay for the cost of travel to work, which remained in the city.

Unlike much of Europe, the UK did not experience a great deal of destruction during the war, but the government recognised that the quality of life for many working class people was low, in terms of health, education and employability, and that important measures needed to be taken (Figure 3.3). The standard of health (physical and mental had been found to be very poor among recruits. 40% nationally and 60% in some areas had been rejected on acount of poor health. In the 1918 election, the Prime Minister, Lloyd George, said that he wanted to create 'a land fit for heroes to live in'. Under the 1919 Housing and Town Planning Act, the government provided subsidies for housing. These subsidies were very generous and allowed local authorities to embark on large-scale house building. Two main subsidies were available: the Wheatley subsidy for local authorities and the Chamberlain subsidy for private builders. These subsidies continued into the 1930s and were the main source of funding for low income housing.

The availability of subsidies led to the nationwide development of many council house estates. The estates could hardly have been more different from the inner city housing. They were built at an average density of 26 houses per hectare. They included three bedrooms, kitchen, bathroom and a garden. But these developments could only take place on unbuilt land, thus cities expanded outwards.

In the 1920s and 1930s building societies began to lend money, in the form of mortgages, on a large-scale. This enabled people with regular employment to borrow money to buy a property at very low interest rates (Figure 3.4). **Decentralisation** of the population took place, with many people from the inner city moving out into suburban locations – inner city populations declined slightly and the suburban population doubled.

Private housebuilding in the 1930s intensified. In 1930, over 100 000 houses were built – the most that had ever been built in a single year. In 1935 and 1936, 275 000 were built in each year and even at the start of World War II, over 200 000 houses were built annually. During the 1930s, over 2.7 million houses were built in England and Wales. There were a number of reasons for this boom in private housebuilding:

- lower costs of living
- very low interest rates
- expansion of building societies
- willingness of local authorities to provide utilities such as sewers, electricity, gas and water
- increased public transport.

Overall, during the inter-war period about 4.3 million houses were built. Of these, 31% were built by local authorities, 11% by private developers with state assistance (such as housing associations) and 58% by unaided private enterprise. Until 1939, there were very few constraints upon development. This led to:

- urban sprawl
- impacts on farming
- transport and congestion costs
- social costs.

For example, much of the land taken over by the new suburbs was good agricultural land. In Dagenham, Essex, some of the best market gardening areas of the county were

**Figure 3.3** *'The home I want'. C3 refers to the health status of many army conscripts (C3 meant unfit for service) caused by poor housing conditions, overcrowding and malnutrition. A.1. refers to the quality of life that people aspired to* Source: Reiss, R., 1919, Homes fit for Heroes, Hodder and Stoughton

**Figure 3.4** *The impact of estate agents – lending money and selling an image* Source: Ward, S., Oxford Brookes University

converted to urban land uses. Urban sprawl to the west of London had the same effect. As cities became larger, it took longer to get to work. Increasingly, more people travelled by car. Indeed, the number of motor vehicles increased from 2 million in 1928 to 3 million in 1939.

Suburban life did not benefit everyone. For the poorest people, living costs, with mortgage repayments instead of rent and travel costs, had increased. In addition, it cost more to heat the larger houses. A survey in Stockton in the 1930s, showed that the health conditions of the poor actually deteriorated in the suburbs. This was linked to the extra costs they had to meet and less money being spent on food.

Suburban areas were also criticised because of the lack of community spirit. They were seen as cold, soulless, impersonal and class conscious. In some areas, walls were built separating richer housing estates from poorer ones – the 'Cutteslow Wall' in Oxford is a good example. So great was the feeling among some people that suburban areas were socially destructive, that increasing attention was directed towards high density housing schemes. Financial pressures were having an effect – it was very expensive to house people in low density suburban developments, and it was much cheaper to accommodate them in high rise tower blocks.

There were fears that many cities, particularly London, were growing too rapidly. By 1939, one-third of all houses in England and Wales had been built since 1918. New planning regulations were brought into being: the *Restriction of Ribbon Development Act*, 1935, for example, tried to impose controls on the spread of developments along major routes. The implications for suburban growth were clear – uncontrolled suburban sprawl was about to be contained.

## Suburban society

Books written in 1957 and 1960 by Willmott and Young, *Family and kinship in East London* and *Family and class in a London suburb*, describe the differences between inner city households and those in the suburbs. In the inner city, extended families (three generations of a family or more) lived in rented, cramped accommodation. Society was dominated by relationships between mothers and daughters. Inner city areas were densely populated by all age groups. By contrast, suburban areas were mostly middle class and owner occupied. Households were smaller and nuclear families (based around father, mother and their children) were the norm. The suburbs were less densely populated than inner city areas and it was more difficult to make friends. In addition, many of the people moving to the suburbs were young or middle aged, and middle class. Hence, there was a lack of age- and class-diversity.

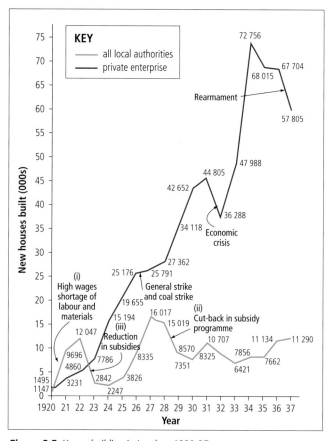

**Figure 3.5** *House building in London, 1920-37*
Source: Jackson, A., 1973, Semi-detached London, George Allen and Unwin

# Inset 3.1
# Suburbanisation in the USA

In the USA suburbanisation followed racial lines (Figure 3.6). The percentage of blacks in the suburbs has remained constant at about 5% of the total population. Moreover, black suburbanisation has tended to be in the inner suburbs, and has involved movement into housing left by whites, whilst white suburbanisation has been at the edge of the city and into new housing. For example, in Chicago as late as the 1960s, less than 2% of new homes were sold to blacks, and 3% of new apartments rented to blacks.

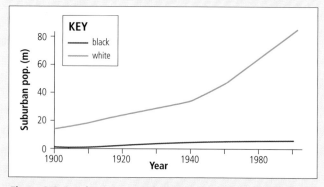

**Figure 3.6** *Racial variations in suburbanisation in the USA, 1900-1970*
Source: Muller, 1976 (diagram taken from University of London Examination Board, 1984)

## URBAN PLANNING
## IN THE EARLY TWENTIETH CENTURY

In 1909 the first British town planning legislation was passed – the Housing and Town Planning Act. Under the 1909 Act local authorities began to plan for urban areas. Their prime concern was about land use zoning, density of housing developments, and the reservation of routeways for suburban extension. Before 1930 there was very little thought of any large-scale implementation of ideas. This changed dramatically in the 1940s.

## Garden cities

We saw in Chapter 2, Urbanisation in the UK, how Ebenezer Howard developed the idea of the garden city. He was responsible for starting two garden cities – Letchworth in Hertfordshire (1903) and nearby Welwyn Garden City (1920). Letchworth was unique in that it was the first 'new town' not built by an industrialist or a philanthropist. The architect's plan for Letchworth included low density housing, land-use zoning (industry segregated from residential land-use) and a large amount of open space (Figure 3.7). The town proved quite attractive to industry because of its good road and rail links.

In 1903 the population was 508 people. The Garden City Association bought 8400 hectares at Letchworth in 1903 to build its garden city. The first house in Letchworth garden city was built in 1904 and much of the early housing was built by housing associations. In fact there was no local

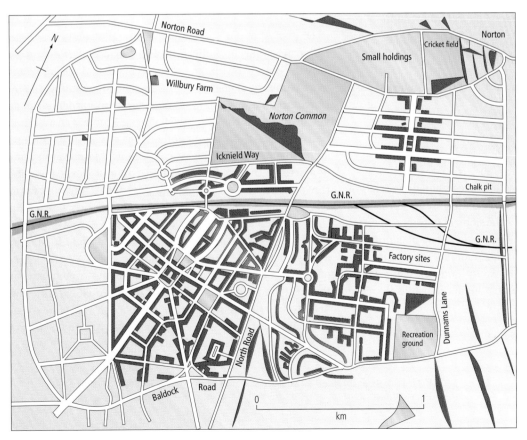

**Figure 3.7** *A plan of Letchworth, the first Garden City*
Source: Letchworth: the first garden city, Letchworth Museums and Art Gallery, 1973

authority provision for housing in the area. Village schools had already existed at the original villages of Norton and William. An independent school was built in 1905 and the present Norton school was built in 1909. Other amenities included a public house (1907), the Cloisters centre for arts, crafts, summer schools and general entertainment (1905), a library (1906), and numerous churches. Each of the villages in the estate had its own parish church. By 1930 there were 19 churches in Letchworth.

| Size of Letchworth (hectares) | | Population size | |
|---|---|---|---|
| 1903 | 8400 | 1903 | 508 |
| 1910 | 10 791 | 1910 | 5324 |
| | | 1920 | 10 382 |
| 1935 | 11 183 | 1930 | 14 454 |
| | | 1940 | 16 868 |
| | | 1950 | 20 321 |
| | | 1960 | 25 515 |
| 1973 | 11 200 | 1971 | 31 540 |

**Figure 3.8** *The growth of Letchworth, 1903-73*
*Source: Letchworth: the first garden city, 1973, Letchworth Museum and Art Galleries*

Letchworth has been described as having 'salubrious surroundings, plentiful greenswards, trees and open-spaces which truly unite Town and Country within predetermined limits of acreage and population. Letchworth garden city is unique in that it came into being almost entirely in the form conceived by its creator.'

However, Letchworth has been subject to a number of pressures:

- the heavy volume of traffic on roads not designed to take it
- the need for urgent industrial expansion
- increased residential accommodation.

### Garden suburbs

**Garden suburbs**, or **garden villages**, combined the ideas of the philanthropists with those applied to garden cities. They were developed as small-scale versions of garden cities and were applied to existing cities, as a form of suburban growth. Some, such as White Hart Lane in Tottenham, and Totterdown Fields, in Tooting, South London, were developed by local councils and built at higher densities than the private developments.

**Figure 3.9** *An aerial view of Letchworth*

One of the most famous private developments was Hampstead Garden Suburb. It was started in 1906 and its growth coincided with the extension of the underground network to nearby Golders Green. The scheme was designed by Unwin and Parker, who had also designed garden cities at Letchworth and New Earswick (York). Hampstead was initially criticised on the grounds that it was a dormitory suburb, not a self-sufficient community. Many of the residents used the Underground to commute into London. However, the suburb was socially mixed, as it attracted some working class people to the area, to work on the Underground and in local shops, and is considered one of the triumphs of twentieth century British design. In fact, in a very short time the garden suburb became a central part of British urban planning: most suburban development in the UK follows the principles of the garden cities, with low density, low rise housing and open space. It was a means of extending the upper class ideal of a family home to less wealthy households, with smaller, owner-occupied homes.

### QUESTIONS

1 Study Howard's diagram of the three magnets (Figure 2.18 on page 31). Compare the advantages and disadvantages of urban and rural lifestyles. Design a poster to represent Howard's message.

2 Plot the data shown in Figure 3.8. Describe how Letchworth's population has increased since 1903.

3 Study Figures 3.7, on page 35, and 3.9. What evidence is there to suggest that Letchworth is a planned settlement? How does Letchworth's street plan differ from that of Bradford in the mid-nineteenth century as shown in Figure 2.9, on page 24?

# Case study:
# Suburban development in London, 1900–39

Up to 1939, London experienced massive growth. More than three-quarters of all new factories built in London were in the suburbs. Suburbanisation and movement to other cities accelerated between the wars. For example, the population increased by 10% in the 1920s, while the size of the built-up area doubled.

Important changes aided this process:
- a shift in employment from manufacturing (blue-collar) to services (white-collar)
- better and more regular wages in the services sector compared with the manufacturing sector
- technological changes leading to improvements in transport.

Between 1914 and 1939, the population of London increased by 33% to over six million people (Figure 3.10); London's built-up area increased three-fold. This growth changed the shape of London. Whereas early growth had been along routes used by the railways, producing a **radial** city, this later growth created a fairly circular city. The reason for this change was due to transport:
- electric trains were more efficient than steam trains and could stop at more regular intervals
- buses allowed for infilling between the radial routes.

London was thriving compared with some of the old industrial areas which were affected by recession, overseas competition and rising unemployment. London had a greater share of employment in service industries, its manufacturing base was more diverse and there were more growth industries, including electrical and mechanical engineering. Migration from the declining, peripheral regions, such as the North East, into London, reinforced the

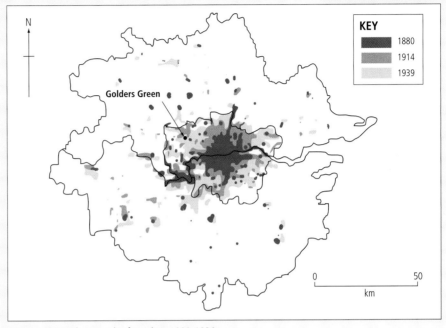

**Figure 3.10** *The growth of London, 1880-1939*
Source: Hall, P., 1992, Urban and regional planning, Routledge

capital's growth and **primacy**.

Up to 60% of the increase in London's population between the wars was due to in-migration, mostly from other parts of the UK. This was largely due to employment related conditions:
- between 1923 and 1934, employment in the South East increased by 44%, compared with falls of 5.5% in the North East and 26% in South Wales
- in 1934, London's unemployment rate was 8.6% compared with 44.2% in South Shields and 67.8% in Jarrow on Tyneside.

## Golders Green:
## unplanned private development

Golders Green shows how rapid development followed the introduction of the railway into a suburban area. At the end of the nineteenth century, Golders Green was a small hamlet in a very rural location. Even in 1906 there were only a few middle class houses in the hamlet. It was, however, an

important crossroads, between Hampstead, Hendon and Cricklewood, and developments were clearly on the horizon (Figure 3.11, see page 38). Gas lighting had been erected along the Finchley Road and the Underground Electric Railways Company had obtained a site for a station at Golders Green.

Attempts to build a station at Golders Green in the late nineteenth century had failed for financial reasons. Between 1900 and 1906, an American syndicate financed and built a tram link between Charing Cross and Golders Green, serving the Hendon and Finchley populations. An underground railway extension from Hampstead to Golders Green was opened in 1907.

## QUESTIONS

1 Describe the growth of London as shown in Figure 3.10.
2 What problems does the uncontrolled sprawl of cities have on (i) the environment and (ii) the economy?

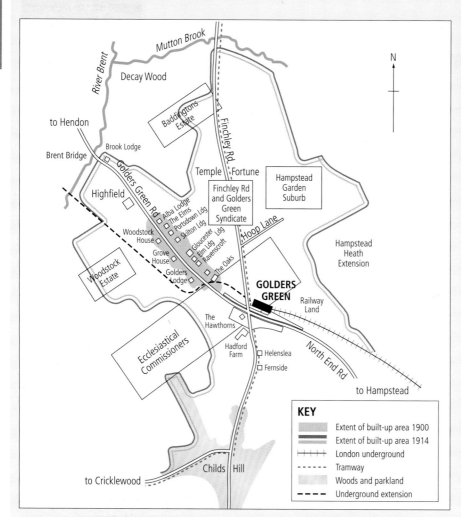

**Figure 3.11** *The Golders Green Estate, 1900-14*
*Source: Jackson, A., 1973, Semi-detached London, George Allen and Unwin*

was the fifth busiest underground station in London with over a million passengers every month. In addition electric trams operated from 1909 and a bus station was opened in 1913. Transport was crucial for the growth and success of Golders Green.

Amenities and utilities were needed to cater for the suburban population. These were quickly provided:

- shopping parade (1908)
- church, bank and post office (1909)
- second shopping parade (1911)
- cinema (1913)
- school (1914)
- police station (1916).

Golders Green grew rapidly and by 1925 the population had reached 13 400. However, there were claims that suburban life was a 'lonely, dull routine'. Traditional family values seemed to be disappearing and were being replaced by an empty, individualistic, materialistic mentality.

| Year | No. of houses | Year | No. of houses |
|------|------|------|------|
| 1905 | 19 | 1911 | 744 |
| 1906 | 14 | 1912 | 486 |
| 1907 | 73 | 1913 | 514 |
| 1908 | 340 | 1914 | 477 |
| 1909 | 461 | 1915 | 432 |
| 1910 | 562 | | |

**Figure 3.12**
*The growth of house-building in Golders Green*
*Source: Jackson, A., 1973, Semi-detached London, George Allen and Unwin*

Between 1904 and 1906, the area was drained, roads were lit, and the ground prepared for housing development. Land prices escalated. The first houses were built in 1905 and building increased rapidly from 1908. By the end of 1910, 18 kilometres of new sewers and 8 kilometres of new roads had been laid. There was no overall plan at Golders Green. There was no local authority control apart from the usual standards that related to road widths and the provision of utilities. The street layout reflected the pattern of land ownership. Houses were packed into small areas as the plots of land were sold off and there was little regard by the developers for open space.

The first people to move to Golders Green were businessmen, managers, and senior white collar workers. It was a very conservative area and developed a reputation for being *petit-bourgeois*. Snobbery was commonplace, and although residents could not afford servants, maids were common. It also developed a strong Jewish community; the first synagogue was built in 1922.

Described by Jackson as 'Half-timbered, tiled and gabled, and cottage in appearance', the Golders Green houses set the trend in suburban houses for the next 30 years. Although gardens were quite small, due to the cost of land, houses were quite expensive and attracted mostly middle class people.

Transport facilities continued to improve. In 1907, an underground train stopped at Golders Green every 12 minutes, by 1908 every 10 minutes, and by 1909 every 3 minutes at peak times. This was the upper limit of technology at the time. By the 1920s, Golders Green

## QUESTIONS

1 Study Figure 3.12. Use the figures to draw a graph which shows the growth of new housing in Golders Green. Describe the graph you have drawn.

2 What traditional family values were disappearing from suburban life? Why should they disappear?

# Case study:
# Suburban Manchester

The population of Manchester increased dramatically from 544 000 in 1901 to 766 000 in 1931. This led to increasing population densities in the inner areas and put great pressure on the available housing. The first substantial suburban housing development was built at a 24 hectare site at Burnage (Figure 3.13), 8 kilometres from the city centre. It followed many of the principles of the garden village – the concept that every house should have the maximum amount of light and air, and a pleasant outlook. One hundred and thirty-six houses were built around a circular road pattern with a density of 26 dwellings per hectare; the houses had hot and cold running water and electricity. However the rents were set too high for the working classes to afford, and thus the development did little to rehouse the poor from slum areas. Another

development was a private development at Chorltonville in 1911. Between 1927 and 1929 Manchester Corporation built on average 2500 houses a year, but suitable sites were in short supply and therefore a new solution had to be found.

In 1926 Manchester City Council purchased 8800 hectares at Wythenshawe. The plan was to create a self-contained satellite town for 100 000 people on the southern edge of Manchester with areas set aside for low density housing, including single-family homes, parks and open spaces, shopping centres, community facilities, agriculture and industries, surrounded by a green belt. These were serviced by a network of tree-lined roads and parkways. 25 000 households would be decentralised, largely from inner city slums.  20% of

the houses were to be built privately, but, in effect, Wythenshawe became the country's first municipally owned satellite town. Given its size, it really represents the UK's first new town. It was planned by Barry Parker, who had planned Letchworth with Raymond Unwin in 1903.

By 1935 the population of Wythenshawe had reached 35 000 people. There was a desperate need for new housing and this led to the emphasis being laid on residential construction, whilst the provision of social facilities fell short of what had originally been envisaged. By 1964, the original goal of 100 000 people had been reached but the relentless pressure for provision of new houses left an estate without basic social amenities.

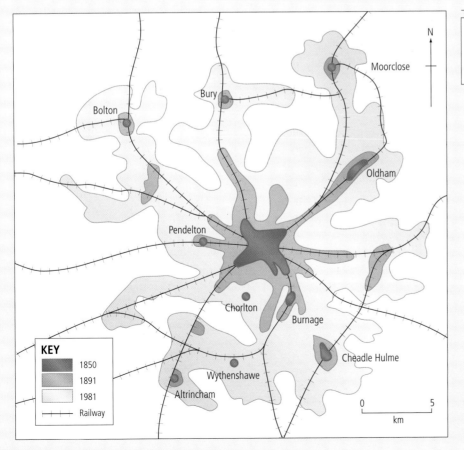

**KEY**
- 1850
- 1891
- 1981
- ┼┼┼┼ Railway

0 ———— 5
km

### QUESTION

1  Describe the growth of Manchester, as shown in Figure 3.13.

***Figure 3.13*** *Suburban development in Manchester*
Source: Knapp, B. et al, 1989, Challenge of the human environment, Longman

## TOWARDS A COMPREHENSIVE PLANNING APPROACH IN THE UK

The move towards a comprehensive planning approach in the UK from the late 1930s, seeing urban planning as part of regional and economic planning, was due to a number of concerns, such as:

- negative effects of suburbanisation
- regional inequalities in the UK
- deindustrialisation of traditional industries such as shipbuilding, iron and steel, and textiles
- long-term (life-time) unemployment
- the growth of consumerism and changes in the central business district (CBD), with congestion, inflated land prices and lack of space
- the threat of war (larger industrial and urban areas were easier to bomb).

The Barlow Commission (1940) was established 'to inquire into the causes which have influenced the present geographical distribution of the industrial population of Great Britain and the probable direction of any change in that distribution in the future; to consider what social, economic or strategical disadvantages arise from the concentration of industries or of the industrial population in large towns or in particular areas of the country; and to report what remedial measures if any should be taken in the national interest'.

The nature of planning changed considerably, largely as a result of the Greater London Plan in 1944, as we shall see in Chapter 4, Green Belts and Chapter 5, New towns .

### Suburbanisation and planning after World War II

During World War II, the bombing of UK cities and the lack of investment in them interrupted the process of suburbanisation. After the war, urban sprawl was limited by:

- the creation of Green Belts
- the introduction of general planning controls
- the building of new towns beyond the Green Belt to take overspill populations.

These are considered in depth in Chapters 5 and 6.

Since 1945 suburban development has consisted of:

- increasing density of housing
- infilling of green spaces
- redevelopment of older areas.

## SUMMARY

In this chapter we have seen how urbanisation in the nineteenth century developed into suburbanisation in the twentieth century. There were many benefits of suburban development – better housing, higher standards of living and a growth in the economy. But there were costs – social, economic and environmental ones. Suburbanisation has been one of the most important geographic processes of the twentieth century – the design and density of housing today owes much to the garden city of the early 1990s. Many of the problems remain! As we will see in Chapter 4, issues on the Green Belt are as important and significant today as they were at the peak of suburbanisation.

## QUESTIONS

1 What are the causes and consequences of suburbanisation? Give examples to illustrate your answer.
2 Describe the advantages of suburban housing over the inner city slums that it replaced.
3 Describe the links between garden cities and garden suburbs. How have the ideas been used in modern town planning?

### Suggestion for extended (project) work

1 Find out from a local library in an urban area how housing developments took place in the early part of the twentieth century. What differences are there between private and public housing developments in your area?

## BIBLIOGRAPHY AND RECOMMENDED READING

Cullingworth, J. and Nadin, V., 1994, *Town and country planning in Britain*, Routledge
Dennis, R., *1986, Suburban London in Clout, H. and Woods, P., (eds.) London: problems of change*, Longman
Hall, P., 1988, *Cities of tomorrow*, Blackwell
Hall, P., 1992, *Urban and regional planning*, Routledge
Hoskins, W., 1955, *The making of the English landscape*, Hodder and Stoughton
Jackson, A., 1973, *Semi-detached London*, George Allen and Unwin
Letchworth Museums and Art Gallery, 1973, *Letchworth the first garden city*
Unwin, R., 1912, *Nothing gained by overcrowding*, GCPTA
Willmott, P. and Young, M., 1960, *Family and class in a London suburb*, Routledge and Kegan Paul
Young, M. and Willmott, P., 1957, *Family and kinship in East London*, Routledge and Kegan Paul
Ward, S., 1994, *Planning and urban change*, Paul Chapman Publishing

# Chapter 4
# Green Belts

In this chapter we look at the origins of Green Belts, the impact of economic, political and demographic change on them, and some recent changes in Green Belts surrounding Birmingham. Finally, in a decision-making exercise, we examine in detail pressures on Oxford's Green Belt.

## GREEN BELTS IN THE UK

There are fourteen Green Belts in England, covering over 2 million hectares, or nearly 15% of the country (Figure 4.1).

In addition, there are five Green Belts in Scotland covering 335 000 hectares and two in Northern Ireland. To designate land as Green Belt is a lengthy process: the land is first classified as Green Belt by a local authority, central government then approves the broad outlines and the local authority defines the exact boundaries in its Local Plan. During that time the proposed Green Belt (the Interim Green Belt) is subjected to many pressures. Many of the problems associated with controlling development in Green Belts stem from the conflict between development and conservation.

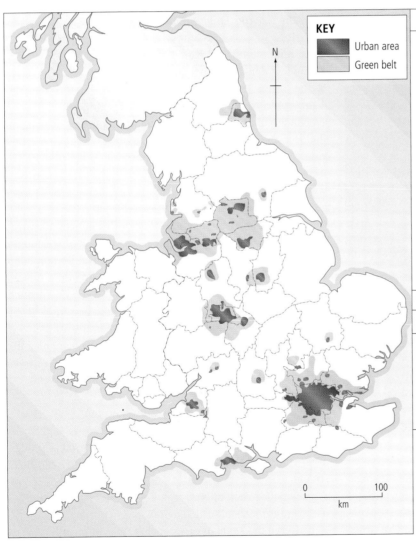

| Green Belts in England | Size (hectares) |
| --- | --- |
| Tyne and Wear | 91 000 |
| Lancaster and Fylde Coast | 2610 |
| York | 22 700 |
| South and West Yorkshire | 363 600 |
| Greater Manchester, Central Lancs, Merseyside and the Wirral | 341 000 |
| Stoke on Trent | 57 000 |
| Nottingham, Derby | 91 000 |
| Burton-Swadlincote | 910 |
| West Midlands | 12 000 |
| Cambridge | 12 000 |
| Gloucester, Cheltenham | 9100 |
| Oxford | 45 500 |
| London | 545 000 |
| Avon | 100 000 |
| **Total in England** | **2 043 310** |

| Green Belts in Scotland | Size (hectares) |
| --- | --- |
| Aberdeen | 26 600 |
| Ayr, Prestwick | 3200 |
| Falkirk/Grangemouth | 3900 |
| Glasgow | 135 000 |
| Lothian/Edinburgh | 16 400 |
| **Total in Scotland** | **168 480** |

*Source: Cullingworth, J. and Nadin, V., 1994,*
*Town and country planning in Britain, Routledge*

**KEY**
■ Urban area
▢ Green belt

**Figure 4.1** *Green Belts in England and Scotland*
*Source: Ward, S., 1994, Planning and urban change, Paul Chapman*

---

## QUESTIONS

**1** Study Figure 4.1 which shows the distribution of Green Belts in England and Scotland.

**a)** Describe the location of Green Belts. How does this relate to the size of urban area? What exceptions are there?

**b)** Why have some small cities been given Green Belts whereas some larger cities have not?

## THE ORIGIN OF GREEN BELTS

In the late nineteenth century, Ebenezer Howard proposed 'the limitation of the spread of towns, and their permanent separation, by zones of country land generally immune from building'.

However, the first significant steps towards creating a Green Belt were not taken until the inter-war period when, in 1927, Raymond Unwin suggested the idea of a Green Girdle around London to stop uncontrolled urban growth (Figure 4.2). By 1935 London County Council started buying up land to prohibit it being developed. It also provided grants to surrounding counties to buy up land. This was declared as land upon which development would not be permitted. In 1938, the *Green Belt and Home Counties Act* was passed and by 1939, 8000 hectares had been bought. By 1945, another 12 000 hectares were secured. Local authorities still own most of this land (about 20 000 hectares in total) and have been able to maintain a substantial Green Belt through the use of powers of development control.

*Figure 4.2* *The M25 – located entirely on Green Belt*

In the 1940s, planners were faced with the massive task of **decentralising** people from the congested inner parts of London to the outer rings. The inner areas were overcrowded with much old, poor quality housing. The outer rings were still close enough to London to allow commuting. Up to 1 million people in London had to be decentralised. Until 1939, the solution had been to build peripheral estates,

thereby increasing urban sprawl. In the *Greater London Plan* (1944), however, Patrick Abercrombie proposed a Green Belt, eight kilometres wide, to stop the outward growth of London.

The *Greater London Plan* was the most famous and influential of all wartime plans. Unlike other plans, it focused upon the metropolitan region, i.e. London and its surrounding hinterland, not just the city itself, and considered a wide range of problems and solutions. It highlighted four of the main concerns which were to dominate post-war planning for London:

- decentralisation of population and industry
- containment of urban sprawl
- redevelopment of inner urban areas
- regional planning, namely linking London with the surrounding region.

In the *Greater London Plan*, London was represented by four rings:

1  an inner, tightly developed ring
2  the low density suburban ring
3  the Green Belt
4  an outer, country ring.

The width of the Green Belt had an important bearing on the overspill problem. Since the outer edge of the Green Belt represented the outer limit of commuting in the mid 1940s, new self-contained communities outside the Green Belt would be created to rehouse the people being moved from central London, and provide them with jobs. It was a solution very close to the original ideas of Ebenezer Howard, namely self-sufficient communities for living and working.

The plan proposed a ban on new industrial development within the inner area, especially Central London, although factory relocation would be allowed. The Green Belt around London was to be enlarged and it would be enforced by planning controls rather than public ownership.

Green Belt policy was adopted in 1955, which enabled the idea to be applied on a national level. Local authorities were required to draw up plans for Green Belts which would:

- stop urban sprawl
- prevent neighbouring towns from merging
- preserve the special character of towns.

This definition has remained largely unaltered, although other functions have been added. In particular, Green Belts should:

- provide for recreation
- safeguard agricultural activities
- preserve the special, historic character of towns
- assist in urban regeneration.

Although these are positive aspects of Green Belts, there have been some unwanted side effects.

## Inset 4.1
## Some side effects of Green Belts

Green Belts have been quite successful in preventing urban sprawl and preventing development on the urban fringe. But there have been some undesirable side effects:

- development is forced further out into the countryside
- buildings in cities are more densely packed
- land prices escalate in areas close to the Green Belt
- housing developments are moved beyond the Green Belt
- there is an increase in commuting and traffic-related pollution
- more roads need to be built for commuter traffic.

The situation in Scotland is slightly different. Scottish Green Belts have a greater emphasis on environmental functions and the provision of recreation. These include:

- maintaining the identity of a town by establishing a clear definition of its physical boundary
- providing for countryside recreation
- maintaining the landscape setting of towns.

Within Green Belts generally, some development is allowed. This includes agriculture and forestry, outdoor sport, cemeteries, institutions, such as schools, standing in extensive grounds and other uses 'appropriate' to a rural area.

The Green Belt policy has had widespread appeal and no other planning circular has been as popular with the public. Even the term 'Green Belt' appeals to most people. It has also found favour with the environmental lobby. Its popularity, however, has not made it any easier to reconcile conservation and development and there are many misconceptions about Green Belts.

## Inset 4.2
## Popular misconceptions about Green Belts

- you cannot build anything on Green Belt land
- all Green Belt land is attractive
- the public has unlimited access to Green Belts
- once land is designated Green Belt, it will always be Green Belt
- Green Belt land is owned by the government

After World War II, pressures for new housing development grew as:

- the number of households increased more rapidly than the population
- car ownership spread.

Increased mobility and suburban sprawl reinforced each other.

Between 1955 and 1960, sixty-nine proposals to form Green Belts were submitted to the government. By 1963, over 14 080 square kilometres of England was covered by Green Belts. However, one-third of this was around London. This was, in fact, the only Green Belt that had passed through all three stages and had formal recognition of its status. All the major English conurbations had proposed Interim Green Belts. Other proposals came from smaller cities, such as Bristol-Bath and Nottingham-Derby, and from historic centres such as Oxford and York. Very often there was a political purpose in proposing the Green Belt, mainly to retain a political identity; for example, Cheshire County Council stopped the expansion of Merseyside, and Northumberland County Council did the same to prevent the spread of Newcastle. Several small towns, such as Swindon, Scarborough and Teeside were unsuccessful in establishing Green Belts.

Green Belt legislation was modified in 1957 and it became clear that Green Belts would only be granted to areas where pressures for growth were strong, and to large towns and cities. It also identified 'white land' within the Green Belt inner boundary which could be developed at a later date.

Throughout the 1960s Green Belts were put under a great deal of pressure and much of the land was developed. This was due to:

- high population growth in the early 1960s
- a shortage of houses
- escalating development costs in cities.

Over 600 hectares a year were lost from London's Green Belt between 1960 and 1980.

In 1964, Richard Crossman, Minister of Housing and Local Government, granted requests to build in the Green Belts in Kent (New Ash Green), Birmingham (Chelmsey Wood) and Sheffield (Stannington). He argued that Green Belts could strangle a city and that green 'fingers' or 'wedges' were a more appropriate design. Other alternatives included land-use zoning, and less restrictive Green Belts. However, no changes were made to the general policy.

In 1965, Crossman claimed that Green Belts were not performing the recreational role outlined in the original Green Belt proposals. One outcome was the creation of country parks – areas of countryside reserved specifically for urban recreational needs, within easy reach of city populations. By 1974 there were 111 country parks in England and Wales, covering 15 000 hectares, and 141 official picnic sites.

Between 1970 and 1974 Green Belt policy under the Conservative government became more popular, with tightening of controls, and less pressure to develop Green Belt land. This trend continued into the 1980s. As population and economic forecasts indicated less growth, pressures on the Green Belt were thought to be reducing. This was the case with industry, but demand for housing increased. This was due to:

- a reduction in average household size
- demand for larger private housing.

In 1974 less than half of the 14 500 hectares of Green Belt had received government approval. By 1987 over 18 000 hectares were approved. Most of the extensions were to existing Green Belts but some areas such as north-east Lancashire, the Fylde Coast, and Burton upon Trent were new.

There was a political bias to the use and development of Green Belts. The typical resident of Green Belt areas was Conservative-voting and relatively wealthy. Many of the Home Counties urban fringe residents and councils did not want large influxes of poorer, inner city people who might vote for the Labour party. Moreover, the local population would then have to provide resources for the newcomers through higher rates.

Under the Conservative government, 1970-74, the Green Belt gradually became primarily a mechanism to control urban development. In the South East it became part of an overall restrictive growth strategy. However, in 1979 with the arrival of the Conservative government under Margaret Thatcher, a general de-restriction of land use controls applied to local authority Green Belt land. Attempts to allow developments on Green Belts were linked with the Conservative government's desire to allow more private development and less state involvement.

In the 1980s, the most important additions to Green Belt policies were related to urban regeneration. The idea was to restrict growth in **green field sites** so that developers would have to use the **brown field sites** (derelict/abandoned land) in inner urban areas; this would help to regenerate the inner cities. This policy proved to be popular with planners as it united inner and outer cities in defence of Green Belts.

---

### QUESTION

**1** Describe and explain how the idea of Green Belts has developed since the late nineteenth century.

---

## PRESSURES ON GREEN BELTS

Today, in the 1990s, Green Belt policy commands even wider support than it did in the 1950s. The policy has changed little since its inception – the 1988 Department of Environment (DoE) booklet is almost the same as its 1962 predecessor.

For many people the most important aspect of Green Belts is the preservation of the countryside and the provision of green areas. A recent survey showed strong support for the Green Belt:

- 82% thought that Green Belts should be preserved at all costs
- 77% felt that shopping centres should not be built in Green Belts
- 60% did not think that industry and office development should be allowed, even if they created jobs.

Nevertheless, demands for new housing and employment have been largely met on Green Belt land (Figure 4.3). For example, Birmingham's National Exhibition Centre and the Nissan car plant at Washington are both on former Green Belt land, and most of the new housing developments, notably the Blackbird Leys estate in Oxford, are on Green Belt land (although the status of this land is in dispute) (Figure 4.4).

There are many pressures to use Green Belt land. These include:

- a shortage of residential land
- the need for more employment
- allowing industry to take advantage of the opportunities in the South East provided by the M25
- allowing regional growth in the South East
- the very high prices that developers are prepared to pay for land with planning permission.

**Figure 4.3** *Up to about four million houses need to be built by 2016. Although there are calls to build on 'urban brown field sites' it is often easier for developers to use green field and green belt sites as illustrated*

**Figure 4.4** *Suburban developments on Oxford's inner Green Belt*

**Figure 4.5** *Mineral working – a conforming land use?*

Moreover there are many pressures on Green Belts from 'appropriate developments' such as agriculture, sport, mineral extraction and transport (Figure 4.5). Some land uses which conform to development restrictions have created severe problems. These include:

● intensification of agriculture
● diversification of agriculture
● mineral workings
● sports stadia.

Consequently, many parts of the Green Belt are run down and unattractive.

There are great pressures on Green Belts for development. The M25 is built almost entirely on London's Green Belt. Completion of the M25 motorway has attracted the attention of developers for commercial and industrial purposes. The south-east of England continues to attract large-scale developments, such as Stansted Airport, Heathrow's fifth terminal and the Channel Tunnel. Many of the high-tech industries located in the South East experience considerable difficulties in recruiting staff because house prices in the region are usually higher than elsewhere in the country.

There has also been a noticeable increase in the demand for new housing in the South East. Estimates for 1981 to 1991 were as high as 720 000 (DoE) and 820 000 (Consortium Developments). Between 1991 and 2001, it is thought that a further 460 000 new homes will be needed in the South East, an increase of 14% (Figure 4.7, see page 46). Many of these are in the Thames Gateway – the area stretching from the East End of London to the Medway Towns and Southend (Figure 4.6).

In August 1997, the Labour government brushed aside environmental opposition and approved the building of a £1.5 billion semiconductor plant on a site on Birmingham's Green Belt. The government argued that the loss of 60 hectares of Green Belt was justified by the urgent need for high-technology investment in the West Midlands. The new plant could create as many as 4000 new jobs. Several international electronics groups, such as Phillips, are keen to invest in the region. Indeed, the German manufacturers, Siemens, who located their £1 billion investment in the North East wanted to locate in the Midlands but could not find a suitable site. If Green Belt land is to be made available, then the regeneration of the Midlands economy may be made easier. In addition to the industrial site, the

Plans for a 'Golden Corridor' of development could create as many as 182 000 jobs and 128 000 houses. Even the lowest estimates are 85 000 jobs and 60 000 houses. The aim is to regenerate the area east of London, an area associated with poor communications and high rates of deprivation. At the same time it would relieve pressure to the west of London. Although the area includes Green Belt, the Environment Secretary Michael Howard said 'there is no danger of us concreting over the Green Belt. It is not necessary'.

**Figure 4.6** *A Golden Corridor of new jobs and homes*
*Source: adapted from Daily Mail, March 1993*

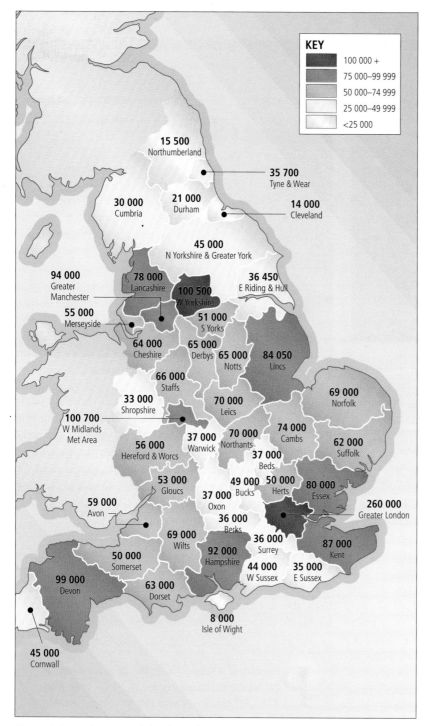

**KEY**

| | |
|---|---|
| | 100 000 + |
| | 75 000–99 999 |
| | 50 000–74 999 |
| | 25 000–49 999 |
| | <25 000 |

15 500
Northumberland

35 700
Tyne & Wear

30 000
Cumbria

21 000
Durham

14 000
Cleveland

45 000
N Yorkshire & Greater York

94 000
Greater
Manchester

78 000
Lancashire

100 500
W Yorkshire

36 450
E Riding & Hull

55 000
Merseyside

51 000
S Yorks

64 000
Cheshire

65 000
Derbys

65 000
Notts

84 050
Lincs

66 000
Staffs

33 000
Shropshire

70 000
Leics

69 000
Norfolk

100 700
W Midlands
Met Area

56 000
Hereford & Worcs

37 000
Warwick

70 000
Northants

74 000
Cambs

62 000
Suffolk

37 000
Beds

53 000
Gloucs

49 000
Bucks

50 000
Herts

80 000
Essex

59 000
Avon

37 000
Oxon

260 000
Greater London

36 000
Berks

69 000
Wilts

36 000
Surrey

87 000
Kent

50 000
Somerset

92 000
Hampshire

44 000
W Sussex

35 000
E Sussex

99 000
Devon

63 000
Dorset

8 000
Isle of Wight

45 000
Cornwall

**Figure 4.7** *New houses needed in the UK by 2016*
Source: Daily Mail, August 1996

government announced a £400 million relief road for northern Birmingham to be built on Green Belt land – transport is, however, permitted in Green Belts, whereas industrial development is more rigorously controlled.

Parts of the Green Belts have been spoiled by rubbish tips, gravel extraction and quarrying, disused railway lines, and derelict buildings. In addition, farming on the urban fringe is often blighted by vandalism, pollution and planning controls. This may cause farmland to be underused so that, in time, it becomes run down and derelict. It can then have its Green Belt status removed and developers can use it for other purposes.

In addition:

- disused hospitals become vacant – due to changing government policy, large sites have become available for extensive and expensive private development, such as the Shenley mental hospital site in Hertfordshire
- changes in farming, such as pick-your-owns and recreation facilities, create additional pressures. These are related in part to the increased volume of traffic on the road but also changes to buildings.

However, in the mid 1990s some of the pressures on the Green Belt from agriculture and mineral working have been lessening, as many sand, gravel and chalk pits have reached the end of their productive life. The quality of some public land, especially on the inner edges of the belt, is not very high, and positive steps are now being taken to improve and restore it. These include:

- developing country parks
- creating community forests
- land use management
- upgrading of footpaths
- improving public access.

---

## QUESTIONS

**1** Study Figure 4.7. Where is the demand for new housing highest? What are the implications of this for Green Belt land? Use examples to support your answer.

**2** Why is there an increased demand for housing if Britain's total population is staying at approximately the same level? Give at least **two** reasons.

**3** What is more important – economic development or environmental protection? Use examples to support your answer.

# Case study and decision making exercise: Oxford's green belt

Oxford has one of fourteen Green Belts in England. Most of it was created in the 1950s and it extends for about six miles from the built-up area. It includes river meadows, fields and flanking hills. It was deliberately drawn tight around the city in order to protect Oxford's unique green setting. However, there have been many problems in trying to maintain the inner Green Belt, which still has only unofficial status and some development has taken place (Figure 4.8). This is partly as a result of conflicting interests in the Green Belt. Moreover, Oxford's Green Belt is divided between five district councils. This gives developers greater chance of obtaining planning permission from one of the districts.

Many people have made the mistake of assuming that Oxford's Green Belt forms a protective corridor around the city. It does provide a green frame or back-ground for its historic buildings, but it is not immune to development. The belt is being continually pushed back, or cut into by roads and sports facilities. There is a strong case for more housing, shopping, park-and-ride schemes and job creation, but whether this should take place in the Green Belt is under fierce debate.

Much land in Oxford's Green Belt has already been developed:
- the Pear Tree park-and-ride and service station covers 14 hectares of Green Belt (Figure 4.8)
- there is a substantial housing development at Blackbird Leys
- a golf course at Hinksey Hill opened in the mid-1990s
- there are plans to establish an inter-faith Centre at Westminster College
- the University has decided to build a world class business centre
- there are plans for an international centre for Islamic Studies, complete with minarets that would alter Oxford's historic skyline.

Now that Oxford's last piece of derelict brown land has been developed, the pressures on the Green Belt are greater than ever, yet Oxford's Green Belt has never had a proper management policy, partly because it is covered by five different local councils. The Oxford Preservation Trust has proposed the creation of an Oxford Green Belt Watchdog, similar to those which oversee the Green Belts around Cambridge and London. The Watchdog would include interested parties such as the Council for the Protection of Rural England and the Countryside Commission.

Superstores and science parks used to be seen as the biggest threat to the Green Belt. Now, housing, roads, golf courses and recreation facilities are seen as bigger threats. Developments on Oxford's Green Belt include an all-weather athletics tracks at Horspath and a proposed sports fields at Kidlington

(Stratfield Brake). Oxford United's new sports ground is located on Green Belt land and large areas of the Cherwell Valley are seen as particularly vulnerable to the expansion of college sports grounds (Figure 4.8). Park-and-ride schemes were intended to reduce traffic problems in the city centre but have added to the pressure to release more Green Belt land.

But a much bigger problem for conservationists is whether much of the Green Belt land is worth saving. The current agricultural value of the land is quite low, and the land is often poorly farmed. Some landowners are even allowing their land to deteriorate so that it can be removed from the Green Belt and sold to property developers. Some land is misused, attracting dumping. Deteriorating environments encourage councils to take more land out of the Green Belt when Structure Plans (local plans) are revised.

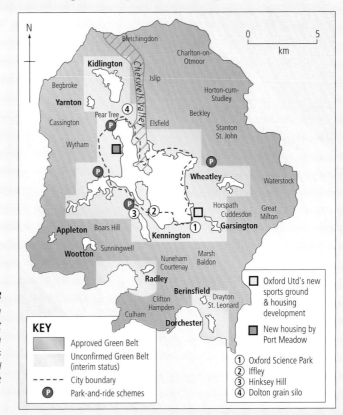

**Figure 4.8**
*Sites of pressure on Oxford's Green Belt*
Source: updated from Scargill, I., 1984, Oxford's Green Belt, Oxford Preservation Trust

**KEY**
Approved Green Belt
Unconfirmed Green Belt (interim status)
- - - - City boundary
Ⓟ Park-and-ride schemes

☐ Oxford Utd's new sports ground & housing development
◼ New housing by Port Meadow

① Oxford Science Park
② Iffley
③ Hinksey Hill
④ Dolton grain silo

**Figure 4.9** *Summertown, Oxford. Notice the use of the Green Belt for recreation at the bottom of the photograph and for farming at the top. The linear shape of Summertown (on a gravel terrace) means that all traffic is concentrated on just two roads*

Pressure to use the Green Belt comes not just from developers. University colleges own considerable amounts of land in and around Oxford and they are very keen to take advantage of the inflated land prices. For example, Oriel College plans to develop 7 hectares of meadow, in the Green Belt close to the village of Iffley (Figure 4.8), into a sports ground, citing the government's budget cuts as their reason. If Oriel College builds on the Green Belt, it is likely that other colleges will follow suit. The riverside meadows, much of which is owned by the colleges, and which give Oxford its unique rural setting, are very vulnerable.

The 30 hectare Oxford Science Park on the edge of Oxford is an on-going development within the Green Belt. It has been developed as a partnership between Magdalen College, Oxford and the Prudential Assurance Company Limited.

Companies that have located there include Sharp Laboratories of Europe and Rand Information Systems Ltd. Sharp Laboratories of Europe were established in 1990 as Sharp's first overseas based Research and Development centre. The custom-built factory was opened in 1992. Their activities include research into optoelectronics and information technologies. Rand specialise in software systems, and they have based their European headquarters at Oxford.

In 1996 Oxford City Councillors allowed plans to go ahead for another proposed project – a Unipart factory site at Horspath, surrounded on three sides by Green Belt land. The crucial problem for the local residents is that the factory will be clearly seen and spoil the area:

- car parking will be allowed on the site
- a 15 metre high factory will be built just 240 metres from the existing houses.

Villagers claim that a process of **'step by step industrialisation'** has destroyed the character of Horspath. Arguments continue as to whether it is in fact inside or outside the Green Belt. Planners claim that as long ago as 1975, a decision was taken to remove Horspath from Oxford's Green Belt; over twenty years later the decision has still not been fully ratified. Oxford United's new stadium is being developed on Green Belt land. Its existing site is too small and safety improvements cannot be implemented. The new 15 000-seater stadium is at Minchery Farm, on the edge of Oxford, and includes a conference centre, a banqueting centre and a fitness centre. There are nearly 2000 parking spaces and spaces for 15 coaches. Other leisure facilities include a hotel and leisure pool which will be built on neighbouring land. In addition, Oxford United have to contribute to:

- the upgrading of the A4074 Sandford interchange
- parking controls in Littlemore and Blackbird Leys
- a new all-weather pitch near the new stadium.

However, in April 1997, funds ran out, and work on the stadium stopped. The result is hardly an appropriate use of Green Belt land (Figure 4.10).

There are plans to build a fifth park-and-ride service into Oxford. However, local residents and the local council are fighting to keep the proposed Kidlington park-and-ride out of the Green Belt. The Gosforth and Water Eaton Parish Council want to protect their environmentally sensitive site, which is vulnerable to vehicle pollution as well as development pressure.

*Figure 4.10* Oxford United's new stadium – funds 'ran out' – hardly an appropriate use of Green Belt land.

Traffic planners are keen to build the 400-space car park at the Dolton grain silo, a disused derelict site, just off the A4165 Oxford Road. They argue that the car park would ease congestion and form an integral part of the Oxford Transport Strategy. This scheme aims to keep traffic out of the city centre. For planners, the grain silo is the best site. The Water Eaton Parish Council want the car park to be located north of Kidlington. This is a very good example of where the local and regional role of the Green Belt has become confused – Oxford City Council wants the park-and-ride to be located at Dolton, but the local residents do not want a park-and-ride on their doorstep. The residents are fighting a local issue, but the Green Belt is a regional plan to contain urban problems.

## QUESTIONS

1 Oxford's Green Belt is divided between five district councils. What problems could this cause? Which interest groups may see this as a positive aspect and why?

2 Briefly explain two contrasting reasons why Oxford colleges are keen to sell their Green Belt land.

3 Explain how Green Belt land can be declassified.

4 How will the new Oxford United stadium affect the Green Belt land?

5 State two contrasting ways in which Oxford's Green Belt has been useful to planners in their attempts to attract and develop industry in Oxford's Science Park.

6 Carry out a questionnaire to find out the views of people in your home area about Green Belts. The following questions will help you to get started:
   • should Green Belts be preserved at all cost?
   • should shopping centres be built in Green Belts?
   • should Green Belts be used to provide low cost housing?
   • should job creation be allowed to take place on Green Belts?

7 'The UK needs more housing, shopping, park-and-ride schemes and job creation. This is far more important than the Green Belt.' Do you agree? Give reasons for your answer.

## SUMMARY

The original function of the Green Belt was to control urban sprawl around London. At the same time that the Green Belt around London was created, a ring of new towns was set up beyond its outer limit and the government of the day organised the dispersal of thousands of people from the bomb-devastated areas of inner London to these towns. Since then Green Belts have been designated elsewhere in the UK. These have grown in size and experienced increasing pressure for development. These pressures are likely to increase. The key issues for the twenty-first century are likely to be:
• should Green Belts be preserved at all costs?
• will landowners continue to run down Green Belt land so that it can be declassified and sold for development?
• are Green Belts seen in a regional context or a local one?
• are the pressures for development national, regional or local?

## QUESTIONS

1 How successful has the Green Belt policy been in achieving its aims? Use examples to support your answer.

2 'Green Belts are 'local issues' for the middle class'. Using specific examples, discuss this statement.

## BIBLIOGRAPHY AND RECOMMENDED READING

**Cullingworth, J. and Nadin, V.**, 1994, *Town and country planning in Britain*, Routledge

**Hall, P.**, 1988, *Cities of tomorrow*, Blackwell

**Hall, P.**, 1992, *Urban and regional planning*, Routledge

**Munton, R.**, 1983, *London's Green Belt: containment in practice*, Allen and Unwin

**Munton, R.**, 1986, The Metropolitan Green Belt, in Clout, H. and Woods, P., (eds.) *London: problems of change*, Longman

**Scargill, I.**, 1984, *Oxford's Green Belt*, Oxford Preservation Trust

**Ward, S.**, 1994, *Planning and urban change*, Paul Chapman Publishing

# Chapter 5
# New towns

In this chapter we look at post-war developments in New Towns, and focus upon the difference between first generation New Towns and second generation New Towns. We also look at New Towns and planned settlements in Egypt and Hong Kong as well as those in the UK.

We have already seen that 'new towns' were developed in the nineteenth century by wealthy philanthropists, in order to improve the living conditions of their workforces. In the early twentieth century, urbanisation had led to overcrowded conditions in the major conurbations and after World War II there was a period of planned rebuilding – New Towns were developed to house the overspill populations (the excess population that could not be housed in large cities).

At the same time, there was unplanned growth in many smaller cities, and in other cities where planning permission had previously been given for housing developments. It is important to bear in mind that planners – especially early planners – needed to predict the future, and plan for conditions that would exist in twenty or even thirty years time. With that in mind, it is fair to say that they have been quite successful.

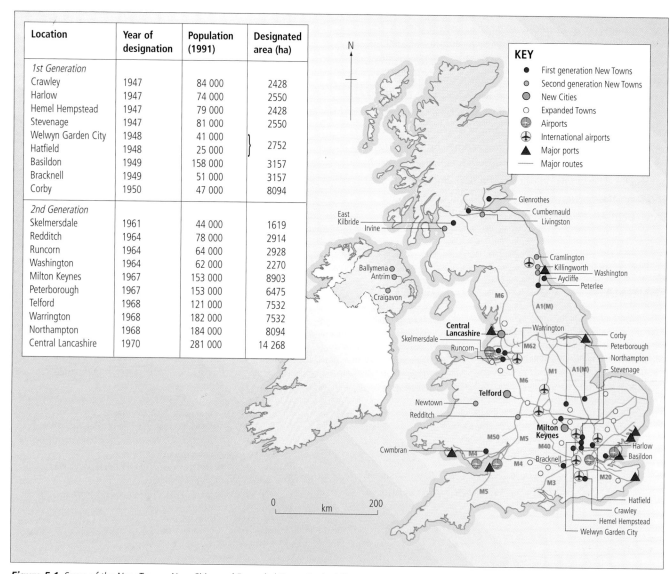

| Location | Year of designation | Population (1991) | Designated area (ha) |
|---|---|---|---|
| *1st Generation* | | | |
| Crawley | 1947 | 84 000 | 2428 |
| Harlow | 1947 | 74 000 | 2550 |
| Hemel Hempstead | 1947 | 79 000 | 2428 |
| Stevenage | 1947 | 81 000 | 2550 |
| Welwyn Garden City | 1948 | 41 000 | 2752 |
| Hatfield | 1948 | 25 000 | |
| Basildon | 1949 | 158 000 | 3157 |
| Bracknell | 1949 | 51 000 | 3157 |
| Corby | 1950 | 47 000 | 8094 |
| *2nd Generation* | | | |
| Skelmersdale | 1961 | 44 000 | 1619 |
| Redditch | 1964 | 78 000 | 2914 |
| Runcorn | 1964 | 64 000 | 2928 |
| Washington | 1964 | 62 000 | 2270 |
| Milton Keynes | 1967 | 153 000 | 8903 |
| Peterborough | 1967 | 153 000 | 6475 |
| Telford | 1968 | 121 000 | 7532 |
| Warrington | 1968 | 182 000 | 7532 |
| Northampton | 1968 | 184 000 | 8094 |
| Central Lancashire | 1970 | 281 000 | 14 268 |

**KEY**
- First generation New Towns
- Second generation New Towns
- New Cities
- Expanded Towns
- Airports
- International airports
- Major ports
- Major routes

*Figure 5.1* *Some of the New Towns, New Cities and Expanded Towns in the UK*
Source: Commission for New Towns Annual Report 1995-1996

| Location features | | | |
|---|---|---|---|
| Crawley | Close to Gatwick Airport and Gatwick Distribution Centre (warehousing). M23 and M25 to Heathrow, M4 and Channel ports. | Redditch | Close to several motorways running north/south and east/west. A strong and varied industrial and commercial base. |
| Harlow | Close to Stansted (London's third international airport), M25 and M11 to Cambridge, the Midlands and the North. | Runcorn | At intersection of M6, M56 and M62, close to Manchester International Airport, with rapid access to Liverpool and west coast ports. |
| Hemel Hempstead | Well-established industrial base. Within easy reach of M1 and M1/M25 interchange for London airports, M4 and Channel ports. | Washington | Close to A1 (M) with rapid access to east coast ports. Nissan's UK manufacturing plant abuts the town boundary. |
| Stevenage | Strong industrial base. Direct access to A1(M), link to M25 for M1, M4, M211, M13, London airports, Channel ports. Near Luton Airport and an important point on London-North high-speed railway. | Milton Keynes | Alongside M1 and only 35 minutes from London by rail. Expanding commercial and industrial base with a range of multi-national companies. |
| Welwyn Garden City | Close to A1(M) link to the M25 for M1, M4, M11, M3 and London airports, Channel ports. | Peterborough | Alongside A1 and only 50 minutes from London by rail. Flourishing commercial and industrial base. Good connections with east coast ports. |
| Hatfield | Close to A1(M) link to the M25 for M1, M4, M11, M3 and London airports, Channel ports. | Telford | Alongside M54 for direct link to M6 and easy access to Birmingham International Airport, Intercity rail network and NEC. Strong international industrial centre. |
| Basildon | A13, A127 arterial routes to London, M25 and east coast ports. Rapid access to Stansted Airport and Tilbury Docks. 30 minutes by train to Fenchurch St. | Warrington | At intersection of M6, M56 and M62, close to Manchester International Airport, with rapid access to Liverpool and west coast ports. |
| Bracknell | High technology 'M4 corridor'. Close to Heathrow Airport. M25 to Gatwick, Channel ports and other motorways. | Northampton | A strong industrial base with a broad range of national and international companies. Close to M1, almost midway between London and Birmingham. |
| Corby | Equidistant between London and Birmingham. Easy access via the new A14 road to M1, M6, A1 and east coast ports. | Central Lancashire | The largest New Town site in UK, includes Preston, Leyland and Chorley. Astride M6 and bordered by M61. |
| Skelmersdale | Adjacent to M58 linking into M6. Greenfield industrial and commercial development opportunities with financial assistance available. | | |

## THE NEED FOR NEW TOWNS IN THE UK

By the early twentieth century, urbanisation had led to over-crowded conditions in the major conurbations. In addition, many of these houses were sub-standard and many were damaged in World War II. Suburbanisation had led to sprawl around the cities and an increase in commuting.

New Towns were seen as the solution to the 'urban problem'. There were three main components in the plans to re-house the UK's population:

- New Towns and New Cities (larger New Towns)
- Expanded Towns
- satellite communities.

Since 1945, thirty-two New Towns have been designated, in two main phases (Figure 5.1). The First Generation New Towns were mainly located around London. The garden cities of Letchworth and Welwyn Garden City were used as models for the First Generation New Towns. These towns were run and controlled by development corporations appointed by the government. Second Generation New Towns were built in the 1960s by the Labour government. These are located in the East Midlands, Wales, the North East and Scotland and were much larger than the first New Towns.

## FIRST GENERATION NEW TOWNS, 1945-60

In 1945, Louis Silkin, the Minister of Town and Country Planning created the post-war New Towns programme, and the New Towns Act of 1946 passed into law very quickly.

## QUESTIONS

1 Study Figure 5.1. Describe the distribution of First Generation New Towns. How does this compare with the distribution of Second Generation New Towns?

2 Using the Nearest Neighbour statistic (page 13), work out the Nearest Neighbour Index for First and Second Generation New Towns. How do you account for these differences?

The model for such towns was:
- a population of 30 000 – 50 000
- self-contained settlements
- neighbourhoods of mixed social classes.

The Labour Party was particularly attracted to the idea of New Towns, providing an 'ideal world' – such idealism was, in part, the result of post war euphoria and the strong social cohesion that the war had created. In addition, the unemployment of the 1930s and the destruction caused by the war created a desire to improve the urban and economic infrastructure of the country.

The first New Town was designated at Stevenage in 1947. However, the local residents of the pre-existing town of Stevenage objected strongly to the new town and called it 'Silkingrad'. (This was a reference to the despotic style of town planning in Russia, where towns were built and named, or renamed, after dictators, for example the historic city of St Petersburg was renamed Leningrad.) Between 1946 and 1950 eight New Towns were designated in southern England with a further six in northern England. The 'urban problem' was seen as being the excessive growth of London: the main aim of the southern New Towns was to house overspill from London. Elsewhere in the country, a major aim was regional development.

Building the early New Towns was difficult:
- they required major planning and infrastructural works
- there was a shortage of construction materials in the early post-war years
- investment in New Towns was limited
- there was bureaucratic muddle and delay
- there were specific problems, such as local opposition by Cheshire County Council to Manchester's plans for a New Town to be located in Cheshire.

By the early 1950s, only 3100 houses had been built in the fourteen designated New Towns. Moreover the Board of Trade, which was responsible for industrial planning and location, refused permission for many industrial developments in the New Towns. The Board argued that New Towns undermined regional policy for existing cities and peripheral areas of the UK, by taking industrial investment away from those areas. Nevertheless, New Towns remained generally popular with the people for whom they were built.

New Towns reflected the aspirations of younger, skilled, inner city working class people for a better life. Housing was good quality and relatively inexpensive. Moreover, it was linked to having a job: those who had found employment in the New Town were allocated new housing.

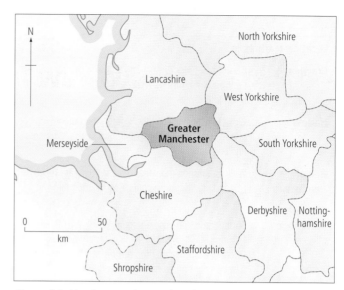

**Figure 5.2** *Manchester and county boundaries*

Unlike other major cities, no New Town was designated for Manchester – sites around Manchester in Lancashire, Cheshire and Derbyshire were investigated, but permission was refused. (A New Town for Central Lancashire was, however, designated in 1970.) Nevertheless, between 1953 and 1973 almost 23 500 new dwellings were built by Manchester City Council on twenty-two **overspill** sites such as Hattersley and Langley, south of Rochdale.

## Expanded towns

However, New Towns were only one arm of the policy which Abercrombie had proposed for Greater London (see Chapter 4). The other aspect was the planned expansion of existing country towns to develop remoter rural areas and thus help to accommodate the overspill. Large, private suburban developments were being built in small and medium sized towns, and in small cities without a Green Belt. The 1952 Town Development Act was passed to allow for industrial development, with grants available from central government. The concept for expanded towns was straightforward:
- the towns would be further from the conurbations than the New Towns
- the towns would have an existing population and existing industries.

Swindon has been the most successful of these in attracting services and manufacturing industry and people. Much of the decentralisation was in fact suburbanisation in areas where Green Belts had not been established. For example, Manchester completed its Wythenshawe estate which had been started during the inter-war years.

---

## QUESTIONS

1 Study Figure 5.2 and explain why Manchester investigated sites in Cheshire, Derbyshire and Lancashire for a possible New Town.

2 What are the implications of county boundaries for urban planning?

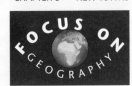

# Case study: **Hemel Hempstead – a First Generation New Town**

In 1947 when Hemel Hempstead was designated as a New Town it had a population of less than 25 000 people. Its location, just 50 km north west of London made it an ideal site. The town was planned to include a large amount of open space, 4.5 hectares per 1000 people (Figure 5.3), with a target population of 80 000 people. The New Town was to consist of fourteen neighbourhoods, an industrial area in the north east of the town, and a town centre. Four families from four London boroughs became Hemel Hempstead's first new residents in 1947.

Since its designation as a New Town, Hemel Hempstead's population has increased by almost 400% (Figure 5.4) and in the 1990s approximately 79 000 people live in Hemel Hempstead. Hemel Hempstead was planned with a classic new town neighbourhood structure. Each neighbourhood consisted of 4000-10 000 people and had its own local shops, pubs, churches and community. About 10 000 new dwellings were built in Hemel Hempstead during the 1950s. They included a wide diversity of housing types and styles, such as starter homes, homes for larger families, accommodation for the elderly, and two- or three-bedroomed homes for low-income families.

**Figure 5.3** *Aerial view of Hemel Hempstead*

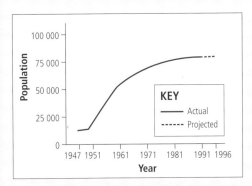

**Figure 5.4** *Population growth in Hemel Hempstead*
*Source: Dacorum Borough Council*

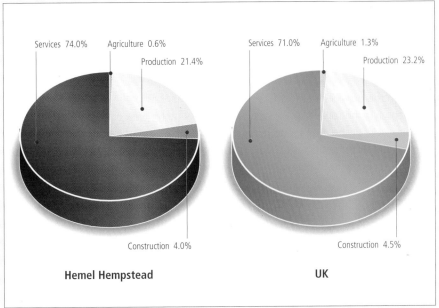

**Hemel Hempstead**

Services 74.0%    Agriculture 0.6%
Production 21.4%
Construction 4.0%

**UK**

Services 71.0%    Agriculture 1.3%
Production 23.2%
Construction 4.5%

**Figure 5.5** *Employment structure in Hemel Hempstead*
*Source: 1991 Census of Employment*

**Figure 5.6** *High-tech industry in Hemel Hempstead*

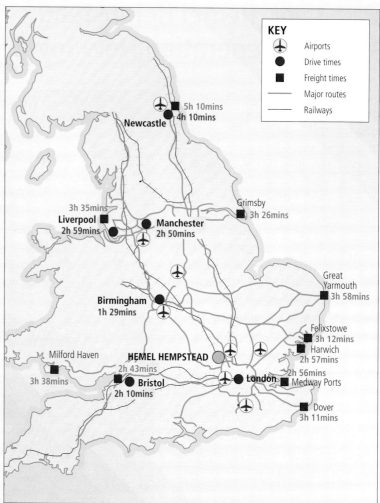

**Figure 5.7** *Location of Hemel Hempstead*
*Source: Commission for the New Towns Annual Report 1995-1996*

Hemel Hempstead is a major employment centre, providing almost 50 000 jobs (Figure 5.5, see page 53). The unemployment rate is about 2% below the national average. It has attracted many large businesses, such as BP and Kodak. The town has a large number of firms in the high technology sector – McDonnell Douglas, Lucas Aerospace, Crosfield Electronics and Bull Information Systems are all major employers in Hemel Hempstead (Figure 5.6).

However, the dominant industrial sector in the town is the service sector which provides 74% of the area's jobs. It has seen a rapid increase since the mid-1980s, particularly in the banking, finance and insurance sector which increased by over 150%. Sports and recreational facilities are an increasingly important sector of Hemel Hempstead's economy – there are a large number of jobs in leisure and recreation. Facilities in Hemel Hempstead include the Dacorum Sports Centre, Rank Leisure World, an eight screen cinema, twenty lanes of ten pin bowling, an ice rink,

two nightclubs and Water World. In the 1990s, Hemel Hempstead town centre was redeveloped, including a complete redevelopment of the town market.

There is a resident labour force of almost 70 000 in the Hemel Hempstead catchment area. In addition, the surrounding area offers an easily accessible pool of labour and there are approximately 470 000 potential employees living within a 30 minute drive of the town centre.
Hemel Hempstead has excellent transport links (Figure 5.7). It is very close to the M1 and M25 motorways so has easy access to many parts of the country. It is on the main Euston railway line with good connections to the north of the UK. It is no coincidence that the main road and rail routes out of London should converge at Hemel Hempstead.

In addition there are three airports within reach: Heathrow, Luton and London City Airport.

## QUESTIONS

1  **Using an atlas, explain why transport routes converge near Hemel Hempstead.**

2  **How useful is Hemel Hempstead's location for economic development?**

3  **What are the disadvantages of Hemel Hempstead's location?**

4  **Explain two reasons why there has been an increase in the leisure industry in Hemel Hempstead.**

5  **Give two reasons why Hemel Hempstead's town centre was redeveloped in the 1990s. Explain your answer.**

**Figure 5.8** *Cycleway in Milton Keynes*

## SECOND GENERATION NEW TOWNS, AND NEW CITIES, 1960-70

In the early 1960s, there was renewed government interest in the idea of New Towns. Between 1961 and 1970, fifteen New Towns and three New Cities were designated. These were mainly in peripheral development areas, unlike the early New Towns which were mostly concentrated in the South East. In particular, the government recognised the attraction of merging New Town and regional growth policies to attract new manufacturing and service industries to disadvantaged regions.

The Second Generation New Towns were not designed as overspill towns but cities with important **multiplier** effects. For example, investment in industrial development brings an increase in employment in the building and other industries and the utilities. The workers need to be housed, clothed and fed, while their children need to be educated and cared for. This increases employment in the service industry. Thus, the initial investment can lead to many increases in employment in other economic sectors.

The later New Towns were very different from the earlier ones:

- larger population sizes, generally with a target population of between 100 000 and 250 000
- higher population densities
- greater architectural variety and creativity
- more private developments and home ownership
- greater awareness of the role of private transport
- large supermarkets instead of shopping parades.

### QUESTION

**1**  In what ways did the Second Generation New Towns differ from the First Generation New Towns? Why was this so?

## Inset 5.1
# Industry and the New Towns and Cities

Britain is one of the most successful countries in attracting inward investment. By 1997, over 1300 companies had invested in the UK. New Towns and Cities have been very successful in attracting their share of this inward investment. Telford has the highest concentration of Taiwanese companies in the UK, and Milton Keynes has the largest number of Japanese companies outside London.

New Towns have had to sell themselves on their merits, since many were denied assistance from the Board of Trade, which believed they would attract industry away from cities. Instead, they gave incentives to areas believed to be in decline. Most New Towns were well able to do this. The growth in population encouraged companies to locate there. The level of home ownership in New Towns created a demand for goods and services – this in turn increased employment opportunities. A multiplier effect existed and New Towns often had above average skilled employment.

Large companies account for only a small proportion of the 50 000 companies operating in New Towns. In Milton Keynes, over 70% of the town's companies employ ten people or less. But these only account for 14% of the town's employment; at the other end of the scale, 1% of the companies employ 35% of the workforce.

Small companies are attracted to New Towns for a number of reasons:

- recruits are easy to train, being younger and less militant compared with the workforce in large cities or old declining areas
- there is a young population structure
- overheads are low
- expansion opportunities are good.

### QUESTIONS

**1**  Briefly explain the advantages of a New Town for the location of industry.

**2**  How do New Towns compare with traditional inner city areas?

# Case study:
# Milton Keynes – a New City

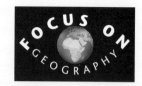

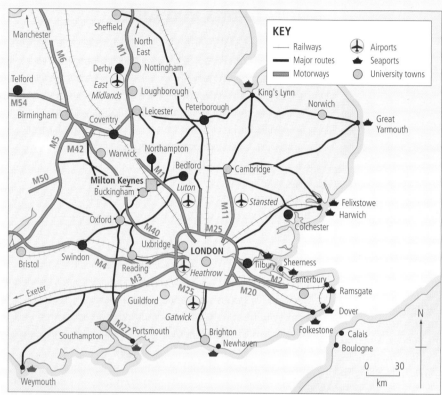

**Figure 5.9** *Location of Milton Keynes*
*Source: Reproduced by kind permission of the Commission for the New Towns, Central Business Exchange, 414-428 Midsummer Boulevard, CMK, MK9 2EA*

**Figure 5.10** *Land use in Milton Keynes, 1992*
*Source: Reproduced by kind permission of the Commission for the New Towns, Central Business Exchange, 414-428 Midsummer Boulevard, CMK, MK9 2EA*

Milton Keynes was designated as a New City in 1967. It covered a site of about 9000 hectares and was planned to accommodate 200 000 people (Figure 5.9). The original settlements on the site comprised four small towns and thirteen villages. These housed about 40 000 people. The Milton Keynes Master Plan identified a number of main principles (Figure 5.10):

- traffic segregated from pedestrians
- a dispersed series of centres
- a high proportion of open space (Figure 5.11)
- opportunities and freedom of choice for people and industry
- public participation in the development of the town.

Milton Keynes was designed to be a low density, high quality urban environment. Housing accounts for 41% of Milton Keynes land use, and on average housing density is about 27 dwellings per hectare. A further 20% of the land has been left for recreational use.

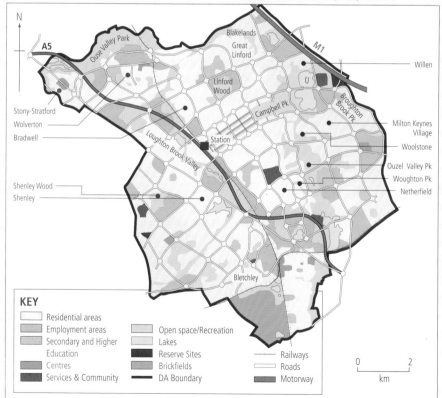

**KEY**

| | |
|---|---|
| Residential areas | Open space/Recreation |
| Employment areas | Lakes |
| Secondary and Higher Education | Reserve Sites |
| Centres | Brickfields |
| Services & Community | Railways |
| | Roads |
| | DA Boundary |
| | Motorway |

0    2
km

**Figure 5.11** *Adding value in Milton Keynes – images of a tranquil environment are used to promote Milton Keynes*
*Source: Reproduced by kind permission of the Commission for the New Towns, Central Business Exchange, 414-428 Midsummer Boulevard, CMK, MK9 2EA*

The main business, commercial, administrative and social centre is in central Milton Keynes. However, it retains a dispersed character, partly as a result of the large number of pre-existing settlements that were incorporated. This also gives it a very different character from most of the First Generation New Towns, which were criticised for their lack of variety of housing, and thus social class.

The road network was designed in a grid pattern dividing the area into neighbourhood blocks. The criteria for the design of the housing within each square were:

- those least likely to have their own car should have access to public transport
- to attract affluent residents there should be attractive, large houses
- open spaces would be used to make the town more attractive and lower the overall housing density
- each neighbourhood should contain a primary school, a shopping centre, a public house, a health centre and a community centre.

Milton Keynes attaches great significance to **sustainability** – environmental, economic and social. For example, it has 1200 energy efficient houses, and 66% of households take part in a recycling programme. All homes built in Milton Keynes between 1986 and 1992 were at least 20% more energy efficient than required by building regulations.

Like any settlement, Milton Keynes has its good and bad points. It has succeeded in many ways:

- it has attracted 3000 businesses
- it employs over 90 000 people
- it has a wide range of commercial and social facilities
- it is home to the Open University.

On the other hand, it has a reputation for being drab (Figure 5.12), and many of its pedestrian walkways, although generally improved, are perceived as underlit and unsafe.

**Figure 5.12** *Milton Keynes' famous concrete cows*

---

**QUESTIONS**

1 Briefly describe three positive aspects of Milton Keynes.

2 Would you like to live in Milton Keynes? Explain the reasons for your answer.

3 To what extent do you think Milton Keynes is a 'city of the future'?

---

## The end of an era

New Towns have had their successes:
- they house over 2 million people in over 500 000 homes
- they have attracted over 1300 foreign companies
- they have created over 11 000 hectares of open space
- 50 000 companies employ over one million people in New Towns
- 120 Japanese companies have set up in New Towns, 50 of them in Milton Keynes
- pedestrianised shopping centres were first developed in the UK in New Towns
- the first science park was at Warrington New Town
- some of the largest and most innovative leisure developments, such as multiplex cinemas and artificial ski slopes, have been built in New Towns
- sustainable energy schemes have been tried and tested in many New Towns
- New Towns have the country's largest recycling schemes
- they have protected large areas of Green Belt from development
- there are over 1100 schools in Britain's New Towns.

Several New Towns can boast outstanding environmental amenities: Telford has the Ironbridge Gorge, a World Heritage Site; Bracknell has over 80 wildlife sites; in the North East, the Washington Wildfowl and Wetlands Centre is a major tourist attraction.

The end of the New Towns era began in the mid 1970s. For the Labour Party, New Towns were becoming a problem because they attracted jobs, skilled workers and public investment away from the inner cities; the Conservatives saw them as part of the welfare state. The Conservative government in the early 1980s saw New Towns as a profitable, publicly owned organisation which could be privatised. By the 1980s, the Environment Minister, Michael Heseltine, began to wind up the New Towns, by privatising them to the Commission for New Towns (CNT).

## NEW TOWNS IN OTHER COUNTRIES

### Egypt's new cities

Cairo has a number of urban problems – notably over-crowding, lack of living space, lack of water, unemployment and poor transport facilities. Egypt has embarked upon a new towns programme to decentralise the population away from Cairo. There are similarities and differences between the UK experience and the Egyptian experience.

Egypt's government has adopted planning policies based on development away from the main city, Cairo. It has devised a strategy for developing **satellite towns** (new towns at the edge of the exisiting centre) and previously unused areas of the country (Figure 5.13).

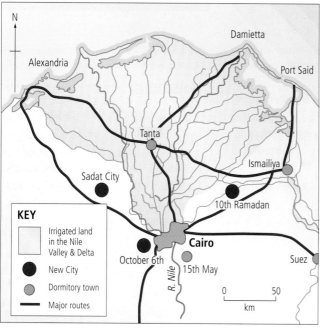

**Figure 5.13** *Location of Egypt's new cities*
*Source: Wood, D., Cairo: urban problems and solutions, GeoActive 156, 1997*

Some of the new cities, such as El Obour and 15th May City, are intended to provide integrated urban development close to, and under the influence of, Cairo, and as such are dormitory towns. Other towns, such as 10th Ramadan City, are designed to be free-standing, self-sustaining developments. In addition, some new cities have been located in previously unused areas in the Sinai desert.

The new cities strategy gathered pace in the mid-1970s and, although successful, it has not slowed growth in Cairo. Unlike the UK, where the New Town policy was aided by a restrictive Green Belt policy, there have been no restrictions on the growth of Cairo. In the absence of any restrictive policy, the New Towns have had to attract development through a mixture of increased salaries for workers, rent subsidies on industrial and residential premises, and tax holidays for new industries.

Sadat City is a New Town situated between Cairo and Alexandria which has been developed as a self-sufficient, independent city (Figure 5.14). It is far enough away from both towns to prevent commuting, but close enough to Cairo International Airport and Alexandria's port to encourage industrial development. Its economic base is mainly industrial, although there are some government departments, university research and development centres, and a construction industry.

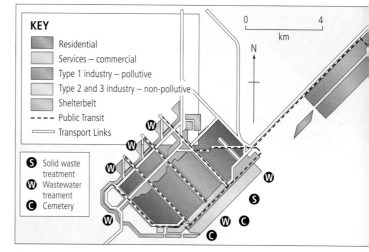

**Figure 5.14** *Land use planning in Sadat City*
*Source: Cairo University & M.I.T., 1979*

Sadat City has a number of special features, notably its neighbourhoods and districts. Each neighbourhood consists of 4000-6000 people and includes a primary school, a nursery, and transport links. Six neighbourhoods combine to form a district which provides preparatory and secondary education, health centres, social services, and religious facilities.

The target population of Sadat City is 500 000. People are attracted to the city by low land costs, job opportunities, cheap housing, higher wages and low taxes. However, the scheme has not attracted many low income households as the cost of housing is still too expensive for them despite the promises of cheap housing.

The 15th May City in Helwan is a New Town twenty miles south of Cairo on the east bank of the Nile. It has become one of the largest industrial developments in Egypt, employing more than 150 000 people in heavy industries, such as steel and cement works. Not enough housing has been provided, however, and up to 60 000 people commute from Cairo to Helwan daily to work.

The 15th May City covers an area of just over 1000 hectares and will eventually house 150 000 people. Unlike Sadat City, there has been a greater attempt to house people with all levels of income. Only 7% of houses are available for high income groups; the majority have been made available for low income (65%) and middle income groups (28%).

Like Sadat City, 15th May City has been divided into neighbourhoods and districts. Six neighbourhoods, each with a population of about 25 000, form a district. Each district provides a secondary school, two preparatory schools and a community green area. Two districts in turn form a 'quarter' which has administrative and commercial facilities.

Egypt's largest New Town is 10th Ramadan City, an integrated, self-sufficient development on the north side of Cairo (Figure 5.15). It has a target population of 500 000 and when finished, will cover an area of over 30 000 hectares. Up to 40% of the land will be residential, 20% industrial, 24% for transport, 10% for open spaces and green areas, and 10% for services and commercial functions.

***Figure 5.15*** *10th Ramadan City*

Each neighbourhood contains about 5000 people and provides a school, mosque and neighbourhood centre. Eight neighbourhoods combine to form a district, which provides a greater range of services and amenities such as a secondary school, more shops, cinema, police station, post office and health clinic. Higher order services, such as hospitals, high schools, and speciality shops, are found in the city centre. Large-scale industrial development has been located on the edge of the town.

## Hong Kong's new towns

Unlike Egypt which has a great deal of land, albeit 95% desert, Hong Kong has very little available land. Nevertheless, the speed and scale of New Towns construction in Hong Kong is impressive. Until the late 1970s, most of Hong Kong's five million inhabitants were crowded into Hong Kong Island and Kowloon, just 83 square kilometres in area. It was, and remains, very densely populated, partly due to the youthful population structure and partly due to influxes of refugees from China and Vietnam. Until the New Towns programme, population growth had resulted in the expansion of squatter settlements on steep, unsafe hillsides (see *Hazards*, in this series, for a discussion of the Hong Kong landslides of 1966).

The New Towns programme was officially started in the mid-1960s but accelerated after 1973. The scheme aimed to rehouse squatters, boat-dwellers and people who were living in substandard housing. The results have been impressive. Over two million people are housed in three New Towns (Figure 5.16, on page 60), the majority in cheap, public housing. Given the lack of flat land in the region, much of the new development has been on land reclaimed from the sea. In addition to the New Towns, there are expanded towns and rural townships. These represent the second and third levels of the New Towns programme. As in the UK, developments in expanded towns have been grafted onto existing towns. Rural townships, on the other hand, were undeveloped, isolated rural settlements which have been enlarged into towns.

There have been some problems. Many of the settlements lacked a full range of services and amenities. Large-scale manufacturing has been introduced into some towns, and this has had a negative impact upon the local environment. Some New Towns in Hong Kong have been criticised for their lack of 'atmosphere' and recreational facilities for young people. On the other hand, they are generally crime-free and lack the social problems of even more densely populated areas.

The example of Hong Kong is an interesting contrast to the UK and Egypt. It is much smaller, has a large migrant/refugee population and it has much steep land. In addition, following the handing back of Hong Kong from UK to Chinese rule in 1997, it remains to be seen if internal migration to Hong Kong will continue, and how the Chinese authorities will manage population and settlement in Hong Kong and Kowloon.

---

## QUESTIONS

**1** How do the new cities in Egypt differ from those in the UK?

**2** Which country do you think has been most successful in its provision of New Towns, and why?

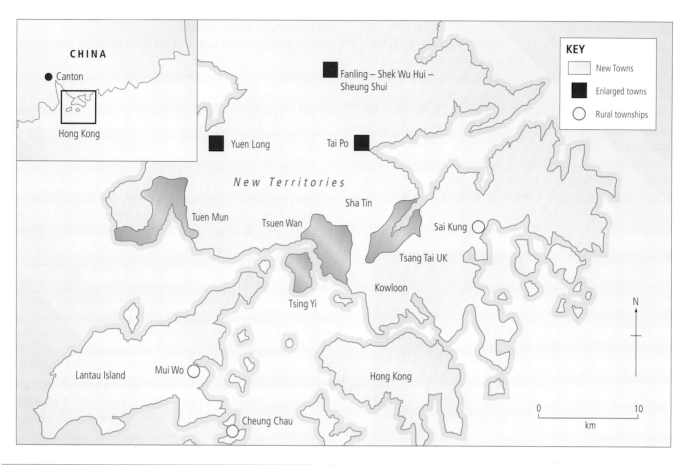

*Figure 5.16*
*Hong Kong's New Towns*
*Source: Phillips, D. R., New Towns bring hope for expanding Hong Kong, Geographical Magazine, December, 1980*

## QUESTIONS

1 Using an atlas, explain why land prices, and population densities, are so high in Hong Kong.

2 How do the pressures for housing in Hong Kong differ from those in **(i)** the UK and **(ii)** Egypt?

## SUMMARY

In this chapter we have seen that New Towns in the UK have had mixed fortunes. They grew in response to a number of conditions that no longer exist or are much reduced. These included:

- polluting heavy industries
- overcrowded living conditions
- low levels of private car ownership.

On the positive side, they house over two million people and they have created many jobs. There is very often a strong environmental focus. But there are a number of problems:

- rigid land use zoning has increased the amount of commuting
- a social balance has not always emerged in some New Towns.

As the number of households in the UK could increase by over 4 million by 2016, there is an urgent need for urban planning solutions to accommodate the required new housing developments.

## QUESTIONS

1 How far did New Towns contribute to inner city decline?
2 Compare and contrast the first generation New Towns in the UK with the later New Towns and the expanded towns in terms of location, size, economic characteristics and land use.
3 To what extent can New Towns be regarded as sustainable towns?
4 'New Towns were just a part of the welfare state, designed to produce enough high quality labourers for the industries that moved there.' Discuss.

## BIBLIOGRAPHY AND RECOMMENDED READING

**Commission for the New Towns**, 1996, *Annual report and accounts 1995-1996*, CNT

**Hall, P.**, 1992, *Urban and regional planning*, Routledge

**Manners, G.**, Decentralising London, 1945-1975, in Clout, H. and Woods, P., (eds.) *London: problems of change*, Longman

**Open University**, 1973, *The New Town idea*, Open University Press

**Ward, C.**, 1992, *New Towns home towns*, Gulbenkian Foundation

**Ward, S.**, 1994, *Planning and urban change*, Paul Chapman Publishing

## WEBSITE

The Commission for New Towns – http://www.cnt.org.uk/

# Chapter 6
# Changing cities

In this chapter we look at the nature of cities and examine some of the changes that have taken place over the last 30 years. We focus upon inner cities and retailing. These illustrate the diverse nature of change in cities. We use case studies from the UK (Oxford), USA (New York and Los Angeles) and the Netherlands (the Randstad) to highlight the differences between densely populated areas, such as the UK and the Netherlands, and less densely populated areas, such as the USA. Large and small cities are compared, whilst the Randstad and Los Angeles are examples of cities which lack a definite centre.

## CHANGES IN UK CITIES

Between 1971 and 1981 all the larger cities in the UK lost populations. Inner city losses exceeded 10% in most larger cities, and up to 20% in Liverpool, Manchester and Glasgow. London's population, which peaked at 8.2 million in 1951, fell to 6.7 million in 1981, a fall of 18%. On the other hand, population gains were found in New Towns, rural districts and smaller towns, especially those within commuting distance of London and the West Midlands. Population decline has been greatest in the central areas of conurbations, especially Greater London (Figure 6.1).

## THE NATURE OF THE CITY

In Chapter 1, Rural and urban settlement, we looked at a number of models of urban land use. Although they differed from each other, they had certain features in common: a central business district, a surrounding manufacturing and poorer residential area (the 'inner city') and an expansion of the city on the urban fringe, the periphery.

| District type | Population 1981 (000s) | Overall change 1981-91 | | Natural change (%) | Net migration (%) |
|---|---|---|---|---|---|
| | | (000s) | (%) | | |
| Great Britain | 54 814 | 1392 | 2.5 | 1.7 | 0.8 |
| Greater London: | | | | | |
| Inner London | 2550 | 77 | 3.0 | 4.4 | -1.4 |
| Outer London | 4256 | 7 | 0.2 | 3.0 | -2.8 |
| Metropolitan:* | | | | | |
| Principal cities | 4324 | -185 | -4.4 | 1.2 | -5.6 |
| Other districts | 8702 | -112 | -1.3 | 2.0 | -3.3 |
| Non-metropolitan: | | | | | |
| Cities | 5598 | 49 | 0.9 | 1.7 | -0.8 |
| Industrial areas | 7440 | 128 | 1.7 | 2.4 | -0.7 |
| New Towns | 2686 | 194 | 7.2 | 4.8 | 2.4 |
| Resort, port and retirement | 3368 | 258 | 7.7 | -4.7 | 12.4 |
| Urban and mixed urban-rural | 9840 | 524 | 5.3 | 2.4 | 2.9 |
| Remoter, mainly rural | 6051 | 452 | 7.5 | -0.5 | 8.0 |

*Figure 6.1* Population change, by district type, 1981-91
Source: adapted from Champion, T. et al, 1996, The population of Britain in the 1990s, OUP

* extended urban area and its suburbs

## QUESTIONS

1 Study Figure 6.1 which shows population changes for different types of settlements.

a) Which type of settlement has increased most in population size between 1981 and 1991?

b) Which types of settlement have recorded negative growth during the period?

c) Which settlements have experienced the greatest amount of (i) in-migration and out-migration; (ii) natural increase (birth rates greater than death rates) and natural decrease (death rates greater than birth rates)?

d) What evidence is there to suggest that British cities are dynamic in terms of population change?

## Economic change in inner cities

The inner city sometimes called the 'zone in transition' or the 'twilight zone'. There are a large number of problems in inner city areas and these include:

- old, poor quality housing
- lack of recreational space
- crime
- graffiti
- air pollution
- decline of manufacturing industry (Figure 6.2)
- visual pollution (Figure 6.3)
- ageing population
- racial conflict
- high percentage of immigrants, which is generally linked with racism
- a lack of services
- road congestion
- dereliction (Figure 6.4)
- unemployment.

Inner city areas are areas of industrial decline and job loss. Although job opportunities in the UK generally have fallen, inner cities have fared the worst. There has been a decline in inner city areas of almost 50% in the number of jobs since 1951. Three significant changes in economic sectors are evident:

1 Since the 1950s there has been a **decline in manufacturing** employment. One million manufacturing jobs were lost between 1951 and 1981 in inner city areas alone.

2 **Gains in the service sector**, especially banking, finance, and insurance, failed to compensate for these losses. Many new jobs were filled by commuters from outside the inner city areas. In 1981, 39% of inner city jobs employed commuters. London's Dockland is an excellent example of an island of highly paid white collar workers in an area of poverty and high unemployment.

3 The majority of new employment was for **women**, mostly in jobs which were part time and low paid. In many cases, employment in inner cities was provided by older, less competitive and less innovative enterprises demanding low skills, easily replaced by new technology.

These changes are part of the decline in restructuring all British economy. The inner cities had much of the oldest and least profitable industrial capacity and did not have locational appeal for new investment. Consequently, they were areas of **disinvestment** characterised by massive **outflows** of capital.

The reasons for industrial decline in the UK include:

- increased overseas competition
- reduced demand
- increasing levels of mechanisation
- reduced need for labour.

**Figure 6.2** *Deindustrialisation – over one million jobs have been lost in manufacturing inner-city areas since 1951*

**Figure 6.3** *Some inner city areas are used for recycling waste, and for refuse collection – this reinforces the negative image of many inner city areas – such as here near King's Cross, London*

**Figure 6.4** *Urban decay, St. Pancras, London (part of the few remaining urban tenements that still remain in London)*

## Immigration and segregation in inner cities

Another feature of inner cities is a high proportion of racial minorities. Why should this be so? Since 1945, immigrants have become an important element in the population of many UK cities. In the early 1950s, the majority of immigrants into the UK were Irish and East Europeans. However, later in-migration has been one of the legacies of Britain's colonial past, with immigrants coming from the New Commonwealth and Pakistan (NCWP). For example, a large number of migrants from the Caribbean came to Britain to work for London Transport in the 1950s, largely in unskilled jobs, which would otherwise have remained unfilled. Other migrants have been Asians, who left India and Pakistan to work in Uganda, another Commonwealth country, and who were then forced to leave Uganda by the then president Idi Amin in 1972. A small number of migrants come from Australia and New Zealand.

Racial minorities now account for about 5% of the UK population. However, their distribution around the UK is not even. They are concentrated in the main urban and industrial areas. For example, people of Asian heritage are concentrated in Greater London (200 000), West Midlands (130 000), West Yorkshire (70 000) and Manchester (50 000)

– the large conurbations which have a great deal of employment in low-paid service jobs, such as in transport and in health services. Industrial towns such as Bradford, Leeds and Huddersfield also have high concentrations of ethnic minority groups – these towns are associated with the textile industry and engineering.

The segregation of people of Asian heritage in Leicester has been well recorded. In 1981, out of a population of 300 000, there were 40 000, or about 14% of the population, mainly concentrated into a few areas, such as Highfields, Evington and Belgrave. These are inner city areas (following Burgess's zone in transition), mostly on the eastern side of the city (following Mann's model of a typical UK city) and also along radial transport routes (following Hoyt's model of sectors). The housing is generally quite poor in these areas and is sub-standard in terms of density, central heating and modern amenities. Housing density is among the highest in Leicester. Much of the industry that originally attracted Asian heritage people, in the 1950s, 1960s and early 1970s was concentrated in and around the CBD and inner city – notably textiles, light engineering and services. The pattern is much less clear cut now.

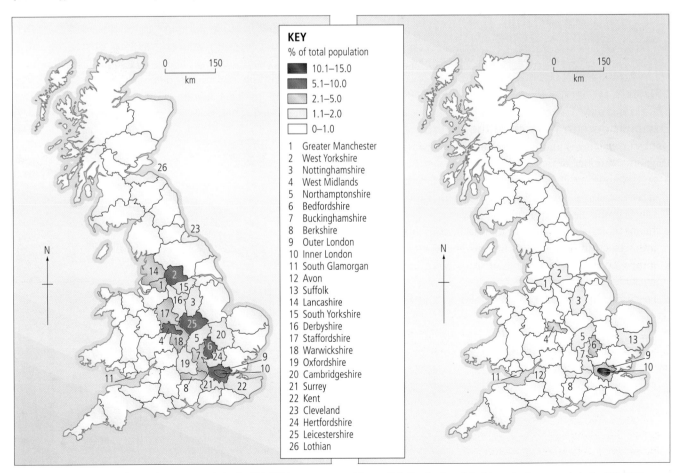

***Figure 6.5*** *Distribution of Asian heritage people in the UK, 1991*
Source: Census 1991, Geofile

***Figure 6.6*** *Distribution of Caribbean heritage people in the UK, 1991*
Source: Census 1991, Geofile

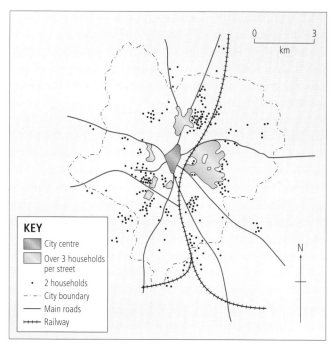

**Figure 6.7** *Distribution of Asian heritage people in Leicester, 1991*
*Source: University of Oxford, Delegacy of Local Examinations*

## QUESTION

1 Describe the distribution of racial minorities at **(i)** a national level (Figures 6.5 and 6.6), and **(ii)** an urban level (Figure 6.7). How do you account for these distributions? Use the models of urban land use in Chapter 1, Rural and urban settlement, to answer this question.

## Economic decentralisation to the suburbs

Unlike inner cities, suburban locations have attracted industries for a number of reasons:

- suburban green-field sites are preferred to urban areas, where there is congestion, few suitable buildings, too much traffic, and high land costs
- firms tap cheap, unskilled female labour in suburban areas because they are less unionised and less militant
- improved access as a result of investment in road networks
- larger production sites are available.

## QUESTIONS

1 Using census data from a CD-ROM, or from your local library, compare an inner city area with a suburban area in terms of deprivation. Use the list of features above to guide you.

2 What are the social, economic, environmental and political problems associated with inner city areas? Use examples to support your answer.

## Retail change in UK cities

Until the 1970s, a threefold-classification of retail outlets in most cities could be described.

1 **Central shopping area** or **high streets** characterised by department stores, chain stores, specialist shops and, increasingly, by pedestrianised malls. Outlets sell mainly high order goods which have a large range and high threshold. The sphere of influence of central shopping areas is generally large.

2 Lower down the hierarchy are **shopping parades** – clusters of shops, usually including a supermarket, off-licence, newsagent and other low order outlets serving nearby residential areas.

3 At the bottom of the hierarchy are **corner shops**, which are generally small, independent outlets, selling a variety of convenience goods, such as food, newspapers, and confectionery (Figure 6.8). They are 'convenient' on account of their long opening hours and wide variety of products carried.

To some extent this picture is still true, although there have been important changes. Modern retailing is changing rapidly as shown by the rapid growth in superstores and retail parks. **Superstores** are large out-of-town outlets, close to residential areas, with more than 2500 square metres of shopping space, ample parking and good road access. DIY, electrical and furniture superstores may cluster to form a **retail park**. Their effect on high street shops has often been very considerable and usually detrimental and, increasingly, government policies favour central shopping areas and neighbourhood schemes over out-of-town developments.

**Figure 6.8** *A low order retail outlet*

The retailing revolution has centred upon superstores, hypermarkets and out-of-town shopping precincts on green-field suburban sites with good accessibility and plenty of space for parking and future expansion. The increasing use of out-of-town shopping centres, on a less frequent basis, has led to the closure of many smaller shops in towns, which depended on frequent convenience trade. The garage retail phenomenon – garages selling a wide range of goods, food, flowers and newspapers – has exacerbated the problem for small town centre shops.

A number of factors explain the changes in retailing:

1 **suburbanisation** and **counterurbanisation** of the more affluent households
2 **technological** change, as more families own deep freezers
3 **economic** change – increased standards of living, especially car ownership
4 **congestion and inflated land prices** in city centres
5 **changing accessibility** of suburban sites, especially those close to ring-road intersections
6 **social changes**, such as more working women.

Retailers have responded in a number of ways. The most noticeable effect is a **polarisation** of retailing: many large retailers have moved into suburban and small town locations in order to capture the younger, more affluent householders, whereas shops in central areas have closed.

For example, the Merry Hill centre, near Dudley, is one of the most successful retailing centres in the UK and has accelerated the decline of retailing in Dudley town centre. Ten major retailers have left high street locations in order to relocate at the Merry Hill complex. It is the UK's second largest retailing centre, containing over 167 000 square metres of retailing space, with a mixture of high street stores and specialist shops, banking, leisure and community services (Figure 6.9). It is the largest tourist attraction in the West Midlands, with 23.5 million visitors annually, of whom 19 million shop there. It is built on the site of the former Round Oaks steelworks, which closed in 1980. Access by car and coach is crucial to its success; it is located on the A4036 with good access to junctions 2 and 3 of the M5.

However, the perceived threat of out-of-town retailing to the town centre has resulted in a variety of attempts to maintain or revitalise retailing in central areas. This is of increasing importance and in some places this has coincided with inner city redevelopment. Renovation may entail full-scale development, as in the case of Princes Square in Glasgow, or it may involve the creation of traffic free zones such as Croydon. However, as a rule, redevelopment only affects small sections of the urban core. Other types of development include covered shopping malls and specialist shopping centres, such as Covent Garden in London.

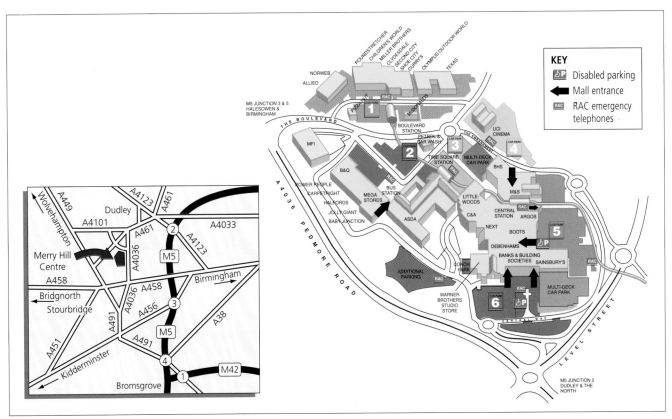

***Figure 6.9*** *The Merry Hill shopping centre*
*Source: Nagle, G. and Spencer, K., 1996, A geography of the European Union, OUP*

*Figure 6.11 Supermarket on the outskirts of Kidlington. Many out-of-town supermarkets offer extensive free parking, as well as having space to expand*

The contrast could hardly be starker. In Merry Hill shopping mall fountains burble beneath glass-domed atriums. Shoppers wander past in weather-proof comfort.

The floors are paved with reconstituted coral and cream marble. Bronze rails gleam beside neo-classical pillars. It is an image of glittering retail success.

Three miles away across the Black Country's sprawl of inter-mingled factories and housing estates, Dudley town centre is expiring slowly.

Boarded up shops present blank facades. The most prominent advertising offers 'closing down sale', 'shop relocation' and 'lease for disposal'.

From his customer-free Millet's store the manager, George Ainslie, looks out bleakly. 'It's completely crucified Dudley, Merry Hill has. There's more people pass my house every day and I live in a cul-de-sac.'

Dudley's decline and Merry Hill's prosperity may feature as a conclusive example of bad planning in the committee's report, but the management of Merry Hill believe they have been unfairly pilloried. Dudley's deterioration long pre-dates the development of the 1.4 million sq ft centre, according to Lesley Marsh, the marketing manager.

'The committee is making comparisons between apples, pears and sausages. We weren't built on a green field site,' she said.

'We have replaced Round Oak steel works, which closed down in the early 1980s, having employed 700 people latterly. We were built in an enterprise zone and we have now created 4000 jobs and attract 25 million visitors a year.'

Merry Hill is now planning further expansion. It intends to create another 2000 jobs in an extra 650 000 sq ft of shops and covered walkways.

*Figure 6.10 The impact of the Merry Hill shopping centre*
Source: The Guardian, November 1994

*Figure 6.12 Dudley town centre*

## QUESTIONS

1 Explain **two** positive aspects and **two** negative aspects of the growth of out-of-town retail outlets.

2 Explain **(i)** the decline of small, independent shops and **(ii)** the growth of large out-of-town retail outlets.

3 How can High Street shopping areas be revitalised? Use examples to support your answer.

4 Read Figure 6.10, a newspaper article on the Merry Hill shopping centre and look at Figures 6.11 and 6.12. What are the 'geographical issues' in the development of out-of-town shopping centres. From the evidence given, evaluate the success of the Merry Hill centre.

## URBAN CHANGE

We have seen that there have been very far reaching changes to cities in recent years. These vary from city to city but all include changes in employment, housing, transport, conservation and finance. These are all affected by national and local government policies. Changes to local political boundaries further complicate the picture.

Although inner cities have been at the top of the agenda for over 20 years they are only part of the urban problem. Other equally important issues include employment, housing, retailing and transport.

# Case study:
# Urban change in a small city – Oxford

Oxford is a small city (population around 110 000), noted for its university and as a centre of tourism. However, it was also an important manufacturing centre – with up to 30 000 people employed at Cowley Car Works. Since the early 1980s manufacturing has declined, but there has been a significant increase in employment in the service industry. Hence the impact of **de-industrialisation** on Oxford has not been as great as in some cities.

As we have seen in Chapter 4, Oxford's growth is limited by its Green Belt. This has created competition for the limited amount of land within the city boundaries. Slum clearances have affected parts of the city centre, such as St. Ebbes, and peripheral estates at Marston, Headington Quarry, Barton, and Blackbird Leys have been built. Since the 1960s, parts of Oxford's inner city, particularly Jericho and St. Clements in East Oxford, have been improved with funding given under the General Improvement Areas Act, as defined by the 1969 Housing Act which awarded grants to landlords to improve their property. In addition, one of the largest public housing developments in Europe in the late 1990s is taking place at Blackbird Leys.

| | |
|---|---|
| **1** | **Traffic:**<br>• congestion on Woodstock and Banbury Roads because of commuting from Woodstock and Witney<br>• parking problems: limited facilities and high costs, e.g. Westgate car park in the city centre<br>• one way system in the city centre, which causes long journeys around the city<br>• narrow streets unsuited to the needs of modern forms of transport, e.g Brewer St., Magpie Lane<br>• lack of access for cars to some streets, e.g. Cornmarket, Gloucester Green |
| **2** | **Housing:**<br>• shortage due to Green Belt planning restrictions<br>• new developments on periphery, notably Barton and Blackbird Leys, on Green Belt land<br>• high cost of land causing high property costs |
| **3** | **Social problems:**<br>• Blackbird Leys (crime, vandalism, joyriding in an area with a large youthful population and high unemployment rate) |
| **4** | **Air pollution, from cars and factories:**<br>• weathering of buildings, e.g. All Souls College, Magdalen College, Sheldonian Theatre<br>• poor air quality |
| **5** | **Services:**<br>• Accident and Emergency (John Radcliffe Hospital) located on the periphery of Oxford |
| **6** | **Schools:**<br>• Many are on the edge of the city and may involve long journeys to school for some groups, for example there is only one Roman Catholic school, and transport to that school could involve a change of 2 or more buses |
| **7** | **Employment:**<br>• redundancies at Cowley: in the 1970s, 25 000 employed at Cowley, in the 1990s approximately 4000 employed |
| **8** | **Zone in transition/inner city area:**<br>• gentrification in Jericho<br>• slum clearance and redevelopment in St. Ebbes and St. Clements leads to population dispersal |
| **9** | **Recreation and open space:**<br>• Oxford is well endowed with open spaces – Port Meadow, Shotover, Christ Church meadows |
| **10** | **Pressures on the periphery:**<br>• out-of-town retailing at Heyford Hill, Park and Ride scheme at Peartree Roundabout, Oxford Science Park. |

*Figure 6.14* Urban issues in Oxford: a summary of examples

**Figure 6.13** Urban Oxford,
showing part of the Blackbird Leys estate

The changes in retailing that many UK cities have experienced have had their effect on Oxford with the closure of many independent specialist shops, for example, the renowned and old-established Needlework Shop in Ship Street. The new retail developments are mainly on the periphery of the city at major road intersections, such as Sainsburys at Heyford Hill. Most of the superstores either sell groceries or are retail warehouses. The main 'branch' of large out of town retailing is located on the Botley Road. It boasts chains of DIY, furniture, carpets, electronics, and leisure retailers, such as Courts, Comet, MFI and Texas. Botley is a very good example of the retail warehouse phenomenon.

There are a number of changes in Oxford city centre which include the proliferation of:

**Figure 6.15** *Urban crime: the Blackbird Leys estate*

- pedestrianised shopping malls, for example, Clarendon and Westgate (popularised from New Town and City developments such as Milton Keynes)

- new shopping centres, such as the Oxford Retail Park on the old Cowley Works on the Eastern by-pass

- emergence of the focus- or niche-retailer exploiting a narrow range of goods / market such as Tie Rack, Sock Shop, and Body Shop. This is a form of **market specialisation**.

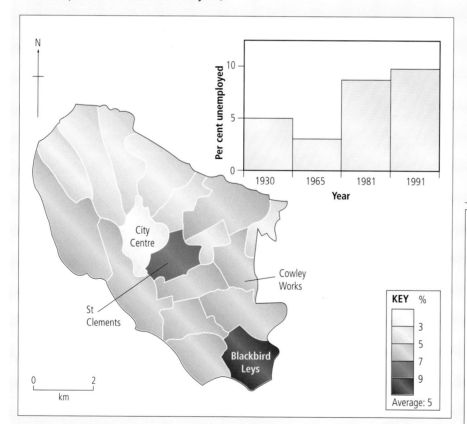

**Figure 6.16** *Unemployment in Oxford – showing concentrations in certain locations and an overall increase*

# Case study:
# Urban change in New York

Unlike Oxford, which is world renowned for its university, New York is known for its cosmopolitan nature, and its concentration of people and economic activities. New York is sited mainly on Manhattan Island but spreads out to Long Island. It is located at the mouth of the Hudson River, on the seaward end of the Hudson-Mohawk valley.

Nearly 18 million people live in the New York built-up area. Four of its five boroughs – Brooklyn, Manhattan, The Bronx and Queen's, would rank amongst the USA's largest cities. New York's annual budget is bigger than any state in the USA and the vast majority of the world's nations.

There are a number of reasons which help explain its spectacular growth:

- historical – New York was one of the first places to be settled by Europeans
- its harbour – this is ice free, experiences little fog and does not require dredging; the tidal range is only 1.5 metres so ships can arrive and depart 24 hours a day
- its location – located at the seaward end of the Hudson-Mohawk gap, New York has very good access to the interior via the Great Lakes and New York State canal, giving it an excellent position for trade (Figure 6.17).
- trading – due to New York's **nodal** position (at a point of concentration of communications) it has developed into a major commercial, financial and industrial centre; this has been further emphasised by the massive internal market in New York's hinterland – over 140 million people .

New York is the largest and most cosmopolitan city in the USA. However, New York's population is declining and changing:

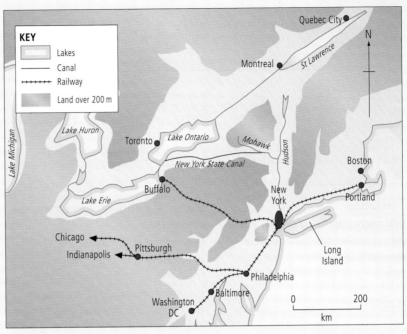

**Figure 6.17** The site and situation of New York City
Source: Young, E. and Lowry, H., 1983, North America, Arnold

- the total population has fallen by over 10% in the last decade
- the white population has fallen from 87% to 65% since 1950
- the middle class population has fallen by 2 million in the past 20 years
- the number of elderly residents has risen by 21% since 1950
- it has the largest black population in the country, 9.1%
- the population of the South Bronx has declined by nearly 50%, since 1981
- almost 1 million New Yorkers receive welfare support.

Most problems of this vast area stem from its rapid economic and social advances which are typical not only of New York, but other large cities as well. They arise from:

- changes in the composition of the labour force
- the high living standards which most US citizens expect
- the social strains set up by the under-educated, unskilled, underpaid and underprivileged minority
- the massive outward migration of the middle class, encouraged by good roads and increased living standards
- the counter movement of lower income families into the inner city.

The policy issues are straightforward:

- provide high quality urban amenities to encourage the middle classes to stay;
- develop welfare and educational programmes to help those who have been trapped by social barriers
- encourage growth in the suburban cities to relieve pressure on the inner cities.

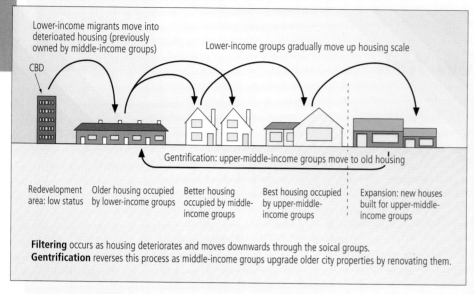

**Figure 6.18** *Filtering and gentrification*
Source: Nagle, G, and Spencer, K., 1997, Advanced geography revision handbook, OUP

In the figure:

Lower-income migrants move into deterioated housing (previously owned by middle-income groups)

Lower-income groups gradually move up housing scale

CBD

Gentrification: upper-middle-income groups move to old housing

Redevelopment area: low status | Older housing occupied by lower-income groups | Better housing occupied by middle-income groups | Best housing occupied by upper-middle-income groups | Expansion: new houses built for upper-middle-income groups

**Filtering** occurs as housing deteriorates and moves downwards through the soical groups.
**Gentrification** reverses this process as middle-income groups upgrade older city properties by renovating them.

## Factors affecting New York and other USA cities

There are a number of issues affecting New York which are relevant to all cities in the USA:

### 1 Centralisation versus decentralisation

The advantages of centralisation include: a greater pool of talent and skills; fiercer competition and more innovation; agglomeration; centralised capital; maximum access and a prestige address. All these advantages apply to Lower Manhattan. However, centralisation causes excessive wear and tear on roads and property, traffic congestion, pollution, constant tearing down and replacing of buildings and intense pressure on living space. These encourage the flight of the middle classes and the inward movement of people from ethnic minorities and poor people, the spread of slums and ghettos, and an increase in ill-health and crime.

Decentralisation spreads the weight of demand out of Manhattan into Long Island, or up the Hudson Valley. It reduces the excessive costs of maintaining the centre, provides green areas and space, and reduces social and class strife.

### 2 Clearance versus rehabilitation in the city centre

Old property is often kept by speculators in an unimproved state to be sold at a later date for office development, multiple stores or as **gentrified** buildings (the upgrading of depressed areas by richer middle-class, young people or 'yuppies'). Often deterioration sets in until slum clearance is necessary to make way for businesses (Figure 6.18).

The inner areas have declined both in terms of population and employment. By contrast, the suburban periphery, which was built primarily as an overflow to the city, has expanded in terms of population and employment. Only 20% of the workers in Westchester

**Figure 6.19** *Most whites have deserted inner city areas and now live in sprawling suburbs*

County (a New York suburb and one of the wealthiest counties in the USA) now commute into the city for their work.

Within New York there is much poverty. Up to 25% of its citizens now live in poverty (as defined by the US Government), and at the start of 1987 there were 50 000 homeless in the city. For example, in the inner city area of the South Bronx the average income is 40% of that of the country as a whole, and one-third of residents are on welfare support (Figure 6.20).

**Figure 6.20** *The South Bronx*

## THE CHANGING FORTUNES OF THE US CITY

The out-migration of business, industries and middle-income residents since the early 1970s from the inner cities in the USA has led to:

- a decline in the populations of all central cities
- a decline in the white population of central cities and an increase in the black population
- a dramatic decrease since 1971 in the average family size – from 3.47 to 3.30 persons – as more and more people live by themselves.

The decline in inner cities was due to a number of inter-related factors:

1 The **post-war baby boom** led to the demand for more and larger houses. Government programmes encouraged the construction of new housing rather than the rehabilitation of older urban housing stock.

2 The **interstate highway system** which was intended primarily as a defence system to enable people and materials to be moved rapidly during emergencies, also enabled commuters to reach the outer suburbs quickly. The construction of these multi-lane highways took large tracts of land from residential and other uses in the inner cities and stimulated the sprawl of the peripheral suburbs.

3 The dominance of the **private automobile** over public transport in cities gave people the freedom to move to the suburbs. From 1945 to 1970, bus rides fell from 23 billion to 6 billion trips per annum.

4 A number of **cultural factors** were also important and had a number of impacts: **a)** The change in factory design from multi-storied mills to horizontal production lines housed in sprawling one-storey buildings required large parcels of land which were difficult to find in the city centres and were expensive. Post-war factory automation reduced the demand for labour in industrial cities and resulted in higher levels of unemployment; labour-intensive industries sought cheaper labour in the newer locations where labour unions were much less strong; the economy moved from one dominated by employment in manufacturing to one dominated by service industries; unemployment increased in inner areas, especially among manufacturing workers. **b)** The movement of white people to the suburbs meant that resident populations of the inner cities were largely people on low incomes, people from ethnic minorities and those either too young or too old to work. Many white people left because crime, public services and environmental quality were deteriorating. The adverse effects of high density living, such as traffic congestion and pollution, also decreased the attractiveness of large cities to both residents and businesses. By contrast, the suburbs were regarded as more attractive, for example, purchasers of residential and business properties reduced their taxes by locating in newer suburban locations.

## Urban revitalisation

In the late 1970s, many US cities, such as Phoenix, Arizona, began to grow again. The 'back to the city' movement was due to a number of factors:

1 Economic:
- the energy crisis of the mid-1970s led to a rapid escalation of energy costs in the large single-family suburban homes
- commuting costs in large cars further strained family budgets
- rapid escalation in the costs of mortgages in the late 1970s and early 1980s placed ownership of the newly built homes beyond the financial reach of 80% of the population
- first-time buyers increasingly looked for smaller, less costly housing units in older urban neighbourhoods – gentrification occurred in many US cities.

2 Demographic:
- average size of households fell as more people chose to live alone, divorce rates rose and birth rates fell
- professional and managerial women postponed marriage and childbirth to concentrate on their careers
- many young people were attracted to living in close proximity to the city centres
- housing units tended to be smaller with a higher proportion of one- and two-bedroom units, rather than the suburban three- or four-bedroom average
- opportunity to renovate and redesign one's living space
- opportunities for home ownership with its considerable tax and investment advantages, through better mortgage relief
- with few or no children, the poor reputation of many urban public schools was not a deterrent to affluent residents who could afford private schools.

3 Leisure opportunities and retail variety:
- the downtown area provides interesting leisure opportunities, consumer choice and services (such as restaurants and dry cleaners which save time).

4 Decline of the older, inner ring of suburbs:
- crime and pollution increased in the suburbs
- some suburbs became too expensive, effectively excluding moderate and even middle-cost housing, making them less attractive to first-time home-buyers.

5 Trends in the national economy:
- during the late 1970s, high inflation rates and slow economic growth encouraged the conservation of existing city centre investments rather than expansion in new areas
- cities already have expensive infrastructures (streets, sewers, water supply) in place; a company expanding in suburbia may be required to provide such services or to pay for part of the cost
- foreign investments in property, offices and industry, for example, in New York and Denver.

## The growth of Los Angeles

We now look at Los Angeles, a US conurbation of over 100 cities with a population double that of London (14 million in Los Angeles as compared with 7 million in London) and covering an area of over 10 000 square kilometres (compared with London with around 1600 square kilometres)! Los Angeles makes an interesting contrast to the other cities that we have looked at because of the number of centres involved and the lack of a unified planning authority (managing the region is therefore almost impossible).

Los Angeles is a huge suburban development and population growth has been rapid. Its growth is linked to a number of industries, including oil, film making, tourism, car manufacturing, defence, electronics and clothing. Not until the 1970s did it have a real centre. This is partly due to the threat of earthquakes which have prevented the construction of tall buildings. Many of the new centres are up to 2½ hours drive from central Los Angeles (Figure 6.21).

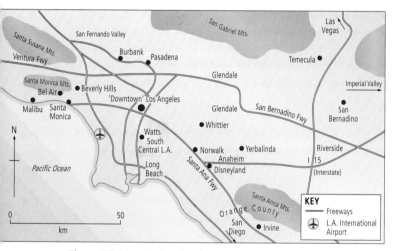

**Figure 6.21** *Greater Los Angeles*
Source: Morris, S.,1997, Los Angeles – urban issues, 1997 Geofile, Stanley Thornes

Los Angeles is one of the most ethnically diverse cities in the USA. Major population groups include Mexicans, Afro-Caribbeans, Filipinos, Koreans and Cambodians. Residential segregation according to ethnic background is very evident. In addition, there are marked variations in socio-economic conditions for racial groups (Figure 6.22) and racial discrimination is widespread. The riots of 1992 broke out in the Watts area which has a high proportion of Hispanics (70%), high rates of unemployment (over 12%), and over three quarters of the population below the poverty line. The area is associated with poor housing conditions, low wages, a lack of public services, and rising crime.

|  | Beverley Hills | Watts | Norwalk |
|---|---|---|---|
| **Age of Housing** |  |  |  |
| Pre 1940 | 35 | 8 | 0 |
| 1940-59 | 31 | 49 | 44.7 |
| 1960-79 | 27 | 27 | 32 |
| Post-1980 | 7 | 15 | 23 |
| **Cars per household** |  |  |  |
| None | 10.7 | 12 | 6.3 |
| 3+ | 16.5 | 16 | 27 |
| **Tenure** |  |  |  |
| Owner occupied | 41 | 35 | 58 |
| Rented | 52 | 63 | 40 |
| Per capita income | $55 463 | $6701 | $10 112 |
| Median income | $48 795 | $23 411 | $45 465 |
| % below poverty line | 6.5 | 28.2 | 8.3 |
| **Occupations** |  |  |  |
| Executive, professional, technical & managerial | 53 | 8.9 | 24 |
| Wholesale & retail | 20 | 7.3 | 10.6 |
| Administrative | 13.4 | 13.9 | 16.6 |
| Service | 8.9 | 12.5 | 14.3 |
| Skilled craft/precision | 3.4 | 39 | 24.6 |
| Transportation | 0.3 | 6.6 | 5.8 |
| Unskilled | 0.5 | 10 | 3.2 |
| **Education (% over 25)** |  |  |  |
| High school | 17.6 | 35 | 71 |
| Graduate | 47 | 3.1 | 12.9 |

**Figure 6.22** *Socio-economic variations in three areas of Los Angeles, 1990*
Source: Morris, S., 1997, Los Angeles – urban issues, 1997 Geofile, Stanley Thornes

# Inset 6.1
# Randstad: a polycentric city region

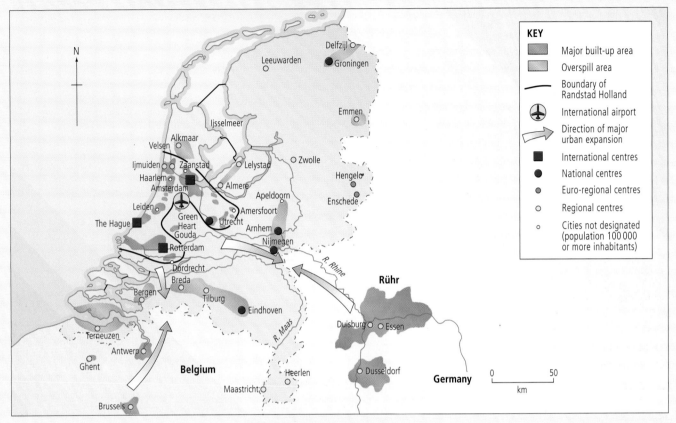

**Figure 6.23** *Randstad, Holland, a polycentric urban settlement, showing overspill and growth areas*
Source: Nagle, G. and Spencer, K., 1996, A geography of the European Union, OUP

Randstad is an interesting comparison with Los Angeles. It contains a number of distinct centres, it is more densely populated, and it has existed for a much longer time. Yet many of the problems are similar – immigration, population increase, suburban expansion and the need for urban planning.

Randstad, meaning 'ring-shaped' or 'rim-city' is a horseshoe-shaped conurbation that comprises four main centres (Figure 6.23). These include Amsterdam, the capital and main financial centre; Rotterdam, the largest port and industrial centre; The Hague, the centre of government; and Utrecht, a conference and trade centre. Randstad has a population of over 6 million people, and an average population density of over 450 people per square kilometre. It accounts for nearly 43% of the Dutch population (but only 16% of the land) and is the fourth largest urban centre in Europe.

Although Randstad is different from most cities, such as London and Mexico City, because it is formed from a number of separate centres, it has still experienced many of the same pressures. Urban sprawl and suburbanisation have created serious pressure on the Green Heart, the rich agricultural area at the centre of Randstad – over 50 000 hectares of good quality land has been lost in urban expansion. The Hague and Amsterdam have lost up to 350 000 people and large-scale counter-urbanisation has resulted in the expansion of many small settlements, such as Alphen and Gouda, near Rotterdam.

---

## QUESTIONS

1 How is urban planning in Randstad affected by the polycyclic nature of the conurbation?

2 Using an atlas, explain why urban growth, suburban sprawl and counterurbanisation pose such great problems in the Randstad.

## SUMMARY

We have seen how widespread and profound the changes in urban areas have been. These have included population decentralisation, in-migration, racial segregation, manufacturing decline and increasing unemployment. Most of these changes have been forced upon inner city areas. Our case studies show very different pictures. New York, on account of its sheer size, has had many more problems. By contrast, Oxford's size and its economic structure have allowed it to escape some of the worst features of urban change. Los Angeles and the Randstad offer another set of contrasts, namely the effect of sprawl and the use of private transport. As we have seen throughout this book, generalisations are not easy. We must study the unique characteristics of each place and combine them with some of the more general features that we can observe in most cities.

## QUESTIONS

1 Study Figure 6.24. What is the evidence to show that rates of counterurbanisation between 1961 and 1991 vary between the regions?
2 Study Figure 6.24. Explain the changing regional distribution of population in the UK between 1961 and 1991.
3 What are the causes and nature of the inner city problem?

## BIBLIOGRAPHY AND RECOMMENDED READING

**Champion, T. et al.**, 1996, *The population of Britain in the 1990s*, OUP
**Department of the Environment**, 1996, *Urban trends in England*, HMSO
**Hudson, R. and Williams, A.**, 1987, *The United Kingdom*, Harper & Rowe
**Lawless P.**, 1989, *Britain's inner cities: problems and policies*, Harper & Rowe
**London Research Centre et al.**, 1996, *Focus on London*, Government Statistical Service
**Matthews, H.**, 1991, *British inner cities*, OUP
**Morris, S.**, *Los Angeles – urban issues*, 1996 Geofile, 299
**Nagle, G and Spencer, K.**, 1996, *A geography of the European Union*, OUP
**Nagle, G.**, 1997, *Service and retail change in the UK*, Geofile, 312
**Robson B.**, 1988, *Those inner cities*, Clarendon Press

| | Population 1961 (000s) | Population 1991 (000s) | % change 1961-1991 |
|---|---|---|---|
| **North** | 3120 | 3019 | -3.2 |
| Tyne & Wear MC | 1244 | 1090 | -12.4 |
| Remainder of region | 1876 | 1929 | 2.8 |
| **Yorks. & Humberside** | 4681 | 4797 | 2.5 |
| South Yorkshire MC | 1303 | 1254 | -3.8 |
| West Yorkshire MC | 2005 | 1992 | -0.7 |
| Remainder of region | 1372 | 1551 | 13.1 |
| **East Midlands** | 3321 | 3919 | 18.0 |
| **East Anglia** | 1469 | 2019 | 37.4 |
| **South East** | 15 994 | 16 794 | 5.0 |
| Greater London | 7993 | 6394 | -20.0 |
| Outer Metropolitan Area | 4345 | 5447 | 25.4 |
| Remainder of region | 3656 | 4953 | 35.5 |
| **South West** | 3689 | 4600 | 24.7 |
| **West Midlands** | 4758 | 5089 | 7.0 |
| West Midlands MC | 2732 | 2511 | -8.1 |
| Remainder of region | 2026 | 2578 | 27.3 |
| **North West** | 6429 | 6147 | -4.4 |
| Greater Manchester MC | 2720 | 2455 | -9.7 |
| Merseyside MC | 1718 | 1380 | -19.7 |
| Remainder of region | 1991 | 2311 | 16.1 |
| **Wales** | 2644 | 2812 | 6.4 |
| **Scotland** | 5179 | 4962 | -4.2 |

Regions containing conurbations are subdivided into:
- Metropolitan Counties which contain the conurbations
- the remainder of the region

In addition, the South East is further subdivided to include:
- the Metropolitan County of Greater London
- the outer Metropolitan area
- the remainder of the South East.

MC – Metropolitan County

*Figure 6.24* UK percentage population change 1961-91 for Standard Regions and Metropolitan Counties
Source: Government Statistical Service, 1993, 1991 Census, Historical tables, HMSO

# Chapter 7
# Urban planning

In this chapter we analyse and assess the effectiveness of the methods used to address the problems of inner city decline resulting from the decentralisation of population and industry from urban areas (Figure 7.1). In general terms, four distinct phases of urban planning can be identified and these are discussed. There is a detailed analysis of planning in Manchester and a look at sustainable urban development.

***Figure 7.1*** *Urban contrasts: redevelopment at Liverpool Street with Hanbury St, off Brick Lane in the foreground*

## PHASE 1 1946-1967: PROVISION OF HOUSING

In 1947 the Labour Government introduced the Comprehensive Development Areas programme (CDA). This was a massive programme of slum clearance and rebuilding aimed at making inner city areas less congested, and environmentally more attractive. Within twenty years, one and a half million properties had been knocked down and the main thrust of urban policy was still towards decentralisation. As we have seen, the New Towns Act of 1946 and the Expanded Towns Act of 1952 encouraged the movement of urban residents to newer, smaller and, by implication, better settlements beyond the major conurbations. At the same time, new council estates were created on the edge (periphery) of cities, and suburbanisation took place in smaller cities and towns.

The CDA policy was not entirely successful. A number of problems became apparent:

- some clearance was so extensive that redevelopment could not keep pace – this led to a serious housing shortage
- vast tracts of derelict and vacant land were left behind
- old communities were broken up and displaced
- tower blocks were hostile and unsuitable environments
- the policy was too limited and failed to tackle economic and social decline
- redevelopment was failing to keep pace with decay – in 1967, 1.8 million houses in England and Wales were unfit for human habitation and a further 4.5 million were in need of repair.

## PHASE 2 1967-1977: SOCIAL AND ECONOMIC POLICIES

The 1968 Urban Aid Programme had two important provisions. First, government subsidies were made available to local authorities to expand services such as housing, advice centres, and nursery schools in deprived areas. Second, **community development projects** were established. These were to combine research into the causes of deprivation with an action programme to encourage self help among the residents of the area. **Inner area studies** demonstrated how economic change, selective population decentralisation, and unequal access to housing had combined to produce concentrations of unemployment in inner areas of London, Liverpool and Birmingham. At the same time, the New Towns and Expanded Towns policies were continuing, but more emphasis was given to the provision of services in urban areas and the attraction of industry and businesses.

Attention began to focus on the complexity of the inner city problems:

1 **Disenchantment** with the effect of redevelopment and decentralisation upon the inner city areas.
2 Increasing concern about the issues of **race and immigration**. Between 1951 and 1966, Britain's African-Caribbean population had increased from just under 75 000 to just under 600 000, and most of the population were resident in inner city areas.
3 **Unemployment** was high – and rising.
4 Slum clearance was very expensive. By contrast, schemes to improve **housing and the environment** were cheaper and more effective mechanisms for urban regeneration than clearance; rehabilitation was socially disruptive but economically more viable.

The late 1960s and early 1970s were an era of experimentation: schemes were often small scale, limited in focus, area-based and needs-led. A shortage of funding reduced their effectiveness.

## Policies for environmental improvement

**General improvement areas** (GIAs) were introduced in 1969, and provided grants to improve both the housing and local environmental conditions. The **housing action areas** (HAAs) introduced in 1974 were an attempt to help the worst affected areas. Their success however was limited for two reasons:

1 The designation of GIAs and HAAs was slow, largely because of **underfunding**.
2 Ironically, urban renewal increased the problems of inner city residents. As housing was upgraded, young, wealthy people moved in, buying run down properties which they gentrified and sold at a considerable profit; this deprived poorer residents of much-needed housing and many were forced to move out.

## Policies for social and economic welfare

During this period a large range of policies and projects provided funding, services and research into the nature of urban problems:

**Educational priority areas** (1967) were area-based programmes in which resources were redistributed to schools in areas of social deprivation; a grant provided 75% of the cost of the projects, the remainder was funded by the local authorities.

**Comprehensive community action programmes** (1974-79) were introduced with the aim of improving delivery and co-ordination of services by local authorities and other welfare agencies in areas of intense deprivation. About ninety areas in Britain qualified for this special assistance.

**Community development projects** (1969-1977) were neighbourhood-based developments and **Inner area studies** (1972-77) were carried out by research teams looking at the problems of the inner areas of Birmingham (Small Heath), Liverpool (Vauxhall) and Lambeth (Stockwell). Their main conclusion was that the inner city problem could not be solved through small scale urban experiments, instead a total approach was needed which would treat the inner city as a region in itself. Research showed that policies confined to specific areas did not necessarily help the most deprived individuals. Moreover, studies which concentrated on deprivation in specific areas overemphasised local causes; local conditions might be important but the root causes of inner city problems were large-scale economic change.

In 1977, the Government White Paper Policy for the Inner Cities outlined four main objectives:

1 strengthening the economies of inner areas
2 improving their physical fabric
3 alleviating social problems
4 securing a new balance between inner areas and the remainder of the urban area.

## PHASE 3 1977-1990: INNER CITY RENEWAL

In this phase, the emphasis moved away from New Towns and Expanded Towns towards comprehensive projects for inner city areas and refurbishment of run-down post-war housing (Figure 7.2). The winding down of New Towns and Expanding Towns was an attempt to halt the continuing decentralisation of people and jobs. The Government White Paper on Inner Cities (1977) concluded that structural (economic) factors were the main cause of inner city poverty. For the first time, inner cities were defined as problem regions. It was argued that emphasis should be given to restoring the industrial base of the city, from which other improvements would follow.

Three principle aims have shaped the form and content of recent policy:

● securing economic regeneration
● improving the environment
● gearing services and amenities to the local community.

Of these, the economic aim has been dominant.

The **Urban Programme** was an important recommendation in the White Paper and led to the creation of **partnership** and **programme areas** in selected inner cities. Here central government entered formal agreements with local authorities and voluntary organisations to produce a coordinated strategy to assist the economic, social and environmental regeneration of the whole inner city area.

The Urban Programme was started in 1968 but expanded after the **Inner Urban Areas Act, 1978**. It was a central government initiative operated by the Department of the Environment (DoE). It had an annual budget of £340 million, allocated to certain local authorities with severe problems. The funds were used for a variety of developments: small factory units, renovations to older units and industrial areas, training of unemployed people, and provision of community centres. Minority (African-Caribbean and Asian, for example) businesses and community groups often received positive discrimination.

The Inner Urban Areas Act established seven **partnership areas** which were to receive between £10 million and £25 million per year from central government. In addition, there were 23 **programme authorities** receiving between £3 million and £6 million a year and 15 other **designated districts** receiving about £1 million each per year. The programme was wound down after 1983. Glasgow was not

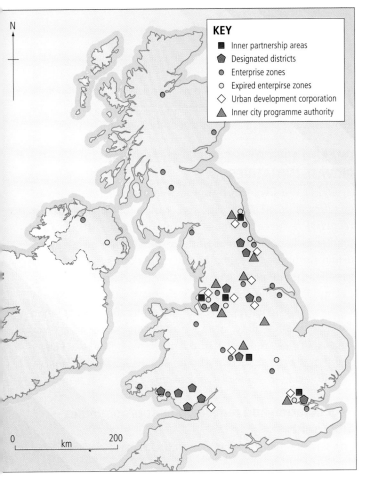

**Figure 7.2** *Government urban initiatives in the UK, 1977-90*
*Source: Carr, M., 1997, New patterns: process and change in human geography, Nelson*

KEY
■ Inner partnership areas
⬠ Designated districts
● Enterprise zones
○ Expired enterpirse zones
◇ Urban development corporation
▲ Inner city programme authority

tracts of derelict land in the inner city. UDCs were answerable directly to central government and had economic and housing powers similar to New Town corporations. UDCs were run by people from business and local government and had extensive powers. They could:

- grant planning permission
- acquire, hold, manage and dispose of land and other property, using compulsory purchase orders if necessary
- build infrastructure for property development
- provide loans and grants
- promote development by advertising.

Three phases of UDCs can be identified:

1 London Docklands (Figure 7.3) and Merseyside UDCs established in 1981
2 1987 – Black Country, Cardiff Bay, Teeside, Trafford Park (Manchester) and Tyne and Wear
3 Post 1988 – Central Manchester, Leeds, Sheffield and Bristol.

During the 1980s, UDCs were the government's most popular means of regenerating urban areas, but this is no longer the case. Funding for UDCs has declined considerably in recent years, as shown in Figure 7.4 (on page 78). In 1993, large financial cutbacks occurred in London and Merseyside, and there was a freeze on funding at Bristol, Leeds, Manchester, and Tyne and Wear. There are contrasting explanations for these cutbacks:

1 UDCs have achieved their aim and therefore do not need continued financial support
2 disenchantment with UDCs' performance. UDCs were highly successful in the boom years of the 1980s, and the London Docklands Development Corporation boasted that for every £1 million of public money invested £10 million of private money was invested (Figure 7.3). However, the recession of the late 1980s and early 1990s halted this. Throughout the UK, urban policies which require private sector property development have had a very low success rate in the early 1990s.

**Figure 7.3** *Redevelopment in London's docklands*

included amongst the partnership areas because it already had its own special agency, the Glasgow Eastern Area of Renewal project (GEAR) established in 1976.

The first partnerships were offered to London's dockland authorities, Hackney and Islington, Lambeth, Birmingham, Liverpool, Manchester, Salford, Newcastle and Gateshead. The key objective of this policy was to strengthen the economies of inner cities, in particular to encourage the retention of jobs. In the first two years of the enhanced Urban Programme, funding rose from £30 million to £165 million.

Eventually, by the early 1990s, assistance was given to fifty-six localities, including most major cities. These partnerships accounted for about 50% of the urban programme funding. About 10 000 small scale projects were funded by the Urban Programme in 1992. However, after 1993 no new projects were supported by the government and there was a decline in funding from £237 million in 1992-93 to just £80 million in 1995-96.

## Urban Development Corporations

Urban Development Corporations (UDCs) have been described as the most important attack ever made on urban decay. These government sponsored agencies were introduced in 1981 with the sole objective of regenerating large

## Deregulation and private sector initiatives

In 1981 the Conservative government declared a number of **enterprise zones**. These were originally intended as an experiment in free market economics. Twenty-five enterprise zones, ranging from 55 hectares to 440 hectares were set aside for commercial/industrial development. The aim was not only to regenerate the national economy, but also to create an urban policy to help cities with acute employment difficulties. The initial eleven areas included the Isle of Dogs, Newcastle/Gateshead, Salford/Trafford, Liverpool/Speke, Clydebank and West Belfast. All were classic areas of urban decline. The second set of designations in 1982 were made at a time of major cutbacks in the steel industry, hence several steel towns such as Workington, Scunthorpe, Flint and Rotherham, were included.

The idea of the enterprise zone stemmed from the concept of freeports – small zones free of government restrictions and subject to relatively low taxation. Substantial advantages for periods of ten years were offered to firms locating there. These included exemption from rates, from development land tax, 100% allowances on capital expenditure for corporation and income tax purposes, exemption from industrial training levies, a simplified local planning system and a general reduction in government bureaucracy.

However, the success rates varied. Some 60% of incoming firms were new start-ups, so the enterprise zones must be considered a moderate success. However, they have had some negative effects. The main ones are the **boundary effect** and their cost. Firms have relocated from just outside the designated area, especially if they could save up to £10 000 per year on rates. The boundary also has a negative shadow effect on areas outside the zones. For example, demand for and value of premises in some adjacent areas has fallen. Many of the zones fail to attract dynamic, innovative small firms. In addition enterprise zones are expensive – it costs up to £168 000 for every new job created!

## Task forces

The Inner Cities Initiative was launched in 1986 and created task forces. These are located in seventeen inner city areas to try out new ideas and approaches in order to unlock development opportunities. Task forces are small-scale teams of civil servants, set up by the DoE, in order to help regenerate local areas. They are set up in deprived areas, such as Moss Side in Manchester, Notting Hill in London and St. Paul's in Bristol – areas with a history of disorder, riots and high unemployment. The purpose of the task force is to saturate the community with aid drawn from existing programmes and support from the private sector and/or local authorities. However, there has been much friction between local authorities and task forces. Local authorities see it as their job to co-ordinate regeneration and regard task forces as increasing centralised control of the planning process.

## PHASE 4 1990 TO THE PRESENT: PARTNERSHIPS AND PRIVATE INITIATIVES

In 1991, the **City Challenge** scheme was established to encourage local authorities to compete for funding. It received a large increase in funding after 1993. City Challenge is open to local authorities with the most severe urban problems. Local authorities and others, such as universities and industries, propose specific urban projects. For example in Leicester, the City Council and De Montfort University designed a project transforming the derelict inner city into a 'showpiece' area with new shops, facilities and houses. Critics argued that government policy had lost steam and that it was asking other organisations for suggestions on how to tackle the inner city problem.

## Regeneration and redevelopment programmes – City Grants

**City Grants**, developed in the 1980s, replace and combine three previous schemes:
1 Urban Development Grant
2 Urban Regeneration Grant
3 Derelict Land Grant.

All of these shared the objective of trying to lead private sector investment into the inner city by:
- developing run down areas

| | £m 92-93 | £m 93-94 | £m 94-95 | £m 95-96 |
|---|---|---|---|---|
| City Challenge | 64 | 214 | 214 | 214 |
| City Grant | 71 | 71 | 71 | 83 |
| Derelict Land Grant (net) | 95 | 95 | 95 | 122 |
| Manchester Olympic bid | 1 | 35 | 25 | 0 |
| Urban Programme | 237 | 176 | 91 | 80 |
| Urban Development Corporation and Docklands Light Railway | 491 | 330 | 293 | 284 |
| Other | 28 | 36 | 32 | 24 |
| **Total** | 987 | 955 | 820 | 806 |

**Figure 7.4** *Changes in government funding, 1992-93 to 1995-96*
Source: Department of Environment/Financial Times, November 1992

## QUESTIONS

1 Account for the distribution of enterprise zones as shown on Figure 7.2.

2 Why have enterprise zones failed to attract dynamic high-tech growth industries?

- redeveloping large industrial sites
- refurbishing large groups of buildings
- replanning derelict land.

Other initiatives include land registers, training, education and employment projects and special projects.

In addition, by the end of the 1990s the whole urban programme is to be brought under one agency, the **Urban Regeneration Agency**. This should overcome the fragmented and piecemeal nature of urban planning to date.

## Criticisms of urban policy

There have been many criticisms of urban policy. These have been made by urban planners, industrialists, investors, MPs and of course, people living in urban areas.

1 **Insufficient funding** – resources have stayed the same or been reduced (Figure 7.4); local authorities' incomes are declining; spending on urban policy has been relatively small when set against the massive expenditure elsewhere in the economy, such as in research and development or defence.

2 Renewed **public sector involvement** is needed. Public sector investment is needed in order to make sites attractive for private development. Local authorities are more likely to be sensitive to local issues and the needs of their citizens.

3 The approach is too **fragmentary** and lacks a clear focus. No less than six government departments are involved, as well as many voluntary organisations and private developers.

4 The continued emphasis on helping **small areas** within cities appears to be unsuccessful – there is a boundary effect and the problem is just displaced.

5 Government policy is ineffective and wasteful. A recent review of urban programme spending suggested that it took between £7000 and £18 000 to create a new job, but that for the £137 million spent between 1981 and 1984 only 5000 jobs were created. This figure needs to be set against a loss of 38 000 jobs in inner city areas.

## Inset 7.1
# Changes in urban policy

Three fundamental shifts in government thinking can be seen since 1946. These are: a movement from local to central control; a movement from public to private sector involvement; and a movement from social to economic concern.

1 Local to central government – the scope of central government has increased whereas the scope of local authorities has lessened. Successive Conservative governments argued that local bureaucracy and red tape delay the take-up of new schemes. Planning controls were seen to hinder the growth of industry.

2 Public to private sector involvement – a free market economy based on minimum local intervention and maximum opportunity to private enterprise. This follows the ideals of the Conservative government, from 1979-97: market-led or demand-led strategies are encouraged and private investors are left to develop what they consider to be profitable land uses. The growth of enterprise zones, CATs (City Action Teams – joint private and local authority), task forces and the City Grant scheme all reflect a strong commitment to private enterprise and the increasing marginalisation of public sector organisations.

3 Social to economic concern – since 1981 economic issues have become dominant. The roots of the urban programme of the late 1960s were social concerns about deprivation and their distinct disadvantage. Since then, the emphasis has switched to encouraging private companies to invest in the inner city – social benefits are thought to accrue from this. Between 1979-80 and 1988-89 spending on social and community projects fell from £197 million to £118 million.

### QUESTIONS

1 Briefly explain how changes in government may affect urban planning.

2 How do governments influence urban policy? Use examples to support your answer.

3 In what ways do you think the Labour government elected in 1997 has changed urban policy? Give reasons for your answer.

# Case study:
# Planning in Manchester

So far we have considered urban planning in a general context. Now we focus our attention upon one city, Manchester, and trace the complex development of urban planning since World War II.

## The City of Manchester Plan, 1945

In December 1940, Manchester was bombed, killing 363 people and seriously injuring a further 455 people. Four and a half hectares of the city were destroyed, and areas such as Market Place and Piccadilly were devastated (Figure 7.5). Thirty thousand homes were damaged and many people were made homeless. Nevertheless, by the 2nd January 1941, approximately thirteen thousand homes had received emergency repairs.

The rebuilding of Manchester really took off after the war. The City of Manchester Plan was an attempt to remove all traces of Victorian Manchester, because of its link with poor living, working and health conditions and to replace it with a modern, international city. There were problems of housing related to overcrowding, and there were nearly 70 000 houses which were unfit for human habitation. Most of these were in areas where the density was over ten dwellings per hectare.

The outbreak of World War II had led to a halt in large scale redevelopment, consequently thousands of temporary prefabricated bungalows were built. Only in 1954 did the Manchester Slum Clearance Programme resume. Before this much had been spent on repairing war time damage. By 1955, up to 70 000 dwellings were declared unfit for human habitation. A five year programme of clearance included the demolition of 7500 properties (Figure 7.6). From 1960 the clearance programme was greatly expanded and four areas were chosen – Hulme, Beswick, Longsight and Harpurhey.

In clearance areas, both high and low rise dwellings were built to repair the previous slums. Compulsory purchase orders transferred ownership to the Council before demolition. The new lower density schemes provided areas of open space. Rapid development reduced population levels by as much as 50%. But the reduction of available housing meant that there was a housing shortage. Alternative accommodation had to be found as the shortage of land available within the city boundaries became more acute.

New neighbourhoods were planned to accommodate the displaced people. These new neighbourhoods were based on the Garden City principle; they had a projected size of 10 000 people and would support churches, shops, playing fields, schools, public houses, community centres, health centres and a branch library. They were designed to be self-contained. A cluster of neighbourhoods would then form a district with a population of about 50 000 – the districts would include health centres, cinemas, public baths, police and fire stations and other social provisions. One such district was Wythenshawe (Figure 7.7).

**Figure 7.5** *War time damage in Manchester*

**Figure 7.6** *Large scale clearances of unfit dwellings in Manchester during the period of post-war redevelopment*
*Source: Manchester Central Library*

Another aim was to remove cross-town traffic from Manchester city centre, not least because atmospheric pollution was seen as one of the greatest threats to public health. This was to be achieved by four new ring roads and an extension of radial routes producing, effectively, a spiders web of communications lines. There was also the construction of the new railway and bus terminal. Like other northern towns, the centre of Manchester was originally developed at a time when land was considered too valuable to be wasted on parks and gardens. Consequently there was a lack of open space in the city centre. In the city centre, the Cathedral was to be restored, tree-lined boulevards were to be created, gardens with fountains and trees were also to be constructed. The 1945 plan for Manchester was very much the reflection of the New Town spirit.

However, many of the proposals were not implemented because of the massive cost involved in the comprehensive clearance and redevelopment. Other proposals such as the redevelopment of inner city housing areas such as Miles Platting, Beswick and Collyhurst went ahead.

## Post-war housing problems and solutions

By the 1960s, pioneering new techniques were introduced using prefabricated concrete panels constructed in factories and bolted together on the site. However there were shortcomings in the approach – many prefabricated panels were prone to damage in transit and sometimes failed to bolt together. However, at the time they were seen as the quickest and most economical way of solving the post-war housing problem. Manchester adopted high rise blocks with relish. Only later did the unsuitability of upper floors for disabled people, children and the elderly become obvious.

**Figure 7.7** *View of Wythenshawe in the 1950s*

## The 1961 Development Plan

The 1961 Development Plan covered fourteen main areas – housing shopping, education, open space, industry, the city centre, minerals, roads, communications, tree planting, public utilities, higher education, cultural areas and health. Compulsory purchase orders were provided to allow comprehensive redevelopment to take place. Over 55 000 dwellings were to be constructed, at a density of 40 habitable rooms per hectare. Retail developments were proposed for Wythenshawe, Blackley and Charlestown (Figure 7.8). Within the central area, the bulk of the development would be concentrated on rebuilding war damaged areas, such as Strangeways, Market Place and Water Street.

## City centre redevelopment

The 1961 Development Plan was updated by the 1967 City Centre map. The proposals were to improve transport, housing, shopping and commercial activity. Transport was to be improved by major roadways and a city centre ring road to run twenty feet below the line of Portland Street. It was hoped to reverse the trend of suburbanisation and reduce the length of travel to work time. Shopping facilities were to be improved. The Arndale Centre, the main shopping centre, was designed on two levels with

a series of malls intersecting in wider squares. However, it took nearly twenty years to implement the plan, and during this period surrounding centres were redeveloped more quickly, thereby taking a substantial slice of Manchester's traditional retail trade.

### Castlefield

One area of Manchester which deserves special attention is Castlefield (Figure 7.9, see page 83). In 1966, British Rail closed Manchester Central Station and in 1975 the Liverpool Road Goods Depot also closed. The Greater Manchester Council bought the area in 1978 and embarked on a campaign to promote Castlefield's rich industrial heritage, which was seen as the key to the regeneration of the area. They also repaired the City Exhibition Hall, a Grade II listed building, which became Britain's first urban heritage park in 1982. In 1983, the first phase of the Castlefield Museum of Science and Industry was opened, and the Air and Space Gallery soon afterwards. Canals and towpaths have been restored. The Granada Company invested and developed its popular Granada Studios Tour in Castlefield at a cost of over £8 million. The Victoria and Albert Warehouses were refurbished as a hotel, and Castlefield has now become one of the major tourist attractions in the North West. The Manchester Arena in the city

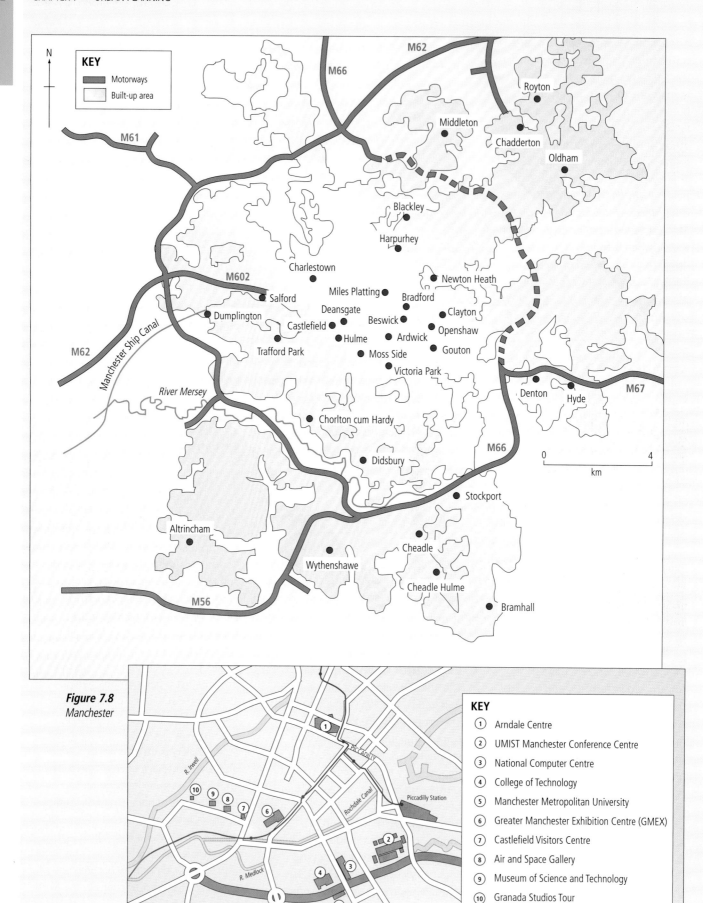

**Figure 7.8**
*Manchester*

*Figure 7.9* Deansgate, Castlefield – a listed building, restored and now used as a recording studio

*Figure 7.10* Hulme Crescents, surrounded by large areas of open space, appeared deceptively attractive when they were built in the mid-1960s

Manchester Royal Infirmary are all situated there. The Precinct currently caters for 35 000 students and extends over 135 hectares, with only 10% of the area still available for development.

## Hulme

Hulme grew rapidly in the nineteenth century to house Manchester's swelling population. It developed chaotically with tightly packed terraces and courts providing cramped and unsanitary accommodation. Few houses had their own toilets, and many had no foundations but were laid on bare earth. Despite this, Victorian Hulme was an important district to Manchester – close to the major areas of employment, with a range of facilities. By the early twentieth century it had become an area of slum clearance. By the early 1960s, all remaining terraced houses in Hulme were bulldozed.

The vision for a new Hulme was planned around the rigid segregation of vehicles and pedestrians – tenants were to be housed in flats and maisonettes on interconnecting decks or streets in the sky. Traditional street life would be replicated far above the hazards of traffic. Shopping facilities were centralised around three precincts – Moss Side District Centre and two smaller neighbourhood sites, Alexandra Road and Princes Road. The best known part of the whole development was the Hulme Crescents – four huge curved blocks of flats and maisonettes linked together by walkways and bridges (Figure 7.10). These were originally compared to their Georgian equivalent in Bath.

By 1972 the redevelopment of Hulme was virtually complete. Over 5000 new homes had been built in less than eight years and over 3000 of those were deck access, making Hulme the biggest concentration of this type of housing in the country. Within months, however, the scheme began to turn into a

centre is Europe's largest multi-purpose indoor entertainment and sports arena. The Arena was originally conceived in 1989 but not developed until 1992, when Manchester was awarded £55 million in support of its bid for the Olympic Games. It has the capacity to accommodate nearly 20 000 spectators and was opened in 1995. The Bridgewater Hall, Manchester's new international concert hall, was opened in 1996.

### Higher Education Precinct

Like many cities, such as London and Liverpool, redevelopment of the central area has included an expansion of universities and colleges. Manchester has developed a Higher Education Precinct to the south of the city centre along the Oxford Road. Manchester University, the University of Manchester Institute of Science & Technology (UMIST), the Manchester Metropolitan University and

nightmare for many of the tenants:
- the housing had been constructed using unfamiliar techniques
- there was poor site supervision
- reinforcing bolts and ties that were supposed to hold panels together were missing
- leaks started to appear
- there was poor insulation and poor ventilation
- high levels of condensation
- huge fuel bills
- the development was unsuitable for families, elderly and disabled people.

The area went into a spiral of decline, with unemployment, drugs, violence and a deteriorating environment. In response to these problems, Hulme City Challenge was launched in April 1992, with the help of nearly £40 million of government money. An ambitious plan was drawn up to build 3000 new homes, new shops, roads, offices and community facilities. The initiative focuses on an area of about 60 hectares which will be cleared, from the mid-1990s and rebuilt in a five year investment costing over £200 million with funding from both public and private sources. Some 1400 properties have been demolished and 50 hectares of land reclaimed. Over 600 homes for rent have been built or are currently under construction and 415 homes have been improved internally.

## The Greater Manchester County Structure Plan

The first Greater Manchester County Structure Plan was adopted in 1981 with revisions being made in 1986. The Plan had four main themes:

1 Urban concentration policies aimed at bringing development back into urban areas rather than on the periphery. This was backed up by strengthening the constraints on green-field development.
2 Investment in areas with the greatest social deprivation.
3 The removal or reuse of derelict land and obsolete buildings, control of air

pollution and the cleaning up of rivers.
4 Resource conservation and amenity – namely the protection of open land and the reduction of energy loss.

The Greater Manchester Council was abolished in 1986 by the Conservative government. As in the rest of the UK there was a return to partnerships between the local authorities and private sector initiatives. There was greater emphasis on entrepreneurship, more limited government investment and extra private investment.

## Conservation listed buildings and urban design

In the early 1990s, there were over 960 listed buildings in Manchester, 50% of which were in the city centre. The first conservation area was designated in 1970 – St Ann's Square and Chorlton Green. Manchester now has twenty-nine designated conservation areas, fourteen of which are in the city centre – largely buildings for the cotton industry. Manchester has sometimes been referred to as Cottonopolis! The most notable conservation area has been the Castlefield area which had over £30 million spent on it between 1979 and 1989.

## Derelict land in East Manchester

East Manchester is one of the key areas in the city where there are opportunities for major change, regeneration, and improvement. The area covers over 16 square kilometres to the east of the city centre and includes the wards of Beswick, Clayton, Bradford, Gorton North, Newton Heath and Miles Platting. In the nineteenth century it was an area of heavy engineering, power, transport and chemical industries; by the middle of the twentieth century the decline in traditional industries hit it very hard. Between 1974 and 1984, 24 000 jobs were lost – at the same time the Victorian terraced housing made way for new council estates such as Miles

Platting (redeveloped in the 1950s) and Beswick (redeveloped in the 1970s). By the 1980s, problems stemming from unemployment, derelict land and lack of investment were addressed through the East Manchester Initiative – a partnership between the council and central government. The basic objectives of the plan were four fold:

1 to assist in the economic recovery of the areas
2 to improve the environment
3 to improve access and mobility
4 to enhance the housing stock.

These objectives revolved around:
- reclamation of derelict land
- reclamation of areas around the Medlock Valley and Rochdale Canal.

The housing strategy was to improve certain areas of existing housing stock. Areas in Miles Platting, Beswick, Clayton and Openshaw were released for new development. Between 1982 and 1991, £50 million was spent on refurbishing Miles Platting alone. In 1992, East Manchester was chosen as a prime location for the major sports and social facilities associated with the Year 2000 Olympic Games bid. The overall objectives of the East Manchester Regeneration Strategy were similar to those put forward in 1983 in the East Manchester initiative:
- stimulating economic and business development
- securing effective land use, and environmental and infrastructural improvement
- encouraging diversity in housing provision and social conditions
- developing skilled and self-reliant communities.

The aim of the regeneration strategy was to provide 2000 new houses and up to 375 000 square metres of new industrial and commercial floor space offering up to 10 000 new jobs. This was to be achieved by encouraging inward investment. There was also a proposal to focus regeneration in a number of specific areas such as housing, retail and leisure uses at Miles Platting. Despite the ultimate decision to take the 2000 Games to Sydney, East Manchester gained enormous benefit from the bid, and key elements of the regeneration strategy have now become a reality:

- £40 million of special government grant to acquire and clear the main 70 hectare Eastland site and to construct the new National Cycling Centre at the Velodrome
- completion of the intermediate ring road – a new dual carriageway linking East Manchester to the national motorway network
- promotion of a new National Stadium, allied to the City's successful bid to host the 2002 Commonwealth Games
- proposed East Manchester Metro Link line promoted by the Passenger Transport Authority.
- completion of major derelict land reclamation schemes, such as those at Ardwick, West and East, goods yards.

## Olympic and Commonwealth Games bids
Manchester put in two bids to host the Olympic Games, the first for 1996 and the second for 2000. It has also made a successful bid for the 2002 Commonwealth Games.

The 1996 Olympic bid was an ideal opportunity to promote Manchester on the world's stage to the benefit of the city, the private sector and ultimately those working and living in the city. The plan envisaged the main stadium arena and swimming pool to be located outside the city, at Dumplington, with other facilities being dispersed around the region at Liverpool, Chester, Wigan and the North West. This seemingly flew in the face of the Olympic ideal which favoured a compact venue with facilities within easy travelling distance of each other and the Athletes Village.
The 2000 Olympic Games bid differed – here development was concentrated on an area of inner city regeneration at

Eastlands in East Manchester. The venue strategy was drawn up to meet three primary considerations:

1  compactness
2  caring for the environment
3  legacy and after-use.

The 2002 Commonwealth Games bid was successful. In 1995 Manchester was awarded the Commonwealth Games, and the Eastland site is the major focus for the Games.

## Central Manchester Development Corporation
In 1998, Central Manchester Development Corporation (CMDC) was set up by the government to regenerate nearly 200 hectares of land and buildings in the southern sector of the city centre. Stretching in an arc from Piccadilly Station to Pomona Docks, it includes six conservation areas with over 90 listed buildings and structures. It also covers:

- a range of housing types
- proximity to the city centre
- three universities
- urban heritage park
- the Museum of Science and Industry
- Granada Studios Tour.

However, decaying buildings, such as warehouses, offices, mills and railway viaducts, contaminated land, and neglected canals typify the area.

The effectiveness of the CMDC's work is already very evident – the Bridgewater Concert Hall and adjacent Great Bridgewater office development (which will provide over 22 000 square metres of office space) were secured in partnership with the City Council. Successful residential developments have also occurred. Castlefield has emerged as a setting for successful housing and office development, and the area now attracts over two million leisure visitors a year. In the eight years of its operation over £420 million of investment has come into the Manchester CMDC area. The Concert Hall, the single biggest project, is an excellent example of the

power of public, private and European partnership in Manchester. In the Woodworth's Street area many of the listed warehouses and sites were ripe for conservation and redevelopment. Many were earmarked for residential use. The result is a village in the city of more than a thousand homes served by pubs, bars, restaurants, taxi firms, post offices, doctors, dentists and even a twenty-four hour shop. The CMDC was disbanded at the end of March 1996.

## The 1995 Manchester Plan
1995 saw the adoption of the new Manchester plan officially known as the Unitary Development Plan. The first part of the plan sets out the City Council's strategic vision and the second part shows how the strategic policies apply at local level. The Plan has two broad aims:

1  to improve the city as a place to live, work and visit
2  to retain and revitalise the local economy.

It plans to maintain and improve the quality of existing homes and provide new housing. Average household size is expected to fall over the next ten to twenty years and the greatest demand will be for single person accommodation.

### Economic development
Manchester is re-emerging as an international city, a centre of decision making, information exchange, professional services, financial institutions, research, media, culture and sport. Manchester has a number of advantages:

- the city centre with its concentration of facilities and attractions
- its role as a centre of business, finance, industry, shopping, tourism, culture and public services and government
- proximity to Manchester Airport – one of the fastest-growing in Europe
- a concentration of media industries
- the presence of major electronic companies

- the Higher Education Precinct – a centre for research and development
- the city's role as a regional centre for leisure and recreation.
- the Olympic and Commonwealth bids which have brought world class sporting facilities to Manchester and the region, and with them an increased awareness of Manchester.

In 1996, over 100 000 square metres of retail and office space were damaged by an IRA bomb blast. Manchester's city centre is second only to London's Oxford Street in terms of volume of shoppers and sales. Ironically, the bomb blast has given planners an opportunity to regenerate the commercial core (Figure 7.11) including the infamously ugly Arndale Centre.

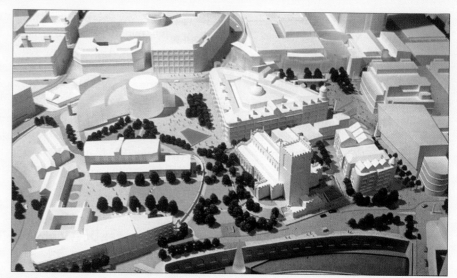

**Figure 7.11** *Designs for Manchester's new commercial core.*
*Printed with kind permission of Manchester Millenium Ltd*

### QUESTIONS

1 Briefly describe the main urban problems in Manchester. Why did they occur?

2 How successful has urban planning in Manchester been? Use evidence to support your answer.

## SUSTAINABLE URBAN DEVELOPMENT

Sustainable development has been defined as development which 'meets the needs of the present without compromising the ability of future generations to meet their own needs' (Brundtland, 1987). It is a form of development whereby living standards are improved, whilst at the same time the environment is used, managed, and conserved on a long-term basis. Sustainable development implies social justice as well as environmental sustainability. Sustainable settlements must therefore include measures to:

- improve basic needs, for example housing and services, such as water and waste disposal
- reduce environmental damage
- promote equal access to resources such as education, health and employment.

This seems an impossible goal although there are many examples to show how settlements can be managed. These include recycling of waste, use of renewable forms of energy, promotion of cycle paths, park and ride schemes, water and energy conservation and insulating buildings. Each of these helps to reduce the waste of a valuable resource.

## Role of local Agenda 21

We saw in *Development and underdevelopment*, in this series, that as a result of the Earth Summit in Rio de Janeiro (1992) national governments are obliged to formulate national plans or strategies for sustainable development. These are called **Agenda 21 statements**. Sustainable development is a local activity because it is **people** who create development, not just governments. Moreover, according to Chambers (1983) all people, however poor, have some ability, however constrained, of changing what they do, in small ways.

Local authorities have a number of roles in sustainable development:

- as a consumer of resources
- as a force for change in the market place
- as a role model for other organisations
- as providers of information
- as providers of services
- as planners
- as local governments and decision makers.

For example, the city of Leicester has used technology to help reduce traffic congestion. It is the UK's first experiment with road tolls in cities. Drivers are charged a small toll for driving on one of the main roads which link the city centre with the M1 motorway. The scheme has won widespread support from the city's environmental lobby and from the business community. The scheme is an attempt to price drivers off the road and on to buses, using the new and much cheaper park and ride schemes and special bus lanes.

## Sustainable urban development in Manchester

Manchester City Council's Agenda 21 statement begins with some simple, but crucial, principles:

1 Sustainability is about the balance between environmental, economic, social and community concerns, rather than just being about environmental or ecological issues.
2 Whatever Manchester City Council does for Agenda 21 must be related to its broad policies for the city, such as urban regeneration, repopulation and so on.
3 There must be visible results from Agenda 21 statements and the council must take sustainability seriously.

Manchester's Agenda 21 includes action in a number of areas. These include:

- monitoring air and water quality
- promoting energy efficiency
- landscaping the environment
- recycling litter
- improving publicity about Agenda 21
- promoting economic development
- introducing more efficient forms of transport, such as trams, and providing cycle lanes
- making grants and awards available for sustainable projects.

Sustainable urban settlements require a balanced land use and an efficient use of space. In urban areas, where the problems appear most intense, it is important to reduce the demand for travel. Efficient transport management is necessary to reduce air pollution, the large scale waste of energy, and the negative impact on human health. A range of measures exists including integrated public transport, road pricing, traffic calming, traffic bans and so on. Reducing energy use through efficiency and conservation measures is necessary. Potential solutions include building design, use of renewable forms of energy, and an improved public transport system.

### QUESTIONS

1 What has your local authority provided in terms of an Agenda 21 statement? All local authorities are obliged to have an Agenda 21 plan. If you telephone, you should be able to contact someone who can send you the details.

2 Briefly explain how we can use energy, water and paper in a more sustainable way. What factors prevent sustainable development?

## SUMMARY

The outcome of more than forty years of government activity is generally disappointing. There is growing agreement that economic growth is a precondition for action on all fronts. Urban policy seems to be afflicted by a stop-go syndrome, and successive governments appear reluctant to continue with early initiatives, especially if they are associated with an opposing political party. Accordingly, there is little continuity. The case study of Manchester illustrates clearly the difficulties of urban planning. Manchester is a very successful city in many respects, yet it has limited resources and has to make difficult decisions about the allocation of those resources, which affects how the plans are carried out.

### QUESTIONS

1 Using examples, examine the effects of structural policies and spatial policies (area-led policies) as a means of developing the inner cities.
2 'The decline of inner cities is irreversible.' How far do you agree with this statement? What are the implications of this for urban planning policies?

## BIBLIOGRAPHY AND RECOMMENDED READING

**Bailey, N., et al.,** 1995 *Partnership agencies in British urban policy* UCL
**Brundtland**, 1987 See WCED)
**Butler, T. and Rustin, M.,** (eds.) 1996 *Rising in the East: the regeneration of East London*, Lawrence and Wishart
**Hall., P.,** 1992 *Urban and regional planning* Routledge
**HMSO,** 1995 *Manchester 50 years of change* HMSO
**HMSO,** 1995, *First steps – Local Agenda 21 in practice*, HMSO
**HMSO,** 1996, *Indicators of sustainable development for the United Kingdom*, HMSO
**Nagle, G. and Spencer, K.,** 1997, *Sustainable development*, Hodder and Stoughton
**Hudson, R. and Williams, A.,** 1987, *The United Kingdom*, Harper & Rowe
**Lawless P.,** 1989, *Britain's inner cities, problems and policies*, Harper & Rowe
**Matthews, H.,** 1991, *British inner cities*, OUP
**Pacione, M.,** 1995, *Glasgow: the socio-spatial development of the city*, Wiley
**Reid, D.,** 1995, *Sustainable development: an introductory guide*, Earthscan
**Robson B.,** 1988, *Those inner cities*, Clarendon Press
**WCED,** 1987, *Our common future*, OUP

## WEBSITES

**Environment Agency home page –**
http://www.environment-agency.gov.uk/
**Friends of the Earth home page –**
http://www.foe.co.uk/
**Manchester Air Quality –**
http://www.doc.mmu.ac.uk/aric/arichome.html

# Chapter 8
# Changing rural settlements

In this chapter we look at changing rural settlements since the 1950s. In the 1950s and 1960s many rural areas were in decline. The case studies of key settlements in the UK and rural planning for the Dutch polders show contrasting attempts to rejuvenate declining rural areas, one long-established, the other reclaimed from the sea. By contrast, the example of rural settlements in Israel shows how political forces can influence rural planning.

More recently, however, rural settlements have been increasing in size. Much of this is due to counter-urbanisation, the movement of people and industry from large urban centres to smaller urban areas and the more accessible rural areas.

## RURAL CHANGE

Rural populations are subject to constant change. Many rural dwellers, particularly the young, leave the countryside to find employment in towns and cities. In most rural areas, especially remote and isolated places, the main movement is one of depopulation. This leads to a decline in the birth rate in rural areas and an increase in the youthful population of urban areas. At the same time, many urban dwellers move to rural areas for retirement or are prepared to commute to work in towns. Hence by increased outward migration and decreased rate of natural increase, the population of many villages becomes increasingly elderly.

The large scale movement from rural areas to urban areas is a feature of both developed and developing countries. Push factors are the disadvantages and problems of country living, such as a decline in agricultural employment due to mechanisation, low wages, poor housing and restricted social and welfare amenities. Pull factors on the other hand, are the perceived advantages of city life such as more employment opportunities, higher wages, better housing and schools, and superior shops and entertainment. However, the evidence for return migration is clear. For many people living in large cities, small towns and rural areas can be very attractive. Due to improvements in transport, they can still benefit from the employment opportunities, shops and recreational facilities of large urban areas but live in small towns and rural areas.

Declining villages have many problems. It is difficult to maintain basic services for those who remain. Decreasing numbers of people leads to the closure of village schools, run-down bus services and the transfer of many services to larger towns. This, in turn, fuels the process of depopulation.

## MANAGING RURAL SETTLEMENTS

### Key settlements in the UK

The **key settlement** concept uses some principles of central place theory (page 10) and assumes that the focusing of services, facilities and employment in one selected settlement will satisfy the essential needs of the surrounding villages and hamlets and that, in the long term, such concentration is more economic than the dispersion of facilities. It has been widely used by local authority planners throughout the UK in areas which differ considerably in terms of population trends. Key settlements tend not to have a slot in the hierarchy of central places, nor have their service areas or spheres of influence been carefully defined or measured.

### Selection of key settlements

In the 1950s to 70s, many rural county councils, such as Devon, Warwickshire and Durham, adopted Key Settlement Plans to provide rural dwellers with essential services and facilities at reasonably accessible locations. The councils selected some settlements as service centres, such as schools and hospitals, for a more efficient use of resources. They ranged widely in size and suitability for other functions. In Hampshire, it was decided that these centres were not necessarily suitable for residential development, since the factors which influence the location of service centres and housing are not always the same. Though the plans have been widely used, from areas of persistent depopulation to those of continual growth, there has been little monitoring of the progress of key settlements or evaluation of their success.

Key settlements vary widely. Some are mostly service centres, some are associated largely with public investment such as schools, hospitals or council estates, and others are concerned with private housing developments. Some have been targeted as centres for industrial or employment growth, although these are normally associated with larger market towns. The main method is therefore to concentrate limited financial resources upon a few selected centres rather than dispersal in a range of settlements. The concept has close links with that of threshold – a certain facility being uneconomic below a critical population size. To reach such a threshold, villages can be linked or grouped and served by an accessible location.

The selection of key settlements depended upon a number of factors:

1 existing social facilities, including primary schools (sometimes a secondary school), shops, village hall, doctor's surgery and public utilities (gas, water, mains drainage)

2 existing sources of employment (excluding agriculture) in or near the vicinity of the village

3 location in relation to principal traffic routes and the possibility that new development might create the need for a new by-pass

4 location relative to bus and rail routes

5 location in relation to urban centres providing employment, secondary schools, medical facilities and specialised services (key settlements are not appropriate close to the main urban centres)

6 location in relation to other villages which will rely on them for services

7 availability of public utilities capable of extension for new development

8 availability and agricultural value of land capable of development

9 the effect on visual amenities.

The concept of key settlements was proposed for the Cambridge area during the inter-war years and has had some success, partly due to the strict control of residential expansion in Cambridge itself, as well as the whole region being a growth area. The policy has also been adopted in areas where depopulation has occurred, such as parts of Devon, in 1964, and Berwickshire, in 1972 (Figure 8.1).

Berwickshire's rural districts were all declining in population and very few settlements were increasing at a significant rate. The need was to stem the population decline and provide modern facilities for those remaining, despite the falling population. The policy proposed **groups** of villages and hamlets, each group having a key centre where some

expansion was allowed.

The Duns group of villages (Figure 8.1) illustrates the working of the policy. The main priority in 1972 was to attract industry to Duns, whose role was to provide employment and housing for its group of villages. More housing was needed due to changes in the population age structure and household structure and to replace old, poor quality housing. All new investment was ploughed into Duns and none into any of the other settlements. The only exception to this was at Swinton, to the south-east of Duns. Swinton was classified as a conservation village where redevelopment of derelict sites would be permitted; however, financing was to come from private developers. For the other five settlements, no deliberate public investment occurred, although private development was permitted. Not much private development took place because of out-migration and continued decline of the area.

If the key settlements concept is to succeed in Berwickshire it will only be at the expense of other settlements in the area: population catchments are too low and thresholds for services and facilities too high.

In Warwickshire (Figure 8.2), a rural area with a relatively stable population, it had been decided that future developments should be concentrated in key settlements. These would absorb not only their own growth, but some of that of other settlements as well. At the same time, such settlements were to be developed to act as service centres for

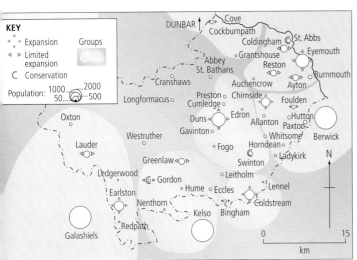

*Figure 8.1* Key settlements in Berwickshire, 1972
Source: Berwickshire County Council

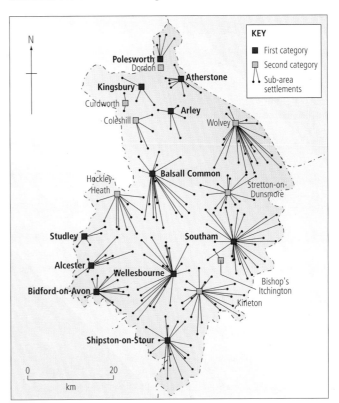

*Figure 8.2* Warwickshire's key settlements, 1973
Source: Warwickshire County Council

these hinterlands. The aim was to identify key settlements in terms of development potential, land constraints and commitments. On the basis of this, it was possible to identify a hierarchy of settlements in which development could be encouraged or restricted.

## THE ZUIDER ZEE PROJECT

Between 1930 and 1968, key settlement policies were developed in the Netherlands as well as in the UK. The Dutch Zuider Zee project (Figure 8.3) used the principles of central place theory.

---

## QUESTIONS

**1** What is a key settlement?

**2** What are the criteria for classifying key settlements?

**3** For a rural area of your choice, classify the settlements into four groups, group A being the most important and group D the least important. Use the criteria adopted by Devon to help you. Justify your choice.

---

| | Weiringermeer Polder | North East Polder | Flevoland Polders Eastern | Southern |
|---|---|---|---|---|
| Development started | 1930 | 1942 | 1957 | 1968 |
| Area (ha) | 20 000 | 48 000 | 54 000 | 43 000 |
| Farmland | 87 | 87 | 75 | 50 |
| Housing/industrial | 1 | 1 | 8 | 25 |
| Woods/nature reserves | 3 | 5 | 11 | 18 |
| Canals/roads/ dykes | 9 | 7 | 6 | 7 |
| | 100% | 100% | 100% | 100% |

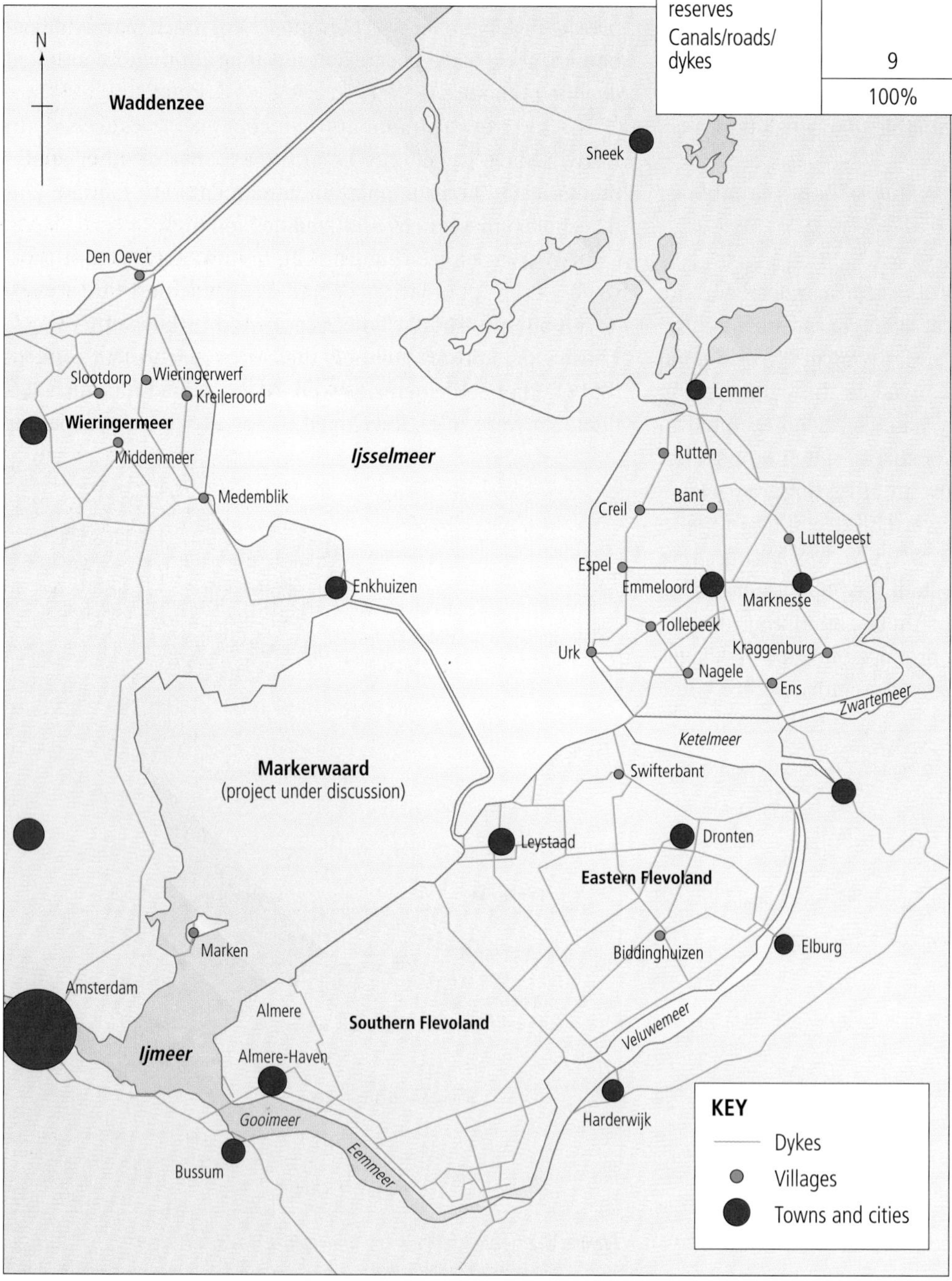

**Figure 8.3** *The Ijsselmeer Polder settlements*
Source: University of Oxford Delegacy of Local Examinations, 1987

KEY
— Dykes
• Villages
● Towns and cities

To solve the problem of shortage of land, the Netherlands instigated a massive plan to build a dam across a large bay on the coast and reclaim the land behind the dam. The first polder (area of land reclaimed from the sea) to be completed was the Wieringermeer, in 1930. The problem was how best to lay out the settlements and the lines of communication. The pattern of roads and canals was largely determined by the division of agricultural land into standard 20 hectare plots. The choice of settlement location could therefore be somewhat arbitrary, for instance, at major road junctions. However, the pattern that developed as a natural/planned process to keep settlements fairly close together was far from ideal. The three original villages were clustered in the middle of the polder, with overlapping service areas. Many villagers outside these areas considered themselves to be too far from the centres for convenience. Population growth on the polder was less than expected, 8000 rather than 15 000. Consequently, many small villages were unable to provide sufficient services and facilities, as they did not have a sufficient threshold population. More recent growth, largely as a result of overspill from Amsterdam 60 kilometres to the south, has taken the population to 12 000. The polder also lacked a definite centre. This is still a problem, as Weiringerwerf is the administrative centre and Middenmeer the commercial one. The continuing development of light manufacturing in the former, may tip the balance in its favour.

In the planning of the North East polder in 1942 (48 000 hectares) an attempt was made to avoid the problems that had occurred in Wieringermeer. The central settlement was located at the intersection of a skeletal road system with smaller service centres on the periphery. In 1948, it was decided that 5 kilometres was the maximum distance that people would be prepared to travel from outlying districts to the villages. A plan was devised to develop eleven villages with populations of 1000-2000 and a main town of 10 000 at Emmeloord. Despite careful planning, a number of problems have occurred. The growth of mechanised agriculture has meant that there are fewer jobs in agriculture than had been expected. Although Emmeloord has developed faster than expected, seven of the villages failed to reach 700 in size, and six of these have declined since 1970. Much of this decline is due to socio-economic changes such as increasing affluence, greater mobility and higher demands on the provision of services.

By 1957, when the Eastern Flevoland had been drained, the planners had learned from their experiences. The settlement plan was to have a number of 'A' centres (with local service functions), a single 'B' centre (with a district service function) and a 'C' centre (with a regional function serving four polders). Indeed, Lelystad was later to become one of the most important towns to accommodate overspill from the urban agglomeration, the Randstad.

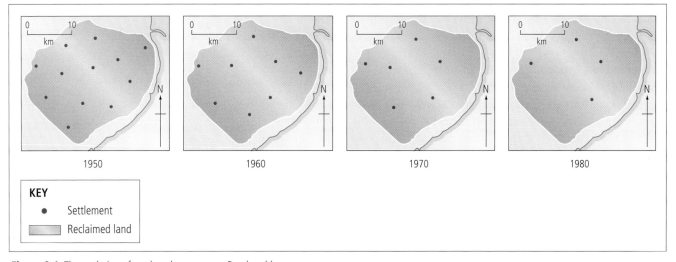

*Figure 8.4* The evolution of rural settlements on a Dutch polder
Source: University of London Examinations, 1990

## QUESTIONS

1 Describe and explain the changes that have taken place with respect to settlement and land use in the Ijsselmeer Polder scheme between 1930 and 1968.

2 Study Figure 8.4 which shows the sequence of changes of central places planned for an area of reclaimed land in an advanced country.

a) How does central place theory help to explain the pattern in 1950?

b) Describe the changes in the provision of central places occurring between 1950 and 1980.

c) Suggest **three** reasons for these changes.

d) Comment on **two** consequences of these changes.

e) Comment on **two** different problems which might arise from the concentration of services into a single high-order centre.

## SETTLEMENT POLICY IN ISRAEL

In Israel, as well as their residential and agricultural functions, rural settlements have had important ideological (cultural-political) significance. The use of civilian settlements, especially agricultural settlements, plays a unique role in the Arab-Israeli conflict. Settlement has been a key element:

- in the expansion of Jewish control over Palestine (pre-1948)
- in the consolidation of that control throughout Israel (1948-1967)
- in more recent attempts to establish long-term control over the West Bank and the Gaza Strip (post-1967).

The creation of a 'civilian presence' can be an important means of ensuring long-term control in circumstances where the land cannot be purchased legally.

Of even greater importance is the functional nature of the settlements. An agricultural village brings far more land under control than a commuter or dormitory village. Also, farming creates a strong bond between the settler and the land, and hence a sense of belonging to the area.

A major component of Zionism (the movement to restore a Jewish nation in Palestine) was the desire to return to the land and to the agricultural origins of the Jewish people. Settlement dispersal was also a major factor in determining the ultimate borders of the state of Israel in 1948-1949. The vast empty Negev desert region was included within the state's boundaries because it was perceived as constituting the future development region for new settlement projects.

### Settlement in the occupied territories

After the 1967 Arab-Israel war, Israeli policies aimed at bringing the region (or part of it) under control were still based around the settlement/colonisation concept (Figure 8.5). Between 1967 and 1989, some 118 new rural and urban settlements, containing about 70 000 people, were established throughout the West Bank and the Gaza Strip. There was a clear concentration in the western margins of the West Bank. The Golan Heights has also been the subject of intensive colonisation by about 30 agricultural villages, aimed at bolstering Israeli control over this peripheral, but strategically important, region along the border between Israel and Syria. The settlement policy can be divided into four major periods: 1967-1976; 1977-1980; 1981-1984 and since 1984.

### 1967-1976

During the period 1967-1976, the ruling Labour government was concerned about defensible borders on the West Bank, Gaza Strip, Golan Heights and Jordan Valley. The small agricultural villages attracted relatively few settlers, but enabled extensive regional territorial control by means of widespread agricultural cultivation. Seventeen settlements,

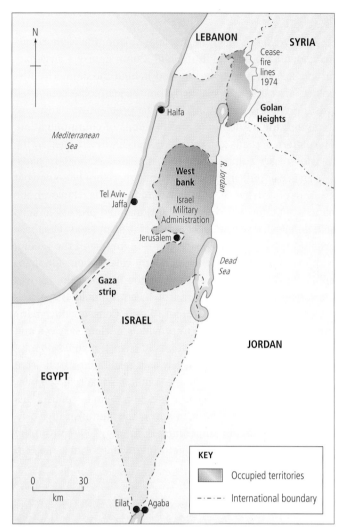

**Figure 8.5** *Israel and the occupied territories, 1990 – political and administrative divisions*
Source: Newman, D., 1990, Israel and the West Bank, CUP

containing about 3000 people, were established along the Jordan valley.

### 1977-1980

Menahem Begin's right-wing Likud party gained control in 1977. The government rejected any territorial concessions on the West Bank. Widespread settlement occurred throughout the region as a means of ensuring territorial control. By contrast with earlier schemes, the Likud concentrated on settling the mountain ridge in the West Bank, the most densely populated area of Palestinian habitation. The creation of settlements in and around the territory densely populated by the indigenous inhabitants, was meant to demonstrate the new government's resolve to retain the whole region under Israeli control.

This period also witnessed the founding of a new type of settlement, the community village or **yshuv kehillati**. Unlike the classic agricultural collectives, the **kibbutzim** and **moshavim** found throughout the agricultural landscape, these community villages were mostly dormitory settlements located within commuting distance of Tel Aviv and Jerusalem. Thus the potential settlers did not have to change their workplace or renounce family independence. Instead, they merely had to change their place of residence, normally from an apartment to a house with a plot of land. Government incentives such as cheap land and large mortgages facilitated the move. In this era about 50 villages were established in the West Bank, accounting for 11 000 people.

### 1981-1984

During the second Likud government, 1981-1984, there was a rapid increase in the pace of development, although the objectives remained the same. Policy makers began to understand that, in order to attract a mass movement of settlers to the West Bank, it was important to emphasise the economic and social benefits rather than the ideological ones, which appealed only to a minority.

Advertising campaigns marketed the idea of private housing in a low density suburb of Jerusalem for the price of an apartment in the city, within commuting distance of the workplaces, and with all the qualities of life that are associated with a small, quiet, garden city. A further 30 settlements were added to the West Bank, bringing the total settler population to 44 000.

Most of the Gaza Strip settlements were established during this latter period. By 1990 there were 16 Jewish communities in the southern section of the Gaza Strip, housing approximately 3500 people.

### 1984 to the present

This period has been characterised by the consolidation of the existing colonisation network, with only a few additional settlements being added. Many of the settlements that were originally established were small, lacking the necessary threshold for the provision of many basic services. The settler population continued to increase annually, mostly through the consolidation and extension of settlements already established. By 1988, the Israeli settler population of the West Bank had risen to 67 000.

Since 1988 there has been a slowing-down in the colonisation process. Many of the existing smaller villages are perceived as small, remote, inconveniently located and unattractive to all but the most ideologically-orientated settlers. Consequently, there has been little growth in these and many remain inhabited by less than 50 families. The continuing uncertainty of the Israeli-Palestinian peace process, and terrorist attacks in Israel, have caused upsurges in nationalism among Israelis. However, in 1997 Israeli ministers suggested that the continued expansion of Israeli settlement on the West Bank could be reviewed if the Palestinians cracked down on terrorism.

---

## QUESTIONS

1  In what ways has Israeli settlement policy differed from that in the UK and in the Netherlands?

2  Explain how and why settlements and agriculture can be used as an ideological or political tool.

---

## RECENT CHANGES IN RURAL SETTLEMENTS IN THE UK

The key factors causing rural change from the 1950s on, are:
- improvements in transport
- higher standards of living
- decreased size of households.

There are a number of reasons for the movement to small towns and rural areas. Three important factors are a growing dissatisfaction with urban lifestyles, an increase in car ownership, and improving technology which has allowed industries to become 'footloose'.

Those who have moved into rural settlements include:
- families who prefer a safer, more pleasant environment
- commuters who prefer living in smaller settlements but whose job is elsewhere
- retired people
- careerists moving to the region as part of their career but whose residence is only short-term
- small-scale entrepreneurs and the self-employed who live in an area they consider offers a good quality of life.

The proportion living in rural areas increased from 19% in 1951 to 21.7% in 1971, an increase of 2.2 million people. Although they may live in rural areas, the newcomers bring with them urban attitudes and lifestyles. In addition, house prices increase. It is not just people that are moving to the rural areas but it is industry and retailing too. It is possible that counterurbanisation (the movement of people and industry from large urban centres to smaller urban areas and the more accessible rural areas), will lead to a more even distribution of population in the industrialised nations in the next fifty years. Indeed, it is difficult to see how inner cities can ever be as attractive to the majority of people as the smaller towns and rural areas.

One of the greatest changes has been brought about by improvements in transport, both public and private. There is a definite relationship between (i) the type and rate of change in rural settlements and (ii) distance from large urban areas (Figure 8.6, see page 94), with the most accessible villages expanding the most.

Many villages have grown at a very rapid rate and have lost their original character, form and function. These are often described as **dormitory**, **commuter** or **suburbanised villages** (Figure 8.7, see page 94).

The villages without good transport links or beyond the distance of commuting have tended to retain more of their

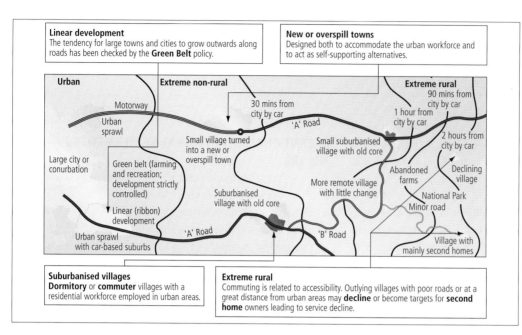

*Figure 8.6 Cloke's model of rural settlements – the relationship between the type and rate of change in rural settlements and distance from large urban areas*
*Source: Nagle, G., and Spencer, K., 1997, Advanced geography revision handbook, OUP*

original character. The size of the population in these villages may not change a great deal but the composition of the population does change; younger people moving out to be replaced by older ones. These villages may become like retirement villages, although lacking in many of the functions that retired people require.

Villages in National Parks or areas of attractive scenery are being affected by the increased incidence of second homes (weekend cottages owned by people whose permanent residence is elsewhere). The Gower is an excellent example of where this has happened. The increase in the number of second homes has led to much conflict in some areas between locals, who are priced out of the housing market, and holiday makers or weekenders, who are made to feel unwelcome and cannot fully enjoy the fruits of their labour (or inheritance).

In the most remote areas, which are not particularly attractive to the second home owners, the problems of decline are greatest. Here there are few opportunities, much out-migration and declining service provision, such as schools. Villages may go into terminal decline and eventually the whole settlement be abandoned.

| Characteristics | Original village | Suburbanised village |
|---|---|---|
| Housing | Detached, stone built houses with slate/thatch roofs. Some farms, barns. Most over 100 years. | New, mainly detached or semis. Renovated barns or cottages. Expensive planned estates, garages. |
| Inhabitants | Farming and primary jobs. Labouring or manual jobs. | Professionals/executives, commuters. Wealthy with young families or retired. |
| Transport | Bus service, some cars. Narrow winding roads. | Decline in bus services as most families have one or two cars. Better roads. |
| Services | Village shop, small primary school, public house, village hall. | More shops, enlarged school, modern public houses and/or restaurant. |
| Social | Small, close-knit community. | Local community swamped. Village may be deserted by day. |
| Environment | Quiet, relatively pollution-free. | More noise and risk of more pollution. Loss of farmland and open space. |

*Figure 8.7 Changes in the suburbanised village*
*Source: Waugh, D., Geography an integrated approach, 1990, Nelson*

## QUESTIONS

**1a)** Using Figure 8.7 describe the main changes that take place when a village is suburbanised.

**b)** Briefly explain **three** reasons why these changes take place.

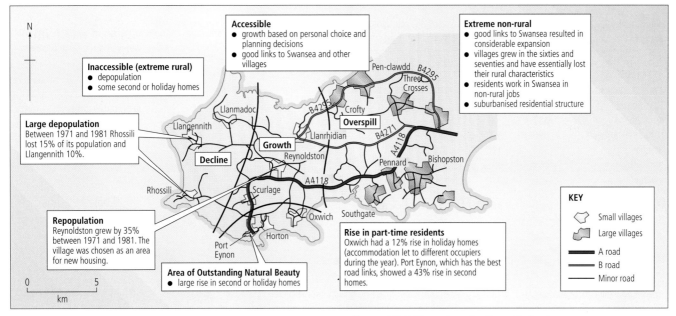

**Figure 8.8** *Settlements on the Gower Peninsula*
Source: Nagle, G., 1998, Geography through diagrams, OUP

## Changing settlements on the Gower Peninsula and the Isle of Purbeck

Many rural settlements are changing due to suburbanisation and counterurbanisation. Villages which are closest to large urban areas are changing the most. This is shown clearly by the example of the Gower Peninsula (Figure 8.8). The Gower Peninsula is in south-west Wales, to the west of Swansea. It is an Area of Outstanding Natural Beauty (AONB). In the last thirty years there has been a dramatic change in the villages on the Gower (Figure 8.9). Some have grown while others have declined. The key factors influencing growth and decline are:

- closeness to Swansea
- accessibility
- natural beauty
- planning decisions.

Figure 8.10 shows the change in age structures of the population in the villages of the Isle of Purbeck, in Dorset. A number of trends can be seen:

- the continued growth of Swanage, partly as a commuter settlement
- an increase in the retired and elderly population
- an increase in the number of second homes in the area, especially in the more scenic parts
- the decline of council housing.

| | Population change 1971-81 % | Second homes % | Holiday homes % |
|---|---|---|---|
| Reynoldston | +34.7 | 1.3 | 1.3 |
| Port Eynon | +18.2 | 43.4 | 4.0 |
| Horton | +7.4 | 13.2 | 5.9 |
| Llanrhidian | +0.4 | 1.7 | 1.2 |
| Llanmadoc | -3.3 | 1.1 | 6.5 |
| Scurlage | -3.8 | 1.3 | 0.0 |
| Oxwich | -6.0 | 17.0 | 12.0 |
| Llangenith | -9.7 | 4.5 | 7.1 |
| Rhossili | -14.6 | 18.4 | 7.4 |

**Figure 8.9** *Population change on the Gower, 1971-1981*
Source: Nagle, G., and Spencer, K., 1996, Investigating geography, Hodder and Stoughton

| Age | 1971 | 1991 | Change | Age | 1971 | 1991 | Change |
|---|---|---|---|---|---|---|---|
| 0-4 | 455 | 489 | ..... | 50-54 | 420 | 413 | ..... |
| 5-9 | 495 | 467 | ..... | 55-59 | 545 | 507 | ..... |
| 10-14 | 895 | 438 | ..... | 60-64 | 655 | 585 | ..... |
| 15-19 | 590 | 481 | ..... | 65-69 | 735 | 681 | ..... |
| 20-24 | 500 | 464 | ..... | 70-74 | 600 | 646 | ..... |
| 25-29 | 360 | 490 | ..... | 75-79 | 430 | 573 | ..... |
| 30-34 | 290 | 484 | ..... | 80-84 | 270 | 461 | ..... |
| 35-39 | 350 | 434 | ..... | 85-89 | 105 | 242 | ..... |
| 40-44 | 405 | 578 | ..... | <90 | 40 | 107 | ..... |
| 45-49 | 410 | 565 | | | | | |

**Figure 8.10** *Changing age structures in Swanage, 1971-91*
Source: Kemp, D., 1996, Environmental studies in Purbeck, Globe Education, Dorset County Council

## QUESTIONS

**1** Study Figures 8.8 and 8.9.

**a)** Choose a suitable technique to show the distribution of second homes and holiday homes.

**b)** Describe the distribution of **(i)** second homes and **(ii)** holiday homes.

**c)** Using an atlas, explain the distribution of second homes and holiday homes.

| Parish | Size (ha) | 1961 | 1971 | 1981 | 1991 |
|---|---|---|---|---|---|
| Arne | 2483 | 1066 | 1062 | 1050 | 1159 |
| Church Knowle | 1183 | 391 | 341 | 338 | 332 |
| Corfe Castle | 3745 | 1381 | 1292 | 1347 | 1341 |
| East Holme | 433 | 55 | 73 | 70 | 58 |
| Kimmeridge | 402 | 87 | 70 | 77 | 96 |
| Langton Matravers | 896 | 950 | 953 | 902 | 910 |
| Steeple | 1364 | 115 | 115 | 119 | 97 |
| Studland | 2053 | 635 | 620 | 432 | 473 |
| Swanage | 1120 | 8120 | 8556 | 8647 | 9041 |
| Tyneham* | 1201 | 0 | 0 | 0 | 0 |
| Worth Matravers | 1098 | 580 | 576 | 518 | 605 |
| *Areas outside the Isle of Purbeck:* | | | | | |
| Wareham | 285 | 3098 | 4368 | 4577 | 5639 |
| Purbeck District | - | 32 075 | 36 688 | 40 414 | 42 383 |

*Figure 8.11* Population changes in the Isle of Purbeck, 1961-91
Source: Kemp, D., 1996, Environmental studies in Purbeck, Globe Education, Dorset County Council

*The villagers of Tyneham were removed during World War II by the Ministry of Defence so that the area could be used as an army firing range. They have never been allowed back to their village.

*Figure 8.12*
Settlements in the Isle of Purbeck parishes
Source: Kemp, D., 1996, Environmental studies in Purbeck, Globe Education, Dorset County Council

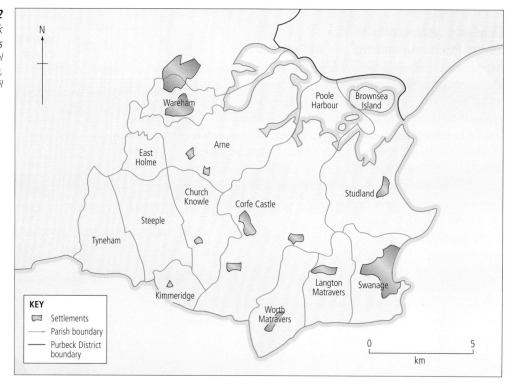

## QUESTIONS

**1** Study Figure 8.10, on page 95.

**a)** Work out the population change for each age group between 1971 and 1991. (Use the formula: (1991 figure – 1971 value)/1971) x 100% value to find percentage change.)

**b)** Which age groups have increased **(i)** the most? and **(ii)** have decreased?

**c)** What evidence is there to suggest a change in the age structure of the Swanage population?

**2** Using an atlas, suggest which settlements commuters from Swanage work in. Give reasons for your answer.

**3** Using an atlas explain why Swanage might be attractive to elderly people.

**4** Study Figure 8.11 which shows population changes in the Isle of Purbeck between 1961 and 1991.

**a)** Which areas have increased the most in percentage terms?

**b)** Which places have decreased in size?

**c)** What evidence is there to suggest that population change varies with **(i)** settlement size? **(ii)** accessibility to centres of employment? **(iii)** potential for retirement such as coastal or scenic landscapes?

**5** Make a copy of Figure 8.12, a map of the parishes of the Isle of Purbeck, and show how population change (1961-91) varies over a small area. Explain the contrasts that you have shown.

# Inset 8.1
# Investigating rural settlements

A number of aspects of rural settlements can be investigated. These include:

- the growth of a settlement
- the suburbanisation of a village
- the sphere of influence of settlements
- the impact of transport developments or closures on a settlement
- the changing function of a settlement.

The choice will depend upon the type of village chosen and its geographical and historical pattern of development.

## Sampling

Sampling is the selection of data for analysis. It is necessary to sample because it is impractical and sometimes impossible to use all the relevant data available. There are three main types of sampling:

1 **Random sampling** – data selection is left completely to chance. Each place has an equal chance of being used. Normally, random number tables are used to generate the survey points. It is a very fair way of taking a sample but can be somewhat time–consuming.

2 **Systematic sampling** – data selection is made in a regular way. This could be every tenth house, every ten metres, every ten years and so on. It is a quick way of taking a sample. However, it may overlook important features and does not always provide the detail which is sometimes necessary.

3 **Stratified sampling** – data is selected at preset places which are divided into sub-areas or sub-sets known to contain a significant characteristic. For example, in a village we may take an old area, an area of modern building, and an area of early twentieth century development.

These methods can be used to decide upon point samples, area samples, line samples (transects) and temporal samples (certain years, for example) (Figure 8.13).

## Methods of data collection

1 **Census data** is collected every ten years with the exception of 1941 because of World War II. It provides a wide range of data on features such as household size, occupation, housing tenure and so on. When using census data it is best to use them over a long period of time as these show greater contrast (Figure 8.14, see page 98). Similarly the use of ten year gaps such as 1891, 1901, 1911 and so on shows trends in the development in village growth (Figure 8.15, see page 98).

2 **Ordnance Survey maps** show how a village has grown over a period of time. Most county libraries contain maps which date back to the eighteenth and nineteenth centuries – these are useful in that they can show what a village looked like at a very early stage. It is best to show the pattern of growth in a settlement over as long a period as possible (Figure 8.16, see page 98).

3 **Kelly's Directories** provide data on the number of services and industries in villages. They can be used with surveys based on observations to show the changes in services and rural based industries.

4 **County Planning Reports** show how county plans, village and transport developments change over time. For example, the reports of the Berkshire highways and planning consultants (BABTIE Reports) show how transport patterns in the county have changed over a long period of time. These can then be related to changes in the settlement pattern.

5 **Old photographs, postcards and other memorabilia** can be used to show how settlements have adapted to change. These can be linked to Mitchell's idea of open and closed villages, integrated and disintegrated settlements (see Chapter 1, Rural and urban settlement).

Primary data collection includes surveying a village. This covers land use, the age of the buildings, the type of buildings, their function, the amount of land they cover and any geographic patterns. It is important to record the number of services and the type of services.

Questionnaires and surveys are also important. Simple questionnaires can be asked to determine the proportion of people that work in the village or work in a nearby town, that use local services such as shops, that use local schools, that use local general practitioners (GPs) and so on. It is possible to determine the sphere of influence of a particular service, such as the milk delivery round, by the use of questionnaires.

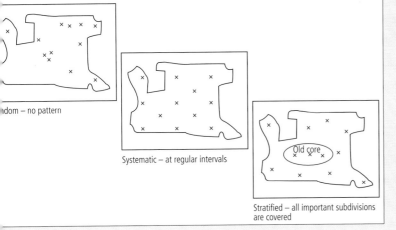

ndom – no pattern

Systematic – at regular intervals

Old core

Stratified – all important subdivisions are covered

*Figure 8.13* Types of sampling

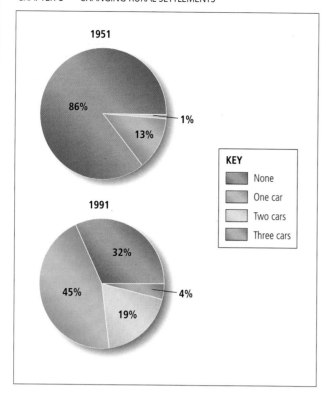

1951

86%

1%

13%

1991

32%

45%

4%

19%

KEY

None

One car

Two cars

Three cars

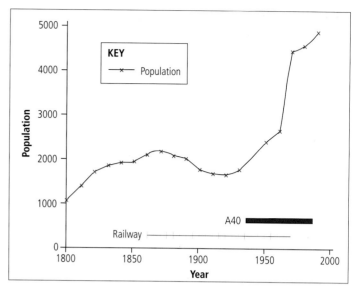

**Figure 8.15** *Population growth in Eynsham, Oxfordshire, 1801-91*
*Source: Russell, J., 1996, Suburbanisation of Eynsham, A Level project*

**Figure 8.14** *Changes in car ownership, 1951-91*
*Source: Phipps, J., 1995, Suburbanisation of Hermitage, A Level project*

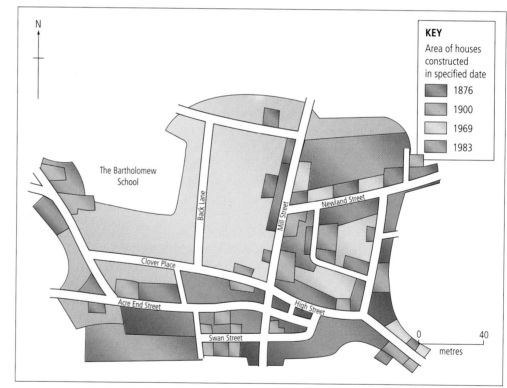

**Figure 8.16**
*The growth of Hermitage, Berkshire*
*Source: Phipps, J., 1995, Suburbanisation*
*of Hermitage, A Level project*

## QUESTIONS

**1** Study Figures 8.14, 8.15 and 8.16 which show changes in rural settlements.

**a)** Describe how Hermitage has developed since 1876.

**b)** How has the population of Eynsham changed since 1800?

**c)** How has car ownership in Hermitage changed between 1951 and 1991? What are the implications for village growth?

**d)** What effect did the railway (1860-1965) have on the growth of Eynsham's population? How does this compare with the effect of the A40 (post 1930)?

## TRENDS IN RURAL AREAS IN THE UK

There have been a large number of changes in rural areas. These include depopulation, fewer farms, changing agricultural land base, counter-urbanisation, long-distance commuting, teleworkers, and retired migrants. In addition, new roads, airports, housing schemes and theme parks have been constructed. The implications of the revised Common Agricultural Policy are very significant. Quotas, reduced prices, extensification and set-aside have led to reductions in farm incomes. Consequently, farming households have been forced to find other ways of generating income.

### Housing

The most notable feature of housing in rural areas during the 1980s was the decline in council house building. The poorest groups are dependent on some form of public sector provision, but by 1991 new council houses accounted for less than 7% of all new housing in the countryside. Rented property is often only available as tied accommodation in particular occupations. The majority of housing for sale was on the open market. This had important implications for the type of person who could move into rural areas, as well as the type of person who was forced to leave rural areas.

---

### QUESTIONS

1  What type of housing are private developers likely to provide? Give reasons to support your answer.

2  Explain why there are fewer houses available for low-income groups in rural areas.

---

### Rural economic activities

Rural economies have been forced to adapt to the decline of agriculture as a large-scale employer. New technologies, improved communications, and the shift of population to rural areas has allowed a wide range of economic activity to locate in small towns and rural areas. The result has been an increasing similarity in the economic profiles of rural and urban areas, although in remoter and less accessible areas, land-based industry remains of greater importance. For the first time since the industrial revolution, technological change is allowing rural areas to compete on equal terms with towns and cities for employment.

The great majority of rural jobs are in service industries and manufacturing. Small firms in these sectors are the chief source of employment and wealth creation in the countryside. The rate of growth of new firms is generally higher in rural counties than elsewhere, and rural firms perform on average as well as or better than their urban counterparts.

Registered unemployment in rural areas is generally, though not universally, below average for the UK . However, wages in rural areas tend to be lower, as are female activity rates, while part-time working is more prevalent and growing faster. There are, however, fewer young people in remote areas and there is continued out-migration of young people in search of housing and jobs.

### RURAL SERVICES IN THE EARLY 1990s

The Rural Development Commission's 1991 survey of services in rural parishes revealed that:

- 39% had no shop
- 40% had no post office
- 51% had no school
- 29% had no village hall
- 73% had no daily bus service
- fewer than 10% had a bank or building society, a nursery or day-care centre, a dentist or a daily train service.

Where they existed, services tended to be concentrated in larger villages and market towns. Overall, the services which most people take for granted are few and far between in the countryside. With the lack of public transport, rural people are heavily reliant on cars to reach essential services, recreational or other facilities.

Population changes have led to most rural areas having above average numbers of elderly people and below average numbers of 16-20 year olds.

### Some key services

In 1991, 61% of settlements with under 300 population had one or more weekly mobile shops. A significant minority of people – about a quarter – still depend on a local shop for their everyday needs, but the proportion varies widely in different areas.

Many rural primary schools closed in the 1960s and 1970s, especially in smaller villages of under 200 people. By 1991, only 40% of parishes had a primary school and these usually had a population of over 500 people.

By 1991, only 16% of parishes had a permanent GP surgery (they are most common in parishes of more than 1000). The number of consultations per GP are lower than those in towns, even for those villages with a surgery, and are lowest in remoter villages with no surgery.

The availability of and access to childcare facilities both pre-school and out-of-school, is patchy and poor. In 1991, only 5% of parishes had an out-of-school childcare group and a nursery.

In 1991, only 27% of parishes had a daily bus services and only 7% had a rail service. Although by necessity car ownership is higher in the countryside than in the towns, significant numbers of people, especially amongst the elderly and women, have no or limited use of a car.

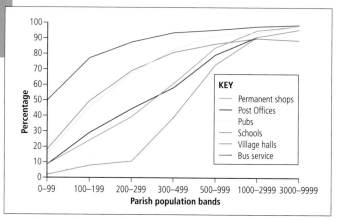

***Figure 8.17*** *Population size and provision of services*
*Source: Rural Development Commission, 1993*

## QUESTIONS

**1** Study Figure 8.17 which shows population size and availability of services.

**a)** What proportion of settlements with less than 100 people have access to **(i)** a bus service **(ii)** a village school, and **(iii)** a post office?

**b)** How does this compare with settlements which have 500-999 people and those with 1000 to 2500 people?

**2** What appears to be the critical size of settlement to sustain a range of services? Support your answer with evidence.

**3** Choose any two of the following groups **(i)** low income groups; **(ii)** the elderly; **(iii)** the infirm; **(iv)** people without access to a car; **(v)** youth. What are the implications of declining rural services for the two groups that you have chosen.

## Sustainable rural settlements

Sustainable rural settlements should fulfil at least four requirements:

- People should live and work locally, and villages and small towns should provide for the varied needs of people in a wide range of circumstances.
- The economy of all rural areas should provide a broad range of job opportunities and make the most effective contribution to the national economy.
- Residents should not be disadvantaged as a result of living in rural areas, and rural communities should have reasonable and affordable access to services.
- Development should respect and enhance the environment.

Businesses in small towns and rural areas can get advice from the Rural Development Commission. For example, help is available regarding:

**1** energy audits where cost savings and environmental benefits are often readily achievable

**2** advice on the implications of recent and forthcoming environmental legislation

**3** green business and marketing opportunities.

Sustainable initiatives in rural settlements include encouraging people who visit the countryside to 'leave the car behind'; to stay in village or on-farm accommodation; to use local hiring facilities for bicycles, horses, surf-boards, fishing, specialist clothing; to support local markets, fairs and cultural events; and to buy local crafts and products. Measures such as these could help to sustain some rural settlements and to deflect some of the environmental opposition to rural development.

## SUMMARY

In this chapter we have seen that rural populations are changing. The population of rural UK is forecast to grow during the 1990s at twice the rate of the UK as a whole. This is creating a great stress upon rural settlements. In addition, the number of elderly people in the countryside is expected to grow very rapidly, and this will give rise to a greater need for some local services, especially care and health services.

Much of the pressure stems from changes in household structure. Household size has declined in recent years and is set to reduce even further into the next century. This means, for example, that even in rural areas where population growth is relatively low, demand for housing may be high. Counties with substantial rural populations are noticeably in the forefront of this trend.

The growth in transport and improvements in technology have had a radical impact on rural settlements. There has been a huge increase in the amount of commuting, working from home, second homes and holiday homes. These have all added to the general suburbanisation of the countryside.

## QUESTIONS

**1** How have pressures on rural areas changed between the 1950s and the 1960s? Use examples to support your answer.

**2** Describe and explain what is meant by the term 'suburbanisation of the countryside'.

**3** Explain two ways in which the principles of central place theory have been used in rural planning.

**4** What are the main 'problems' in rural areas in the 1990s? Justify your answer.

## BIBLIOGRAPHY AND RECOMMENDED READING

**Clout, H.**, 1972, *Rural geography – an introductory survey*, Longman

**HMSO**, 1995, *First steps – Local Agenda 21 in practice*, HMSO

**HMSO**, 1996, *Indicators of sustainable development for the United Kingdom*, HMSO

**Kemp, D.**, 1996, *Environmental studies in Purbeck*, Globe Education/DCC

**Pacione, M.**, *Rural geography*, PCP

**Pacione, M.**, 1983, *Progress in rural geography*, Croom Helm

**Phillips, D., & Williams, A.**, 1984, *Rural Britain: a social geography*, Blackwell

**Rural Development Commission**, 1993, *English rural communities*, RDC

**Rural Development Commission**, 1993, *Rural services: challenges and opportunities*, RDC

**Rural Development Commission**, 1993, *Rural sustainable development*, RDC

**Woodruffe, B.**, 1976, *Rural settlements policies and plans*, OUP

## WEBSITES

**Environment Agency home page –** http://www.environment-agency.gov.uk/

**Friends of the Earth home page –** http://www.foe.co.uk/

# Chapter 9
# Cities in the developing world

We saw in Chapter 1 that rates of urbanisation are much higher in economically less developed countries (ELDCs) than in economically more developed countries (EMDCs), and over the next decades urban centres in the developing world will expand greatly. In this chapter we examine the rate and scale of that growth, its links with economic development, the reasons for urbanisation, and the characteristics of developing world cities, notably slums and squatter settlements, and the informal sector. We also look at the models which describe and explain urban patterns in the developing world, including land-use models similar to those for the developed world, and statistical analyses, such as the rank-size rule. Finally, we look at the links and contrasts between cities in the developing world and those in the developed world, and we assess the emergence of the world city.

## URBAN AREAS WORLDWIDE

The United Nations has standardised its data to recognise settlements of over 20 000 people as urban, over 100 000 as cities, and over 5 million as large cities. About 45% of the world's population lives in urban areas. Approximately three-quarters of the population in EMDCs is urban compared with 25% in ELDCs. However, the rate of urbanisation in developing countries is much faster than in developed countries, hence developing countries account for an increasing share of the world's urban population.

Urbanisation in ELDCs is diverse and there are important regional variations. For example, many parts of Latin America are as urbanised as Europe, with the urban proportions of Venezuela and Argentina in particular being extremely high. By contrast, Africa is much less urbanised, with many countries having less than 10% of their population in urban areas. Within Africa, North Africa is far more urban than Central and Southern Africa. Asia appears to have a more regular distribution, with approximately 25% of Asians living in urban areas. It does, however, vary between the newly industrialised countries (NICs), such Taiwan and South Korea, where nearly 50% live in urban areas, and the large countries, such as China and India, where less than 25% are urban.

## CITIES IN THE DEVELOPING WORLD

When looking at large cities in the developing world, there are at least five key points to consider:

1. Each city is unique – it has its own set of economic, social, political, environmental and cultural conditions that combine to determine the rate and character of growth and provision of housing, employment and services.
2. Cities with high rates of population growth have distinctive housing and infrastructure problems and a range of responses to these problems (Figure 9.1).
3. The formal sector is unable to provide sufficient housing and employment opportunities so the informal sector is increasingly important in the overall housing and job markets.
4. Natural population increase is becoming a more significant factor in the growth of cities in the developing world.
5. The development of housing, infrastructure and services in every city is different. Great care must be taken in making generalisations about the characteristics of developing world cities.

### Rate and scale of growth

Urban growth in Europe added 45 million people to urban areas throughout the whole of the nineteenth century. In Brazil, alone, between 1950 and 1975 more than 45 million people were added to urban areas. In the same period the total urban population of ELDCs grew by 400 million!

***Figure 9.1*** *Urbanisation in the developing world, Rio de Janeiro*

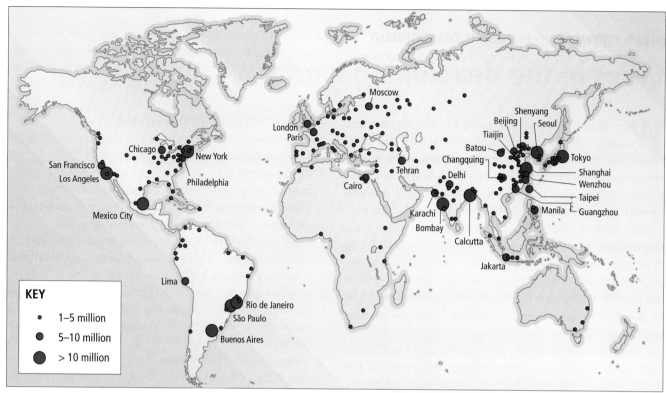

**Figure 9.2** *Distribution of the world's largest cities*
Source: Baker, S., et al., 1996, Pathways in senior geography, Nelson

One of the main trends in ELDCs is that the largest cities are growing the most rapidly. By the year 2000, most of the world's twenty largest cities will be in ELDCs rather than EMDCs. Moreover, in some ELDCs the main city is much greater in size than the second city. This is known as urban primacy and has often been explained by geographers by the use of the rank-size rule (see page 109). For example, in Thailand, Bangkok is nearly fifty times greater than the second largest city, Chiang Mai, and it contains over three-quarters of the country's urban population.

Figure 9.2 shows the changing rank and regional distribution of the world's largest cities between 1950 and 2010. The distribution of the world's largest cities is shown in Figure 9.3. Two key points can be seen:

1 The population of the ten largest cities has increased dramatically. In 1950, the tenth largest city, Calcutta, had a population of 4.4 million, by 2010 the tenth largest city (Jakarta) will have a population of over 17 million.

2 Cities from EMDCs will almost completely be replaced by cities from ELDCs.

| Rank | Agglomeration | 1950 | Agglomeration | 1970 | Agglomeration | 1990 | Agglomeration | 2010 |
|---|---|---|---|---|---|---|---|---|
| 1 | New York, USA | 12.3 | Tokyo, Japan | 16.5 | Tokyo, Japan | 25.0 | Tokyo, Japan | 28.9 |
| 2 | London, UK | 8.7 | New York, USA | 16.2 | São Paulo, Brazil | 18.1 | São Paulo, Brazil | 25.0 |
| 3 | Tokyo, Japan | 6.9 | Shanghai, China | 11.2 | New York, USA | 16.1 | Bombay, India | 24.4 |
| 4 | Paris, France | 5.4 | Osaka, Japan | 9.4 | Mexico City, Mexico | 15.1 | Shanghai, China | 21.7 |
| 5 | Moscow (former USSR) | 5.4 | Mexico City, Mexico | 9.1 | Shanghai, China | 13.4 | Lagos, Nigeria | 21.1 |
| 6 | Shanghai, China | 5.3 | London, UK | 8.6 | Bombay, India | 12.2 | Mexico City, Mexico | 18.0 |
| 7 | Essen, Germany | 5.3 | Paris, France | 8.5 | Los Angeles, USA | 11.5 | Beijing, China | 18.0 |
| 8 | Buenos Aires, Argentina | 5.0 | Buenos Aires, Argentina | 8.4 | Buenos Aires, Argentina | 11.4 | Dacca, Bangladesh | 17.6 |
| 9 | Chicago, USA | 4.9 | Los Angeles, USA | 8.4 | Seoul, Republic of Korea | 11.0 | New York, USA | 17.2 |
| 10 | Calcutta, India | 4.4 | Beijing, China | 8.1 | Rio de Janeiro, Brazil | 10.9 | Jakarta, Indonesia | 17.2 |

**Figure 9.3** *The world's ten largest cities (population in millions), 1950-2010*
Source: United Nations Organisation, 1993, World urbanisation prospects, 1992 revision, New York

---

## QUESTIONS

1 In what ways have the world's largest cities changed between 1950 and 1990? What is likely to happen by 2010? How do you explain these changes?

2 Describe the number and location of large cities as shown in Figure 9.3. Suggest some reasons for this pattern.

## URBAN GROWTH AND ECONOMIC DEVELOPMENT

There is a strong correlation between urban growth and economic development. However, to suggest that one causes the other is not necessarily correct. Levels of development have normally been measured in terms of gross national product (GNP) per head – and we have seen already that this is not necessarily the best measure of development. For example, does a high proportion of people living in urban areas lead to increased wealth, or does increased wealth lead to a high proportion of people living in urban areas? There is certainly a connection between the two factors, but one does not necessarily cause the other.

Urban places perform a number of important functions in the process of development.

1 **Commercially** towns provide the market and exchange centres necessary for the conversion from subsistence to cash crops.
2 **Industrially** towns may provide a stimulus for development – the larger the town the better for skilled and unskilled labour.
3 **Politically** towns may provide a focus for nationalist feeling and also allow for ethnic, tribal and religious intermixing.
4 **Administratively** towns provide economies of scale for health and education.
5 **Socially** the intermixing may weaken ties to traditional rural beliefs and customs.

Although cities make significant contributions to the economic wealth of a nation, they lead to huge problems such as pollution, destruction of ecosystems and poor living conditions. The deterioration is manifested in a number of ways:

- high rates of unemployment and underemployment as urban labour markets are unable to absorb the growing number of job seekers
- insufficient housing and shelter coupled with the growth of slums and squatter settlements
- overloaded and overcrowded transport systems
- air, water and noise pollution
- deteriorating infrastructure (basic services) and shortfall in service delivery such as public transport, waste disposal and health care
- growing inequalities between areas or districts within a city in terms of access to infrastructure and services
- inadequate sanitation and water supplies and associated health problems
- increasing prevalence of social problems, such as rising crime rates, suicide rates, drug and alcohol abuse, family breakdown and homelessness
- general deterioration of the perceived quality of life.

According to the United Nations Centre for Human Settlements, the environmental problems that result from urbanisation are best considered at five different, but closely related, levels. These range from the household level (or the immediate surroundings) for ill health, disablement and premature death arising from contaminated water and inadequate sanitation, to the global level where city-based production and consumption places large burdens on dwindling resources. The range of impacts is shown in Figure 9.4.

**Figure 9.4** *The impacts of urbanisation*
Source: Baker, S., et al. 1996, Pathways in senior geography, Nelson

| | Household/ workplace | Community | Metropolitan area | Region | Continent/planet |
|---|---|---|---|---|---|
| **Key infrastructure and services** | Shelter<br>Water storage<br>Onsite sanitation<br>Garbage storage<br>Stove<br>Ventilation | Piped water<br>Sewerage<br>Garbage collection<br>Drainage<br>Streets/lanes | Industrial parks<br>Roads<br>Interceptors<br>Treatment plants<br>Outfalls<br>Landfills | Highways<br>Water sources<br>Power plants | |
| **Characteristic problems** | Substandard housing<br>Lack of water<br>No sanitation<br>Disease vectors<br>Indoor air pollution | Excreta-laden water/soils<br>Rubbish dumping<br>Flooding<br>Noise stress<br>Natural disasters | Traffic congestion<br>Accidents<br>Ambient air pollution<br>Toxic dumps | Water pollution<br>Ecological areas lost | Acid rain<br>Global warming<br>Ozone layer |

## QUESTIONS

1 Briefly compare the advantages and disadvantages of populations being concentrated in large cities.

2 How do the problems of urbanisation in developing countries differ from those caused by urbanisation in the developed world? Support your answer with examples.

## EXPLAINING URBANISATION IN ELDCs

Vance's model of colonial impact (page 10) is a useful starting point when looking at urbanisation in ELDCs. Initial developments from Europe were made by individual adventurers to obtain valuable objects such as gold and silver. There was very little development of settlements and most of the trade was left in the hands of existing traders. Even when Europeans began to live in developing countries they tended to live in very compact areas near the central part of the city. There was very little planning and very little urban growth. No new hierarchies were created and only in a few places in Latin America were new settlements created.

Settlement development did not really take place until the industrial revolution in Europe. This led to an increased demand for raw materials and also for food for the workforce. Increasingly, urban areas and economic activity in the developing colonies were transferred from inland trading routes to coastal locations. Although manufacturing was limited a large commercial and service sector was required in order to meet the demands of trade and consumer needs from the colony. It is from this stage of **industrial colonialism** that segregation began to appear in ELDC cities.

In the late colonial period, the inter-war period (1918-1939), there was erratic demand for the primary products of the colonies. Many colonies were left to their own devices and the period saw the beginning of rural to urban migration. Many of these migrants began to live in squatter settlements on the periphery of the existing urban area. From 1939 onwards, there was a period of migration from European countries to many of the colonies, due to economic recession in EMDCs and many ELDCs, for example South Africa, Argentina and Rhodesia (Zimbabwe). Many of these new European migrants took up white collar and retail occupations which Europeans had previously been unwilling to undertake. This made it much more difficult for indigenous people to get into high level service employment. One of the results was that many of them migrated to the developed world.

During the 1950s and 1960s, independence spread rapidly throughout much of the developing world. Once the colonial powers had left, there was a great surge of indigenous peoples to the cities, lured by the prospect of better employment and a higher standard of living. This led to high rates of unemployment in cities and an oversupply of labour. By contrast, in the developed world there was an undersupply of labour and this also led to increased migration from developing to developed countries, for example Algerian people to France, Turkish people to Germany and Asian people to the Netherlands.

Given the inability of urban areas in the developed world to provide jobs for many of the immigrants, a new sector developed – the informal sector which included many jobs that were outside regular waged employment. This is also known as **petty commodity production**. These changes are shown in Figure 9.5.

| Chronological phases | Major features of urbanisation |
|---|---|
| Pre-contact | Small, organically patterned towns predominate. |
| 1500 | Mercantile colonialism. Limited colonial presence in existing ports, trade usually in natural products of local region. |
| 1800 | Transitional phase. Reduced European interest in investment overseas, greater profits to be made in industrial revolution. |
| 1850 | Industrial colonialism. European need for cheap raw materials and food. Colonialism takes territorial form, new settlement patterns and morphology created. |
| 1920 | Late colonialism. Intensification of European morphological influence. Extension to towns higher in hierarchy. Increased ethnic segregation. |
| 1950 | Early independence. Rapid growth of indigenous population through migration in search of jobs. Expansion of slum and squatter settlements. |
| 1970 | New International Division of Labour (NIDL). Appearance of multinational corporation (MNC) factories. Further migrational growth. Rise of aided self-help programmes. |

**Figure 9.5** *Stages in colonial urbanisation*
Source: Drakakis-Smith, D., 1987, The Third World city, Routledge

### Neo-colonialism and the New International Division of Labour

In the 1960s and 1970s, many multinational corporations (MNCs) began to shift their production factories to areas of cheap labour. This is referred to as **neo-colonialism**. This means that although the MNCs do not claim any rights over a country (as the UK does over its colonies), the MNC exploits some of the resources of the country (in much the same way as colonial powers exploits their colonies). The movement of production into developing countries can be explained for a number of reasons:

* cost of production – wages, rents, raw materials are lower in ELDCs than in EMDCs
* labour is cheap in ELDCs
* the presence of a large informal sector keeps wages low
* advances in technology, such as the fax and telecommunications, allow production in all parts of the world
* international agencies, national governments and aid agencies are all keen to bring employment to developing countries, hence many grants and other forms of assistance are available; most of this investment tends to take place in cities rather than in rural areas.

## Demographic influences on urbanisation

Migration and natural increase (excess of birth rates over death rates) together fuel the process of urbanisation, varying in relative importance over time.

In general, migration is more important in the early stages of urban population growth, when the proportion of the national population living in towns and cities is low. In the very early stages of urbanisation most migrants are adult males, followed at a later stage by **family reunion**. A typical sequence of migration might have been:

1 migration of breadwinner to a nearby small town, learn some skills and establish an income
2 move on to a larger settlement with a greater range of opportunities
3 families join the initial migrant.

However, such movement no longer dominates migration patterns. Much of this is due to new transport developments which make longer distance travel easier and cheaper, often at the expense of local destinations.

There has also been a shift to **circular migration** – the return flow of urban-rural migrants (often older, more successful peoples, as well as those who have failed in the urban system) at the same time as rural-urban migration. The other marked change in migration trends has been the rapid growth of female migration to the city. Over the last decade or so there has been a massive upsurge in the demand for female labour in the city following the expansion of factories in ELDCs and NICs.

**Figure 9.6** *Poor quality housing, in South Africa, an ELDC*

| City | Population | Peripheral settlements as % of the city's population |
|---|---|---|
| *Africa* | | |
| Dakar | 500 000 | 18 |
| Lusaka | 194 000 | 27 |
| *Asia* | | |
| Calcutta | 6 700 000 | 33 |
| Djakarta | 2 906 000 | 25 |
| Karachi | 752 000 | 33 |
| *South America* | | |
| Santiago | 2 184 000 | 25 |
| Lima | 2 800 000 | 36 |
| Caracas | 1 590 000 | 35 |

**Figure 9.7** *Low quality housing*
Source: based on UN, The extent of peripheral housing: 1978

---

**QUESTIONS**

1 What type of person is most likely to migrate from a rural area to an urban area? Justify your choice.

2 What are the implications of this for **(i)** the rural area and **(ii)** the urban area? Use examples to support your answer.

---

## Migrant housing in ELDC cities

There are two main responses to the housing needs of disadvantaged urban residents: squatter housing and slum formation. **Squatter housing** is on the city fringes and usually comprises structures that are erected illegally, disregarding building regulations, or on land without the permission of the owner. **Slums**, by contrast, are centrally-located, permanent buildings that have become substandard through a combination of age, neglect and sub-division. Many rural to urban migrants initially go to the slums so that they can be close to sources of employment. Later on, as they acquire more money and more family members appear, they move to the more spacious peripheral squatter settlements (Figure 9.6).

The single most distinctive feature of cities in ELDCs is the existence of self-built shelters: slums, shanty towns, and squatter settlements (Figure 9.7).

Figure 9.7 shows the relative and widespread importance of low quality housing. In Mexico City the population in this type of housing rose from 15% in 1952 to 40% in 1970. Their growth rate was between 10-15% each year between 1950 and 1980 whereas the city's overall growth was only 6% per annum.

Slums, in particular, because of their central location, are very closely connected with the central business district (CBD) either as a supplier of workers or as a potential consumer. In the 1970s, John Turner showed from his studies in Latin America that squatter communities are highly organised and contain a normal range of changing family ambitions and priorities. Because they are poor, however, such households are forced to choose between these priorities – the need to balance job proximity, cheap rent and access to services such as education or shops. These govern the type and location of accommodation that families look for.

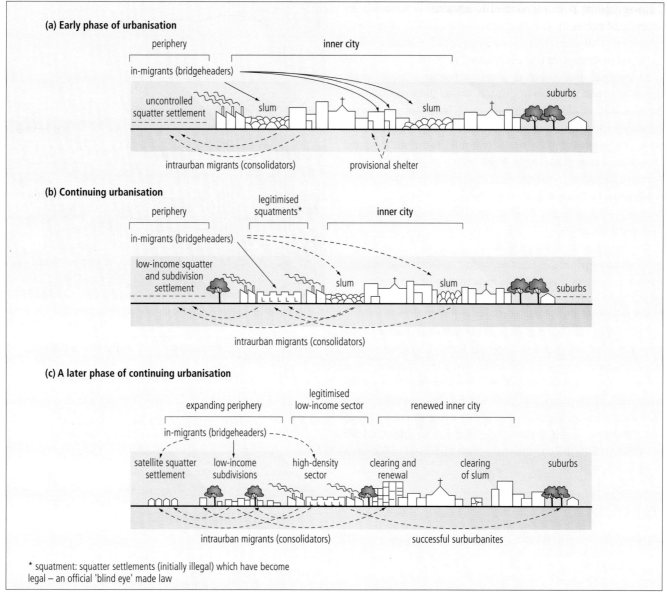

**Figure 9.8** *Stages in squatter settlement formation*
Source: Baker, S., et al., 1996, Pathways in senior geography, Nelson

There are a number of stages in the formation of squatter settlements (Figure 9.8). In the first stage the 'bridgeheader' is the initial migrant. The main aim of the migrant is to gain **employment** and any nearby shelter will suffice. Later, when a regular and more reliable income is secured, the main aim changes to **security of tenure**. Finally, once the legal tenure has been secured, the priority is given to improving the lifestyle by improving **access to services** such as education and health care. Turner claimed that upwardly mobile families would either move to accommodation that satisfied these changing needs or stay in a community that was itself being upgraded.

Turner's model has been criticised, however, in that squatters, like all poor people, do not have a full freedom of choice. They are constrained in where they can locate.

Secondly, it would be wrong to regard squatter or slum settlements as solutions, although they may be partial solutions. Slums and squatter settlements are the result of inequalities in access to resources, not the solutions to inequalities.

Slums of hope and slums of despair are a further distinction:

**Slums of hope** are the self-built houses where migrants are consolidating their position in the informal urban economy: housing is improving, for example, in Mexico City these are the *Colonias Paracondistas*.

**Slums of despair** have little room for improvement becomes incomes are low, rents are high, leasing arrangements are insecure and there are environmental problems, the *Ciudades Perdidas* in Mexico City, for example.

Governments have responded to squatter settlements in a variety of ways:

1 Eviction of the most troublesome squatters in the squatter settlements has occurred. Examples include the bulldozing of the Crossroads Settlement outside Cape Town in South Africa in the 1970s during apartheid, and also the removal of street children in Rio de Janeiro prior to the 1992 Earth Summit.
2 Some governments have developed prestige projects in order to attract international attention, however these do very little to meet the needs of most squatters.
3 New towns have been built, for example those outside Cairo.
4 Housing renewal.

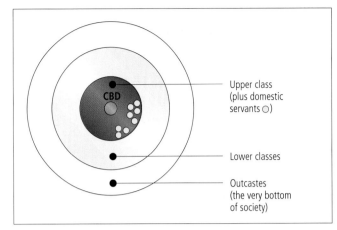

**Figure 9.10** *Model of the preindustrial city*
Source: Potter, R., 1992, Urbanisation in the Third World, OUP, (after Sjoberg)

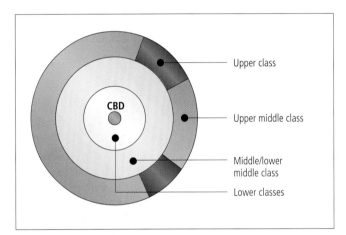

**Figure 9.11** *Model of the industrial city*
Source: Potter, R., 1992, Urbanisation in the Third World, OUP

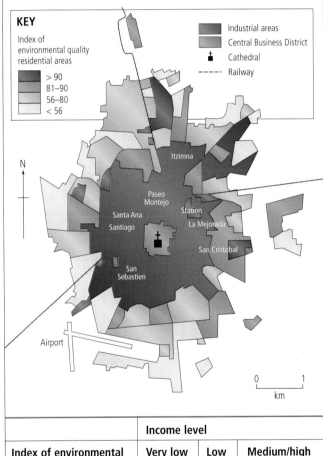

| Index of environmental quality (maxiumum 100) | Income level | | |
|---|---|---|---|
| | Very low | Low | Medium/high |
| 81-100 | 4 | 11 | 16 |
| 58-80 | 32 | 4 | 8 |

**Figure 9.9** *Housing quality in Merida, Mexico*
Source: adapted from Instituto de Verienda, Mexico

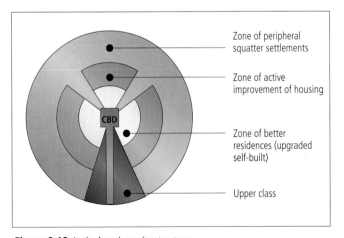

**Figure 9.12** *Latin American city structure*
Source: Potter, R., 1992, Urbanisation in the Third World, OUP, (after Griffin and Ford)

## QUESTIONS

1 Study Figure 9.9 which shows the quality of housing in Merida, Mexico.

a) Describe the distribution of (i) high quality housing and (ii) low quality housing.   b) How do you account for these differences?

## MODELLING CITIES IN ELDCs

There are a number of models which describe and explain the development of cities in ELDCs. As we have seen earlier, all models are simplifications, whereas every city is unique. Hence, we must use caution when we use them. A selection of models is shown in Figures 9.10 and 9.11 (see page 107), and in Figures 9.12 (see page 107) and 9.13. There are a number of key points about cities in ELDCs :

- the rich generally live close to the city centre whereas the very poor are more likely to be found in the periphery
- higher quality land is occupied by the wealthy
- segregation by wealth, race and ethnicity is evident
- manufacturing is scattered throughout the city.

## Primate cities

Cities in the developing world are characterised by a high degree of **primacy**. Urban primacy occurs when the largest or top ranking city, in terms of population size, dominates the rest of the national urban system. There are three main ways in which a city can achieve primacy:

1 **colonial inertia** – a colonial power establishes strategic cities both in the mother country and in the colonised country to function as centres of administration, religious and military influence. This possible pathway to urban primacy applies largely to the primate cities of Latin America and Asia, except China and Japan

2 **export dependency** – export orientated production of primary commodities is focused on gateway port cities reinforcing their economic dominance and promoting primacy

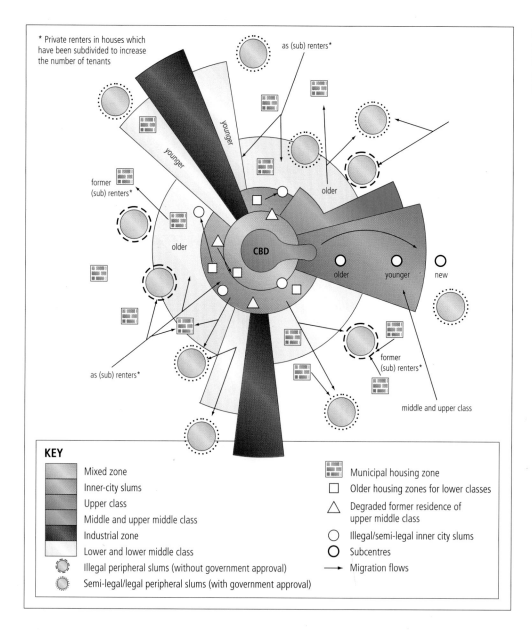

**Figure 9.13**
*Model of internal movements in the Latin American city*
*Source: Potter, R., 1992, Urbanisation in the Third World, OUP*

* Private renters in houses which have been subdivided to increase the number of tenants

**KEY**

- Mixed zone
- Inner-city slums
- Upper class
- Middle and upper middle class
- Industrial zone
- Lower and lower middle class
- Illegal peripheral slums (without government approval)
- Semi-legal/legal peripheral slums (with government approval)
- Municipal housing zone
- Older housing zones for lower classes
- Degraded former residence of upper middle class
- Illegal/semi-legal inner city slums
- Subcentres
- Migration flows

**3  urban bias theory** – the increasing role of manufacturing in the largest city and the effects of mechanisation in rural areas cause massive rural urban migration, promoting primacy.

## The rank-size rule

The rank-size rule states that the population of a given city tends to be equal to the population of the largest city divided by the rank of the given city:

$$Pr = \frac{P_1}{r}$$

where

$Pr$ is the population of the town ranked $r$

$P_1$ is the population of the largest town

$r$ is the rank of town '$r$'

| Brazil 1985 (000s) | | Mexico 1990 (000s) | |
|---|---|---|---|
| São Paulo | 10 099 | Mexico City | 15 047 |
| Rio de Janeiro | 5615 | Guadalajara | 2870 |
| Belo Horizonte | 2122 | Monterrey | 2558 |
| Salvador | 1811 | Puebla | 1157 |
| Fortaleza | 1589 | Juarez | 789 |
| Brasilia | 1577 | Leon | 758 |
| Nova Igauacu | 1325 | Tijuana | 698 |
| Recife | 1290 | Torreon | 689 |
| Curituba | 1285 | San Luis Potosi | 613 |
| Porto Allegre | 1275 | Merida | 532 |

**Figure 9.15** *The rank-size rule, Brazil and Mexico*
Source: Pick, J. and Butler E., 1994, The Mexico handbook: economic and demographic maps and statistics, Westville Press

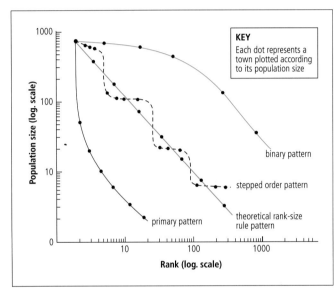

**Figure 9.14** *The rank-size rule; most regions have hierarchies which approach one of these idealised linear progressions*
Source: Wynne-Hammond, C., 1985, Elements of human geography, Unwin

Figure 9.14 shows the main patterns that emerge; the theoretical rank-size distribution follows a straight line. Christaller's hierarchy of settlements shows distinct tiers. The other two distributions show the case of primacy (or a primate distribution), in which one city dominates the urban landscape and is much larger than the second and subsequent towns, and the binary pattern, in which the largest two settlements are quite close in size. (The scale that is used is referred to as a log-log or double log scale. It is used in order to compress the large range of values.)

## EMPLOYMENT IN ELDC CITIES

Since 1970, many ELDC cities have been transformed in order to attract MNCs and their factories. This has been achieved in three main ways:

- administrative reorganisation to allow national governments to assume the function of city authorities
- heavy government spending on modernisation and infrastructure
- the activities of the informal sector have been repressed, especially when they are in conflict with modern industrial processes.

Most development strategists identify industrialisation as a key to economic growth. They focus on investment in the city rather than the countryside. Some argue for heavy industry, others prefer manufacturing, import substitution, export orientation, capital intensive or labour intensive industry. Participation of the female labour force has increased steadily as urban growth has accelerated in the developing world. The reasons for this increase relate to the increased demand for unskilled, short term, non-unionised and, therefore, cheap female labour. Although cheap labour has been an important factor in the investment shift, it is not the only reason – local resources, export facilities and strategic locations always add to the equation.

Most manufacturing tends to be concentrated in large cities, for example, Taipei in Taiwan has one third of Taiwan's industrial establishments of over five hundred employees. Although small cities are less important in absolute terms they still contain a high proportion of manufacturing jobs.

---

## QUESTIONS

**1**  Study Figure 9.15 which provides data for the ten largest towns in Mexico and Brazil.

**a)**  Plot the distributions for Brazil and Mexico.

**b)**  How do you account for the differences?

**2a)**  Using **(i)** an atlas and **(ii)** a local census, work out the rank-size distribution for the UK and your county.

**b)**  Describe the patterns you have drawn.

**c)**  What conclusions can you draw about the rank-size rule from the two diagrams you have drawn? Justify your answer.

Within the city, the distribution of industry is closely related to size of plant. Smaller factories may be scattered throughout the urban area, but where space is at a premium, such as in Hong Kong and Singapore, they tend to be clustered around the CBD. Flatted factories (single-storey low rise factories) have been constructed, providing multiple levels which are subdivided into different units. In areas outside the CBD, most of the larger manufacturing factories tend to be concentrated in industrial estates, usually close to port facilities.

## The informal sector

Since the mid-1970s, the term informal sector has become widely recognised in geography (Figure 9.16). It refers to all activities which are not registered or taxed. It is the equivalent of the 'black market' or 'moonlighting' jobs in the UK. The informal sector covers a wide range of activities such as manufacturing, services, transport and building of squatter housing (Figure 9.17). In some cities it accounts for up to 90% of employment.

**Figure 9.16** *The informal economy*

| Informal Sector | Formal Sector |
|---|---|
| Ease of entry | Difficult entry |
| Indigenous inputs predominate | Overseas inputs |
| Family property predominates | Corporate property |
| Small scale of activity | Large scale of activity |
| Labour intensive | Capital intensive |
| Adapted technology | Imported technology |
| Skills from outside the school system | Formally acquired skills |
| Unregulated/competitive market | Protected markets, e.g. tariffs, quotes, licensing arrangements |

**Figure 9.17** *Characteristics of the formal and informal economy*
Source: Rogerson, 1985, quoted in Drakakis-Smith, D., 1987, The Third World city, Routledge

---

1 **Formal income opportunities**
- Public sector wages
- Private sector wages
- Transfer payments, for example pensions, unemployment benefits

2 **Informal income opportunities: legitimate**
- Primary and secondary activities, e.g. farming, market gardening, building, self-employed craftspeople, shoemakers, brewing and distilling
- Tertiary (service) enterprises with relatively large capital inputs such as housing, transport
- Small-scale distribution, for example, market traders, street hawkers, food and drink sales, bar attendants
- Other services, such as musicians, launderers, shoe shiners, barbers, photographers, car repairs
- Private transfer payments, such as gifts and similar movements of money between people, borrowing, begging

3 **Informal income opportunities: illegitimate**
- Services, such as receiving stolen goods, usury (lending money at an exorbitant rate of interest), pawn broking, drug pushing, prostitution, smuggling, bribery, political corruption, protection rackets
- Transfers, such as petty theft (pickpockets, larceny), burglary and armed robbery, speculation and embezzlement, gambling

**Figure 9.18** *Income opportunities in an ELDC*
Source: Drakakis-Smith, D., 1987, The Third World city, Routledge

Some geographers see the informal sector as a valuable way of relieving the economic problems of the poor by using their energy, together with small-scale assistance or training, to try to help them improve their circumstances (Figure 9.18). This approach led to the **basic needs strategy**. These are the self help programmes which flourished in the 1980s and 1990s in an attempt to overcome the problems of housing, employment and general standards of living in many cities.

## Exploitation of the informal sector

Some geographers argue that the informal economy allows even more exploitation of the poor by the rich. For example, the entrepreneurs who own the equipment or the capital necessary for the operation of a business are often quite wealthy people who work in the formal sector and lend capital and equipment to workers in the informal economy at high rates of interest; the informal sector benefits those in the formal sector, since it keeps prices down for those in regular employment (the formal sector).

---

### QUESTIONS

1 Describe the nature of employment in the informal economy.

2 Explain why informal activities are important in the economy of developing world cities.

## THE RISE OF THE GLOBAL ECONOMY

Rapid technological change has become a central force in the economic readjustment occurring in all EMDCs of the world. The process is known as industrial restructuring and is an essential feature of the post-industrial era. Three dimensions of change are associated with the process of industrial restructuring:

- deindustrialisation – the decline of traditional heavy industry
- reindustrialisation – the growth of small industries in deindustrialised areas
- tertiarisation – the growth of the service sector.

Closely linked with these three changes has been the rise of a highly integrated global market which sees the Triad – North America, the European Union and the Asian Pacific Rim – consolidate their role as major trading blocs in the 1990s and for the early part of the next century.

The global economy should not be confused with the world economy. The global economy refers to those select countries and regions, such as those in the Triad, that are closely linked by access to technology, capital and labour through shared information networks and management structures. By contrast, the world economy refers to the total production of all countries in the world, both the select countries of the global economy and the poorer countries that are not part of the integrated economy, such as Ethiopia, Chile and Afghanistan.

## THE EMERGENCE OF THE WORLD CITY

Cities are primarily focal points or hubs of power based on innovation and communication. Their power reflects the range and intensity of contacts and linkages that the city has with the rest of the world; a city develops a wide range of organisations that generate and control the flow of information. This collection of organisations and their linkages can be viewed as an information structure which provides the city with a comparative advantage in the information economy.

Global industrial change has been both the cause and consequence of the emergence of a highly integrated network of 'world cities' (Figure 9.19). New communications technology, along with the internationalisation of services and finance, is strengthening a small number of cities such as New York, London, Tokyo, Los Angeles and Hong Kong. A number of closely related factors are involved in the evolution of the world city:

- the international division of labour
- networks and hierarchies
- internationalisation
- availability of capital
- immigration
- divisions of wealth and wellbeing
- strains of growth.

*Figure 9.19* The network of world cities
Source: Nagle, G., and Spencer, K., 1996, A geography of the European Union, OUP

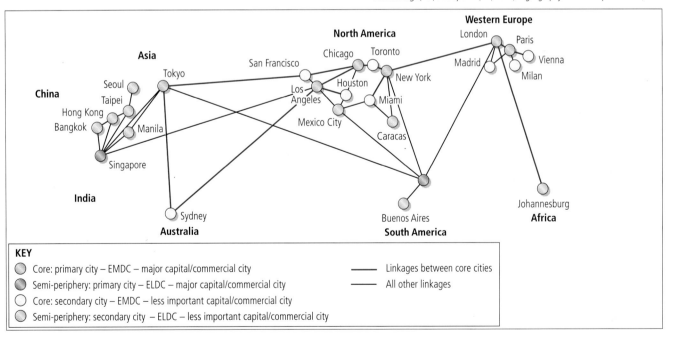

KEY

- ◐ Core: primary city – EMDC – major capital/commercial city
- ◑ Semi-periphery: primary city – ELDC – major capital/commercial city
- ○ Core: secondary city – EMDC – less important capital/commercial city
- ◔ Semi-periphery: secondary city – ELDC – less important capital/commercial city

—— Linkages between core cities
— All other linkages

## QUESTIONS

1  Study Figure 9.19 which shows the distribution and hierarchy of World Cities. How many of these are from developing countries? How do you explain this?

2  In what ways will the map of world cities differ by the year 2025? Give reasons for your answer.

## SUMMARY

Urbanisation and urban form in ELDCs can be contrasted with the process in EMDCs in many ways:

1 Urbanisation in ELDCs is taking place in countries with the lowest levels of economic development rather than the highest, as was the case when urbanisation began in EMDCs.
2 It involves greater numbers of people than it did in EMDCs.
3 Rural to urban migration is much greater in volume and more rapid in ELDCs.
4 Industrialisation lags far behind the rate of urbanisation and consequently most immigrants are forced into marginal employment in the informal sector.
5 Counterurbanisation has yet to be experienced in ELDCs.
6 Fertility rates are greater in cities of ELDCs and net reproduction rates are higher than in industrialised countries.
7 The environment of the inner city core in cities in ELDCs is generally better quality than the environment of the peripheral area; this is the exact opposite of cities in EMDCs.
8 Massive areas of squatter settlements on the city periphery characterise most large cities of the developing world.
9 Urban planning is severely fragmented in time and space and is often poorly organised because of the inherent instability of the political process in many ELDCs.

## QUESTIONS

1 Study Figure 9.20 which shows population size and number of millionaire cities (cities with a population of over 1 million people) for regions in the developing world.
a) Choose an appropriate method to show how the number of millionaire cities has changed from 1950 and is projected to rise until 2000.
b) Why have you chosen this method?
c) Describe the patterns you have shown – which areas have the (i) greatest, (ii) least, (iii) most rapidly changing, number of millionaire cities?
d) How do you explain the rapid growth in the number of millionaire cities?
e) What are the links between national population growth rates and the growth rates of the largest city? What are the implications of this for urban planners?
2 What is the informal economy? Why is it so important in cities in the developing world?
3 'Slums and squatter settlements are the result of inequalities in access to resources, not the solutions to inequalities.' Discuss.

## BIBLIOGRAPHY AND RECOMMENDED READING

**Baker, S., et al.**, 1996, *Pathways in senior geography*, Nelson

**Dickenson, J., et al**, 1996, *Geography of the Third World*, Routledge

**Drakakis Smith, D.**, 1987, *The Third World City*, Routledge

**Gilbert, A, and Gugler, J.**, 1982, *Cities, poverty and development*, OUP

**Pick, J, and Butler, E.**, 1994, *The Mexico handbook: economic and demographic maps and statistics*, Westview Press

**Potter, R.**, 1992, *Urbanisation in the Third World*, OUP

**United Nations**, 1993, *World urbanisation prospects: the 1992 revision*, United Nations

| | 1950 | 1960 | 1970 | 1980 | 1990 | 2000 |
|---|---|---|---|---|---|---|
| *Less developed countries* | | | | | | |
| Population (millions) | 62 345 | 113 446 | 192 932 | 339 373 | 595 130 | 931 835 |
| Number of cities | 31 | 50 | 74 | 118 | 198 | 284 |
| *Regions* | | | | | | |
| Africa | | | | | | |
| Population (millions) | 3 503 | 7 482 | 15 415 | 36 485 | 83 363 | 154 158 |
| Number of cities | 2 | 44 | 8 | 19 | 37 | 57 |
| Latin America | | | | | | |
| Population (millions) | 17 276 | 30 988 | 56 383 | 101 301 | 164 167 | 232 158 |
| Number of cities | 7 | 11 | 17 | 27 | 42 | 57 |
| East Asia | | | | | | |
| Population (millions) | 33 771 | 62 117 | 90 495 | 131 910 | 191 270 | 261 554 |
| Number of cities | 14 | 24 | 31 | 42 | 61 | 82 |
| South Asia | | | | | | |
| Population (millions) | 19 360 | 33 267 | 58 837 | 105 879 | 199 085 | 328 163 |
| Number of cities | 11 | 16 | 23 | 36 | 65 | 95 |
| Australasia | | | | | | |
| Population (millions) | 3 136 | 4 012 | 5 021 | 7 185 | 11 903 | 13 427 |
| Number of cities | 2 | 2 | 2 | 3 | 6 | 6 |

*\* does not equal total of regions*

**Figure 9.20** *The growth and regional distribution of 'millionaire' cities*
Source: Baker, S., et al, 1996, Pathways in senior geography, Nelson

# Chapter 10
# Urban issues in the developing world

In this last chapter we consider urbanisation in the developing world, highlighting the diverse nature of urban settlements. The problems facing urban areas, and the potential solutions, result from a unique set of physical, social, economic, political and cultural factors. Here we look at the range of urban problems in Mexico City, Rio de Janeiro and Bangkok. We then consider urbanisation at a national level and consider the effects of government policy on urbanisation in China.

## URBANISATION IN LATIN AMERICA

Urban growth rates in Latin America have consistently been the highest in the world since about 1970; they have exceeded rural growth rates by about four times. By the year 2000, the region as a whole will be 75% urbanised, which will be roughly equivalent to European rates. However, within Latin America there are very important variations. For example, forecasts for Mexico City, made in 1970, suggested that its population would reach over 30 million by 2010; however, its 1990 population was just under 16 million and it is now only expected to reach 18-20 million by the year 2010. The city's growth rates have slowed because of a sharp decline in fertility as well as a sharp decline in migration. These can be attributed to government and private policies of decentralisation and investment in secondary urban centres. In addition, industrial developments in the north of Mexico have also attracted more migrants there.

### The impact of colonial development

In the sixteenth century Spain founded many of its towns, such as Mexico City, in the highlands of Latin America and in coastal areas, such as Lima and Buenos Aires. These linked the colonies to the Spanish homeland. The form and structure of the city followed patterns of physical and social segregation found in Spanish cities. Important buildings such as the cathedral, governor's residence, commercial arcade and town hall surrounded a central plaza which was itself surrounded by a grid pattern of streets. The residents clustered around the urban core with houses constructed to maximise defence against attack. Indigenous peoples and undesirable land uses, such as smelting and slaughter houses, were located on the periphery.

The Portuguese in the late sixteenth and early seventeenth centuries constructed their towns on hilly and easily-defended terrain where mining was conducted. They also built some settlements along coastal plains. The Portuguese towns were developed as rural service centres as well as colonial centres of administration and control.

Latin American cities in the twentieth century have been better able than Africa, and some Asian countries, to absorb the huge influx of rural migrants because of stronger industrial growth and employment.

Since the 1980s there has been a change in residential patterns. A large proportion of the high class population has moved out of the centre to the periphery creating a high class sector. This high class sector is also the focus of attention for the best shops, prestigious office spaces and entertainment areas. In Brazil, edge towns (elite/high class towns on the edge or periphery of large settlements) have developed on the edge of São Paulo and Rio de Janeiro due to lack of space, high land prices and congestion in the city centre. The edge towns, such as Barra (Rio de Janeiro), are upmarket developments, usually with excellent transport links, such as motorway connections, with high quality services, hypermarkets and are chosen for new office location.

## MEXICO CITY

Mexico City is a primate city. It has a population of approximately 18 million and contains about 25% of Mexico's population (Figure 10.1, see page 114). Guadalajara, Mexico's second city, is only 2 million people strong. Since the beginning of this century, Mexico City's population has increased more than 40-fold; in 1900, there were just 370 000 people, by 1930 it had reached one million, and since 1950, the population has grown by nearly 500%! Mexico City's growth rate has been maintained at about 5% per year since 1945, although recently, since the 1980s, the growth rate has fallen to 2% per year.

The precise figure for the population of Mexico City is uncertain because the built-up area does not coincide with the administrative boundaries and the exact population of many of the shanty towns is unknown.

Mexico City is a classic example of a city beset with problems caused by rapid urban growth:
- unplanned development
- severe pollution from traffic and industry (Figure 10.2, see page 114)
- inadequate provision of housing and services (Figure 10.3, see page 114)
- low quality of life for many people.

Each year about 33% of the addition to the population results from in-migration. This represents 600-1000 people per day or about 400 000 each year entering the city.

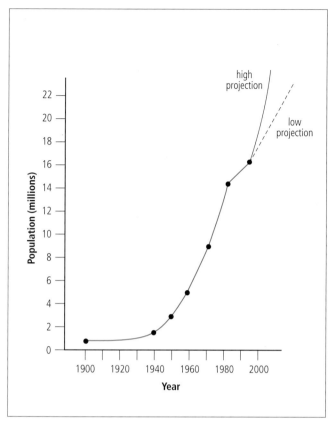

**Figure 10.1** *Population growth in Mexico City, 1900-95*
*Source: Morris, S.,1997, Mexico City – urban issues, Geofile 306, Stanley Thornes*

**Figure 10.2** *Industrial pollution in Mexico City*

**Figure 10.3** *Informal economy in Mexico City – city street traders*

Migrants to Mexico City are characterised by a number of features:

- they are young (15-45 years) – 50% of Mexico City's population is under 18 years old
- the majority are women (121 women per 100 males) – the women get jobs in the clothing business
- large numbers are from the adjacent states of Mexico, Puebla, Morelos, Hidalgo and Tlaxcala, and also from the impoverished regions of the south, such as Guerrero, Oxaaca and Chiapas.

## Housing in Mexico City

Average population density in Mexico City is about 14 000 per square kilometre. This gives an average of about 140 per hectare, although it is as high as 550 per hectare near the city centre. (One hectare is about the size of a rugby pitch!) The concentration of population into Mexico City has forced enormous growth – Mexico City is now 1250 square kilometres in size (Figure 10.4). This has led to the rapid expansion of housing, particularly squatter settlements.

Housing within the city may be divided into a number of categories (Figure 10.5).

Despite the rapid population increases there has been a relatively small amount of housing provided by the state. It is estimated that there is a shortfall of about 800 000 homes in Mexico City, and up to 60% of the population live in settlements that are classified as illegal. Most state housing programmes are geared towards self-help programmes. Deprivation is widespread. A survey has shown that:

- 25% of houses have only one room
- 38% of houses have no water supply
- 25% have no sewerage facilities
- 43% have no bath.

The government has attempted to improve the situation by building new houses, but these are beyond the price range of the poor. Slums and squatter settlements, though often illegal, are gradually being improved.

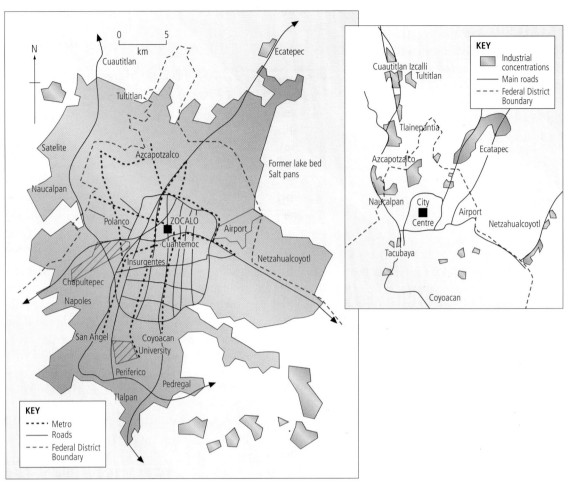

**Figure 10.4** *Mexico City's urban area*
*Source: Morris, S., 1997, Mexico City – urban issues, Geofile 306, Stanley Thornes*

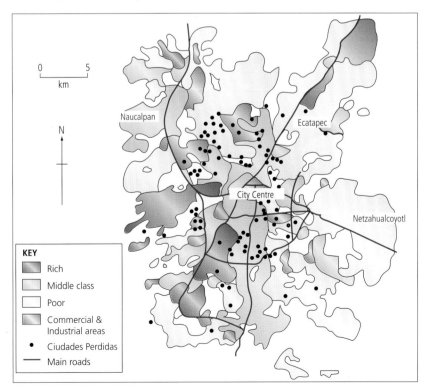

**Figure 10.5** *Housing areas in Mexico City*
*Source: Morris, S., 1997, Mexico City – urban issues, Geofile 306, Stanley Thornes*

### Low income housing in Mexico City

*Vecindades tenements*
In the city centre; one household per room; shared facilities; low rents; no investment; poor conditions; high densities of population; limited redevelopment after the 1985 earthquake

*Ciudades perdidas*
Temporary squatter settlements; no services; low rents; close to the bus station and railways

*Vecindades nuevas*
Small tenements in older settlements, housing 5-15 families

*Colonias*
Settlements on the periphery; established by developers, often with most urban functions.

*Colonias paracaidistas*
Groups of squatters 'capture' the land through invasion

## The economy of Mexico City

Mexico City is the economic core of Mexico. The Federal District of Mexico City produces 28% of the country's industrial output, nearly 50% of its manufacturing, and over two-thirds of its banking services. Mexico City has 33% of the country's jobs in industry and services, and most migrants go to the city in search of higher wages which may be six times as much as those in the countryside.

| | |
|---|---|
| Manufacturing | 39% |
| Services | 36.5% |
| Commerce | 13.5% |
| Transport | 4% |
| Other | 7% |

*Figure 10.6* *Formal sector employment in Mexico City*
*Source: based on data in Dickenson, J., 1996, A geography of the Third World, Routledge*

Nevertheless, economically speaking, Mexico City is poor – less than 33% of the population is economically active. Of these, manufacturing is the most important single source of employment (Figure 10.6).

Industrial growth slowed in Mexico during the 1980s, and unemployment, underemployment and economic marginality are causing increasingly severe problems. Access to jobs is now more selective. Nearly half of the city's population is engaged in the informal sector. The poor share accommodation and use their relatives both as a social security network and to provide child care when women are at work.

## Environmental problems

The concentration in Mexico City of 3.5 million vehicles and 40 000 factories produces 12 000 tons of gaseous waste daily. Smog reduces visibility daily to about 2 kilometres. The city has the world's highest ozone concentration and one of the highest figures for carbon monoxide. In 1994, air quality was officially classified as acceptable on only 20 days in the year! In addition, there is very little green space in the city.

Another problem in the city is that caused by the dumping of hazardous waste (Figure 10.7). There are no legal landfill sites and only five recycling plants in Mexico City. Illegal dumping at Rincon Verde has led to increased risk of diseases in the area, underground fires and pollution of the water table (see *Development and Underdevelopment* in this series, for a case study of water problems in Mexico City).

## Urban form

Mexico City can be split into **zones**, **sectors** and **nuclei** that resemble some of the urban models (Figure 10.5, see page

*Figure 10.7* *Illegal dumping of hazardous waste in Mexico City*

115). The old city core is surrounded by the tenements of the urban poor (vecindades). In general, the poor dominate the north and east the middle classes are found mostly in the south central area, and the highest class is found in the west. Hence, within nuclei there are class variations organised in a preindustrial fashion, namely a centralised elite and a peripheral lower class. The colonial palaces in the city centre and the peripheral poor illustrate the persistence of preindustrial features.

There has been some suburban development to the west and north of Mexico City, and small satellite communities have clustered in the south. There has also been peripheral development of low quality housing. In 1954 the Federal District prohibited the subdivision of land within the city limits. This led to the development of shanty towns on the edge of the city at Naucalpan, Ecatepec and Netzahualcoyotl (Figure 10.8).

*Figure 10.8* *Substandard housing in Mexico City*

## QUESTIONS

1 How far does Mexico City conform to any model of an ELDC city? Explain why lower quality housing predominates in the north and east.

2 Describe the growth of population in Mexico City as shown in Figure 10.1.

3 Describe the distribution of temporary squatter settlements as shown in Figure 10.5. How do you explain their location?

4 Why are Mexico City's problems so intense?

5 Using an atlas, explain why smog should be such a problem in Mexico City.

## URBAN CHANGE IN RIO DE JANEIRO

By the year 2000, with half of the world's population living in urban areas, mega cities (or supercities) will be increasingly important. Of the twenty-one mega cities that will exist by 2000, eighteen will be in Africa, Asia and Latin America. Rio de Janeiro will be one of these mega cities.

### History of Rio de Janeiro

Rio was first settled almost five hundred years ago by the Portuguese. In the 1700s, the gold boom led to the creation of Rio as the new political and economic centre. During the twentieth century, industrial growth caused Rio to spread outwards, and by 1991 it had a population of just under 10 million people. It is composed of fourteen municipios, or state subdivisions (Figure 10.9).

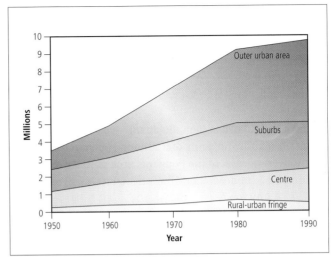

**Figure 10.10** *Population growth in Rio de Janeiro's districts (1950-91)*
Source: Scoble, S., 1994, Urban change in Rio de Janeiro, Geofile 235, Stanley Thornes

**Figure 10.9** *Metropolitan region of Rio de Janeiro. The inset (left) shows the distribution of households with two or less minimum salaries (1980)*
Source: Scoble, S., 1994, Urban change in Rio de Janeiro, Geofile 235, Stanley Thornes

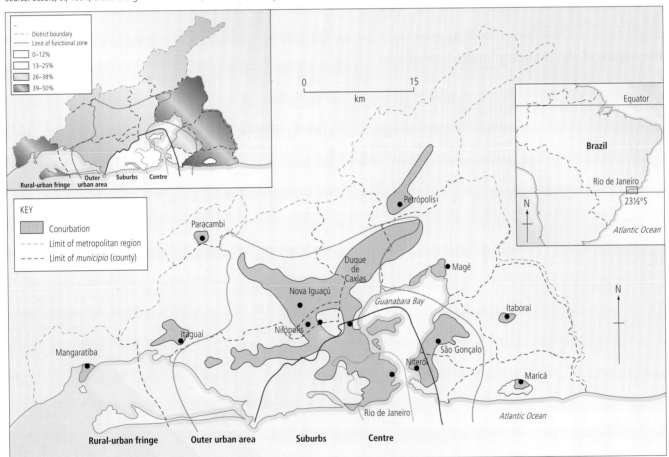

## QUESTIONS

**1** Study Figure 10.9. Describe the distribution of households with less than, or equal to, two minimum salaries.

**2** Describe the growth of Rio as shown on Figure 10.10.

**a)** Which area has grown the most?

**b)** Which type of area has grown the least?

**c)** Explain the pattern that you have shown.

Rio consists of four distinct zones:

1 Centre (Nucleo) – this is the historic core of the city which includes the CBD, the high class residential areas and the industrial port complexes where the city's main functions are located.
Housing is elite, but also with important shanty developments.

2 The older suburbs (Zona Imediata) – this area has a good infrastructure and a mix of traditional and modern industry covering most of the populous area of Rio and Niteroi.
Housing is middle class, but also contains over half of Rio's shanty towns.

3 The outer urban area (Zona Intermediata) – the newer outer fringes of the expanding cities, including Nova Iguacu and Duque de Caxias that are industrial cities in their own right.
Housing is lower class, containing nearly one quarter of Rio's shanty towns.

4 The rural urban fringe (Zona Distante) – a less urbanised zone beyond the commuting zone of Rio.
Housing is lower class.

## The nature of the changing urban environment

Historically the growth of Rio de Janeiro has been predominantly by in-migration, although a rising proportion of growth is now occurring through natural increase. The explosive growth of the outer urban and suburban areas can be explained primarily by in-migration and by natural increase, but also by the decentralisation of lower income residents from the centre or suburbs of the Rio de Janeiro Municipio. The consequence of this change has been the concentration of some of the poorest groups of the population in this zone. The proportion of households receiving two or less government minimum salaries per month (the Brazilian definition of poverty, approximately US$120) is 33% in Nova Iguacu and 31% for Duque de Caxias. The distribution reveals a concentric pattern of levels of wealth, generally coinciding with the four functional zones of the city.

Wide inequalities in the provision of urban services are also evident. Gas, water, waste disposal, pollution control, transport services and electricity networks are poorly provided on the city's margin compared with the central area. During the period of military rule, (1964-85), the urban infrastructure was mainly developed in the wealthy areas of Rio de Janeiro. The concentration of wealth, high quality accommodation, the provision of municipal services, access to the CBD, and the popular beach-front lifestyle characterise the core of Rio. By contrast, the rise of the **favelas** (slums/shanty areas) as an urban feature of Rio, found increasingly in suburbs and outer urban areas, has been rapid from the 1950s. Initially, in the early 1950s, their destruction and the removal of the residents to planned low quality housing estates (**conjuntos habitacionais**) located in the suburbs was the significant policy. The clearance of favela sites for the building of high class apartment blocks and condominiums has served to maintain the status and value of the central area. There is no real policy for the favelas. The authorities have provided token assistance to upgrade conditions in them, but the changes have been very superficial.

## The dilemma of low quality housing

The official definition of favelas is 'residential areas containing sixty or more families in accommodation lacking formal organisation or basic services, who are squatting illegally on the site'. In 1992, just under one million people lived in favelas, 17.6% of the total population. Favela areas occupy 765 sites of varying size, the largest and best known site is Rocinha, with an estimated total population of 80 000 (Figure 10.11).

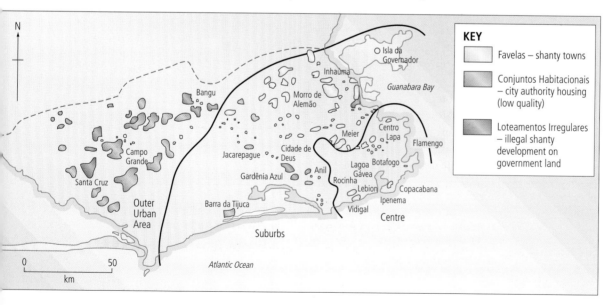

**Figure 10.11** *Location of low cost housing (favelas) and Barra da Tijuca in Rio de Janeiro*
Source: Scoble, S., 1994, Urban change in Rio de Janeiro, Geofile 235, Stanley Thornes

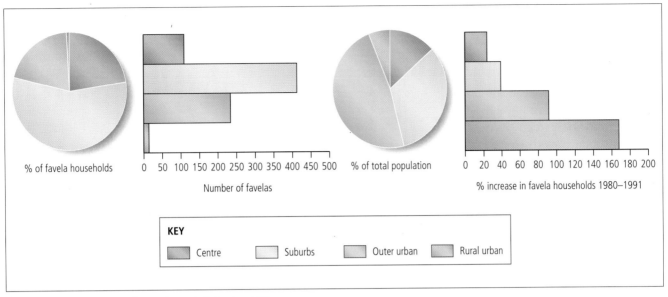

% of favela households

Number of favelas

% of total population

% increase in favela households 1980–1991

**KEY**

Centre    Suburbs    Outer urban    Rural urban

***Figure 10.12*** *Selected data for Rio de Janeiro's favelas, 1991*
*Source: Scoble, S., 1994, Urban change in Rio de Janeiro, Geofile 235, Stanley Thornes*

Favelas are illegal settlements according to the law, holding no land titles, although they are recognised by local authorities. In 1990, a programme of electrification was started as a means of improving conditions in the favelas. Nevertheless conditions remain poor, with low incomes, high unemployment and inadequate infrastructure service. In 1992 there was a cholera epidemic, and many of the favelas regularly suffer from landslides, rock falls and flooding during the summer.

The worst conditions are found in the most recent favela areas. Here spontaneous settlement occurs in the absence of basic services. Long-established favelas such as Rocinha, which date back to 1940, provide a mix of commercial services for a more diverse socio-economic population. In some cases neighbouring favelas have merged to form 'super favelas'. The majority of favela households are located in the suburban zone. Since 1980, the greatest increase has occurred in the western districts of Rio. By contrast, in the centre, where nearly all available land was already occupied, no favelas have been recorded.

It is important to recognise that favelas are only one type of low quality housing available to the urban poor. Almost a million inhabitants live in conjuntos habitacionais, predominantly located in the suburbs and outer urban areas. Most of these were provided by the city authorities. Another type of residential area is the **loteanentos irregulares**, where government land is illegally sold. Within Rio, over 80 000 such plots are currently occupied. This, together with an estimated 600 000 street dwellers, unregistered favelados (favela residents) and those living in abandoned buildings, reveals the scale of the problem.

***Figure 10.13*** *Rio Favela, Brazil*

## QUESTIONS

**1**  Study Figure 10.12.

**a)** Describe the distribution of favelas in Rio de Janeiro.

**b)** Account for the distribution of favelas in Rio de Janeiro.

**c)** Where has growth occurred in the 1980s? Explain your answer.

# Case study:
# Barra da Tijuca

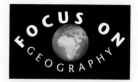

There has been overwhelming pressure to decentralise the population of Rio de Janeiro. In response, in the 1960s the City Planning Authority chose the lowlands of Jacarepagua, an area of flat scrub, marshland, lagoons and coastal spits, as an area for enlarging the urban area by a further 122 square kilometres.

The town of Barra da Tijuca on the coast expanded from 2500 inhabitants in 1960 to 98 000 in 1991, growing by 139% per year during the 1980s. It contains many attractions for Rio's expanding rich middle class with the pleasant environment of mountain views, forest, lagoons and 20 kilometres of beaches to enjoy in an area four times larger than the increasingly congested and polluted central zone, but still only thirty minutes away by motorway.

Barra represents the most recent example of the decentralisation of the rich. In the affluent borough of Barra, there are clusters of eighteen- to thirty-storey apartments with low rise residential areas of eight to ten storeys centred on two commercial cores, Barra and Sernambetiba. There are shopping malls and hypermarkets (Figure 10.14). Between the two nuclei, single family residences add to the mix. 20% of the dwellings are designed as single storey and 10% as two storey. The settlement reflects a motorised, consumer-orientated and wealthy life style. Middle class residents of Barra enjoy a culture centred around the beach, expensive restaurants, shopping centres, leisure centres and clubs which satisfy strongly elitist aspirations (Figure 10.15). The areas are protected by security guards, fences, closed circuit television cameras and guard dogs, leading to an 'imprisonment' of the middle class.

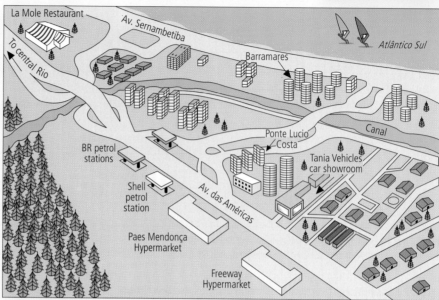

*Figure 10.14* Barra – a new type of ELDC settlement. Important elements of the Barra lifestyle, as described in a property company advertisement for new apartments
Source: Scoble, S., 1994, Urban change in Rio de Janeiro, Geofile 235, Stanley Thornes

The lowlands of Jacarepagua have effectively been divided into two areas, the coast and the inland lowlands, by the development of Barra. This is officially designated through Barra's separate administrative status from Jacarepagua since the late 1970s.

The inland area of Jacarepagua contains areas of conjuntos habitacionais neighbourhoods such as Anil, Gardenia Azul and Cidade de Deus. This area was created from the 1960s onwards. It suffers from remoteness, lack of public transport and services, overcrowding and poor maintenance.

So, in urban Rio there is evidence of decentralisation and there is evidence of the continuing separation of rich from poor. There is a concentration of wealth in the central area and this has been extended to growth areas such as Barra. At the same time, there is a marginalisation of the urban poor into more distant areas which remain unserved by basic urban infrastructure.

*Figure 10.15* Barra – high quality environment in Rio de Janeiro

## URBANISATION IN ASIA

Asia combines a very low level of urbanisation with the largest population in the world. Since the mid-1970s Asia has seen almost two-thirds of the global increase in population. It has also experienced a substantial increase in its rural population, from 1.5 billion in 1970 to 2.1 billion in 1990. This has resulted in Asia having the second lowest level of urbanisation of the continents (44%) in 1990, after Africa (32%). Nevertheless, there are exceptions – the island state of Singapore, for example, is heavily urbanised.

The implications of this basic difference in levels of urbanisation are quite important because the trends in population growth and distribution suggest that urbanisation in Asia could follow two possible pathways:

1 Urbanisation will continue to accelerate, leading to very large rural-urban migration; this would create extremely large, densely populated cities, some of which would exceed 50 million by 2020. This route is unlikely, given that many countries have decentralisation policies and are learning from the mistakes of other countries.

2 Urbanisation will continue and be accompanied by strong rural population growth.

Asia's patterns and trends in the levels and rate of urbanisation are dominated by the six countries with populations that exceed 100 million people, namely, Bangladesh, China, India, Indonesia, Japan and Pakistan. Up to 80% of the Asian population and up to two-thirds of the urban population is concentrated in these six countries.

### Bangkok, Thailand

In 1982, the population of Bangkok was 5.5 million. By 1993, it was over 8 million and Bangkok was the fourteenth largest city in the world. It is continuing to grow very rapidly (Figure 10.16) and rural to urban migration remains high. Part of the reason for the high rate of migration is the availability of jobs in Bangkok. In the 1980s, the economic growth rate of Thailand was about 10% per year, and many of the jobs created were in and around Bangkok.

Bangkok has a number of problems. The most famous is its traffic problem (Figure 10.17), but there are many others, for example a shortage of water, and subsidence. Called the 'Venice of the East', it is sited on the Chao Phraya river. However, there is now a major shortage of fresh water and increasing subsidence due to over exploitation of the aquifers (water bearing rocks). Indeed, Bangkok is sinking by 10 centimetres per year. As it is on a very low lying flood plain, only 1.5 metres above sea level, it could be under water by 2005! The flood water is causing structural damage as well as being almost impossible to drain during high tide or the monsoon. A start has been made by pumping water out of the lower lying areas.

**Figure 10.17** *Traffic congestion in Bangkok*

Refuse collection and the provision of adequate sewage facilities is another huge problem. Much of the informal economy is dependent upon refuse for scraps of food, reuse of materials and peddling of goods, yet there is a detrimental effect on people's health from working through the rubbish tips, as well as widespread air and water pollution. The Chao Phraya river is badly polluted.

There are a million and a half economic migrants living in Bangkok and most of the very poor live in the very worst environments. As the pace of development increases, so the plight of the poor seems to become relatively worse. Drugs and AIDS are huge problems.

A number of schemes to tackle urban problems have been developed by the government, self-help schemes and NGOs (non-governmental organisations). These have helped develop new homes and businesses, and social schemes

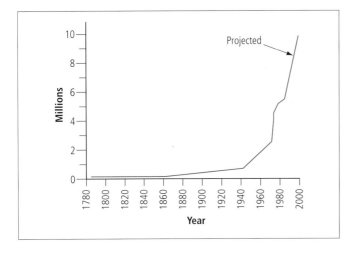

**Figure 10.16** *Population growth in Bangkok, 1780-2000*
Source: Digby, B., 1995, The human environment, Heinemann

such as the kindergarten at Klong Thoi, one of Bangkok's largest slums.

It is thought that in the future Bangkok may become another Tokyo, a government/business centre with decentralisation of industry elsewhere. However, at present, most private investment in Thailand goes straight to central Bangkok (Figure 10.18).

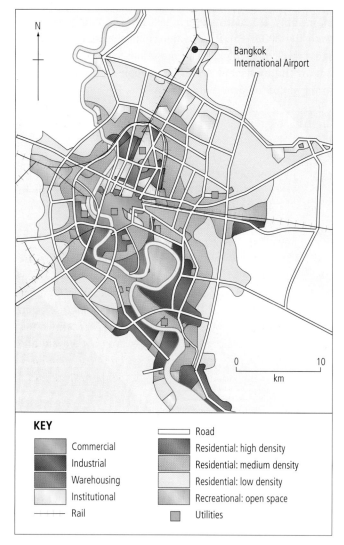

**KEY**

| | | | |
|---|---|---|---|
| ▨ | Commercial | ▭ | Road |
| ▧ | Industrial | ▨ | Residential: high density |
| ▧ | Warehousing | ▨ | Residential: medium density |
| ▫ | Institutional | ▫ | Residential: low density |
| — | Rail | ▨ | Recreational: open space |
| | | ▨ | Utilities |

***Figure 10.18*** *Land use in Bangkok*
*Source: Digby, B., 1995, The human environment, Heinemann*

### Traffic in Bangkok

Thailand is on the brink of imposing severe restrictions on the use of new private cars in traffic-congested Bangkok. Roads make up about 8% of Bangkok's total land area compared to 20–25% in European cities. For instance, areas of similar size in central Bangkok and central London illustrate the difference (Figure 10.19). In addition to less overall road space, the large majority of secondary roads in Bangkok are dead ends leaving main roads to carry an inordinate share of the traffic burden.

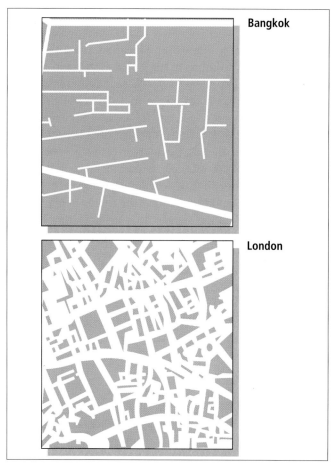

***Figure 10.19*** *Street plans for London and Bangkok*
*Source: Financial Times, March 1996*

# Inset 10.1
# The impact of traffic congestion on development, health and tourism

Bangkok's traffic congestion has worsened steadily. The speed of traffic flow on the main streets fell from 13 kph in 1984 to 8 kph in 1991. It is now little faster than walking pace. Congestion is costing the nation more than US$780 million a year in fuel bills and Bangkok's drivers are being forced to spend the equivalent of an average of forty-four days a year stuck in traffic jams. The rate of loss in business opportunities and other conveniences as a result of the worsening traffic snarls could be much higher. Air and noise pollution are alarmingly high on numerous thoroughfares and cause health hazards to passersby. Worsening traffic congestion and infrastructure shortages also provide a disincentive to investment and business, especially tourism.

Bangkok traffic is chaotic. Thousands of the city's residents must be on the road before dawn each day to reach work or school on time. A mass transit system barely exists; where it does it is inefficient, slow and overcrowded. The only way to move around the city is to risk one's life and damage one's lungs by riding on the back of a motorcycle taxi. These problems can only be solved by long term measures such as mass transit, road pricing, and development control.

One important improvement is the provision of automated traffic lights, installed at a cost of US$40 million; it will eventually replace the city's 569 traffic lights which are currently manually operated by police sitting in booths at each intersection. Already the automatic system has reduced waiting time at many lights from ten minutes or more to just two or three, thus spreading traffic out along Bangkok's limited road space. Nearly 2000 road sensors, backed up by video cameras, measure traffic flow and alter the timing of lights within the system. The idea is to reduce the incidence of gridlock and to prevent a single problem such as an accident from causing delays in the rest of the city; the system will allow the police to enforce traffic regulations rather than be in traffic booths.

The next step is to expand Bangkok's expressway system and to implement three mass transit systems. The first of the three systems, a 25 kilometre elevated rail line through the centre of the city, was finished in 1996. The US$1.6 billion package makes the project the world's first urban mass transit system to be financed without government assistance or pledges to safeguard it.

---

## QUESTIONS

1 Explain **two** contrasting reasons why there is a transport problem in Bangkok.

2 For a city in the developed world, outline the problems caused by traffic. How can these problems be overcome?

3 Is it possible to reconcile development and environmental problems, or is it just the preserve of the wealthy to think about the environment?

4 What are the long-term solutions to the problems associated with shanty towns?

---

## Urban growth in China

We have already seen, in Chapter 5, how the new town policy in Hong Kong was influenced by migration from China, and we questioned how migration and urban planning might change now that China has regained control of Hong Kong and its territories. Here we look at government urban policy at a national level in the world's most populous country, China. (In *Development and underdevelopment* in this series, we examine China's water crisis in urban areas).

When the Communist Party came to power in 1949, China's urban population was about 70 million or 12.5% of its total population (575 million). By 1990, China had an urban population of over 575 million or 51% of the total population (1.15 billion). China's urban population grew by almost 6% per year between 1949 and 1990, which outpaced the growth rate of population, which was just under 2%. Unlike conditions elsewhere, urbanisation in China has proceeded quite slowly until fairly recently. This reflects the population and decentralisation policies introduced by the government. By 1995, however, almost 60% of the population lived in urban areas. This removed China from the group of less urbanised Asian nations, such as Bangladesh (15%), Thailand (17%), India (23%) and Indonesia (22%), and into a group of more highly urbanised countries such as South Korea (57%) and Taiwan (57%).

The urban growth figures are the result of several factors, as well as rural-urban migration:
- the return of people previously sent to the countryside in the 1950s and 1960s (Inset 10.2)
- the reclassification of rural settlements as urban
- the upgrading of some towns to cities.

A distinctive feature of China's urban population is the very high concentration in large cities. Over 60% of the urban population live in cities with a population of more than 500 000 and over 40% live in a metropolis (the main city in a region). In China, there are almost fifty large cities including twenty metropoli, the largest number in any one country. For example, Shanghai's population is 13 million, Beijing has over 10 million and Tianjin has over 9 million.

### Distribution of urban growth in China

The distribution of population and urban settlements in China has been strongly influenced by government policy. One policy which slowed down the growth of a large city was the rural transfer movement (XIAFANG), whereby thousands of factories and millions of urban dwellers were sent to rural areas in the 1950s and 1960s. The reasons for these transfers included:
- national defence
- geographically balanced development
- the elimination of rural/urban differences
- the development of new forms of technology.

In 1980, the Government created four special economic zones in its south-eastern coastal cities to attract foreign investment and new technology. In 1984, another fourteen coastal cities were targeted as 'open cities' for foreign investment and development. Another significant policy reform in recent years was the dismantling of the commune system of agricultural production. This reform enabled many farmers to generate a profit for the first time and led to increasing levels of mechanisation in rural areas. As a result, substantial industrial growth occurred in many small cities and towns. Former commercial centres and market towns in rural areas that traded in handicrafts have become localised industrial centres and a growing proportion of the local labour is employed in industrial enterprises.

A major consequence of this restructuring is a greatly increased migration of many redundant rural workers from farms to neighbouring industrial towns and more distant cities as they search for better jobs and a higher standard of living.

Cities in China are now beginning to experience the urban problems found in many other developing world cities: namely the emergence of slum and squatter settlements and an urban underclass of temporary residents or unemployed people who have little or no access to health care facilities, adequate housing, education or social welfare benefits.

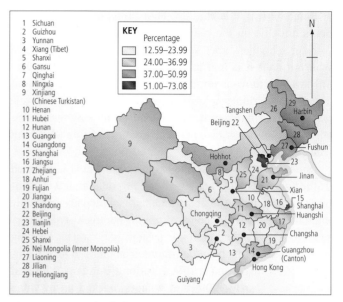

**Figure 10.20** *Levels of urbanisation in China, 1990*
Source: Baker, S. et al., 1996, Pathways in senior geography, Nelson

## QUESTIONS

1 Why has urbanisation been a relatively recent process in China?

2 Study Figure 10.19. Describe the distribution of urbanisation in China.

3 How has government policy affected the urbanisation process in China?

4 How do urban problems in China differ from those in Mexico or Brazil, or any other country that you have studied?

---

## SUMMARY

During the late 1980s and early 1990s, a number of significant changes to the growth and structure of cities in the developing world can be observed.

1 The pace of urbanisation accelerated in Africa and South Asia but it slowed in the Middle East and even more so in Latin America.

2 Many large cities made substantial progress in developing better transport systems which enabled many potential immigrants to commute to work from the countryside. This has helped preserve the basic identity and function of the village which is an important element in the urban system in developing nations.

3 Urban planning is beginning to reduce the concentration of population and industry, creating a more polycentric urban form, this is especially true around large cities such as Mexico City, Seoul and Kuala Lumpur.

4 An increasing number of large cities in the developing world are now peripheral cities in the global economy. Peripheral cities are those that developed either as processing and export centres for the rural hinterlands of developing nations, or as newly emerging industrial production centres for large corporations. As a result of the worldwide economic recession of the early 1990s, the pace of metropolitan growth has slowed.

5 The gap between primate and secondary cities has narrowed as the governments of developing countries focus investment on urban infrastructure and services in regional or secondary cities.

However, despite these encouraging signs, the majority of cities in the developing world will struggle to provide adequate services and facilities for large populations. Communities are becoming more polarised as many large cities of the developing world become part of the global economy. The contribution of the informal economy to the urban economy as a whole has been underestimated. Squatter settlements continue to provide cheap accommodation that reduces pressure for wage rises, thus enabling them to function as a source of cheap labour – largely for the benefit of EMDCs.

## QUESTIONS

1 With the use of examples, discuss whether it is possible to talk of an 'ELDC city'.

2 Describe and account for the environmental problems that are found in cities in the developing world.

3 What are the similarities between cities in the developed world and cities in the developing world?

## BIBLIOGRAPHY AND RECOMMENDED READING

**Baker, S. et al.**, 1996, Pathways in senior geography, Nelson

**Drakakis-Smith, D.**, 1987 The third world city, Routledge

**Elliot, J.**, 1994, An introduction to sustainable development, Routledge

**HMSO**, 1995, First steps – Local Agenda 21 in practice, HMSO

**Morris, S.**, 1997, Mexico City – urban issues, Geofile 306

**Pick, J. and Butler, E.**, 1994 The Mexico handbook: economic and demographic maps and statistics, Westview Press

**Potter, R.**, 1992 Urbanisation in the third world, OUP

**Reid, D.**, 1995, Sustainable development: an introductory guide, Earthscan

**Scoble, S.**, 1994, Urban Change in Rio de Janeiro, Geofile 235

# Glossary

**Agglomeration**    A clustering of people or activities, such as manufacturing and services, which benefit from being in close proximity, e.g. they can share amenities, communication links and labour supply.

**Centrality**    Possessing the advantage of a central location, enhanced by good transport links.

**Conurbation**    A general term used to identify a large, sprawling urban area, e.g. London, where two or more cities have merged.

**Core**    The centre or focus of an area. It usually contains the largest population cluster (frequently the capital city) and the most developed economic base of a region or country.

**Core-periphery model**    The essential differences between the well-developed *core* and less developed *periphery* are the result of initial comparative advantages. The flow of resources between core and periphery generally adds to the differences in their levels of prosperity.

**Counter-urbanisation**    The movement from larger cities to smaller cities and towns; it is a movement down the settlement hierarchy. Counter-urbanisation does not suggest that urban characteristics are being discarded and replaced by rural ones.

**Cumulative causation**    Theoretical process which leads to the formation of core and periphery areas. New economic development in the core often stimulates the local economy and attracts migrants searching for work. The cumulative effect of movements of people and resources increases wealth in the core.

**Deconcentration, decentralisation and deurbanisation**    Terms used to describe the movement of people and/or employment from a small number of large, dominant centres to a more dispersed pattern of location. A policy used frequently by governments to achieve a more balanced distribution of development.

**Deindustrialisation**    The absolute decline in manufacturing employment, largely caused by the replacement of labour by machines and automation, e.g. use of robots in car manufacturing plants reduces greatly the need for labour.

**Development**    Frequently considered to mean the growth and modernisation of an economy, and an increase in per capita income and *gross national product* (GNP). While these are important aspects of development, increasing recognition must be given to improving the quality of life of a population, e.g. education, health care, cultural values and housing.

**Enterprise zone**    Vacant, and often derelict, land within or near urban areas in which industrial development is encouraged through a series of financial and planning measures.

**Form**    The shape of a settlement.

**Formal/informal sector**    The formal sector consists of large-scale capitalist enterprises with fixed conditions of employment and job security; it includes government, manufacturing and services; the informal sector consists of small-scale, labour-intensive activities with job insecurity, multiple occupations and low monetary returns.

**Gentrification**    Process whereby older buildings and neighbourhoods within the *inner city* are converted to more fashionable areas with modern dwellings and modernised and refurbished older buildings. This usually involves the younger and more affluent members of society and often results in established residents moving to alternative housing areas.

**Green Belt**    A policy used by urban or regional planners to break up the continuous spread of the built-up area surrounding major cities, e.g. London. Certain restrictions are placed on new developments within Green Belts.

**Gross domestic product (GDP)/gross national product (GNP)**    GDP is the total value of all finished goods and services produced by an economy in a specific time period, usually one year; GNP is GDP *plus* income accruing to residents of a country from abroad, *less* income accruing to foreign residents investing in the country.

**Hierarchy**    The different levels of settlements as characterised by number of outlets, range, choice and services.

**Hinterland**    The area surrounding an urban centre and which is served by that centre, e.g. providing services and goods.

**Inner city**    The part of the city centre that includes the central business district and a small area of land immediately surrounding it. In the UK, this area has frequently experienced significant changes in land-use patterns since the 1970s, e.g. office developments, road improvement schemes, urban renewal and the relocation of established populations.

**Multiplier effect**    Where development in one activity generates additional employment and wealth in other activities, e.g. motor vehicle assembly creates a demand for many inputs (lights, tyres, windscreens, brakes, etc).

**Neo-colonialism**    The reassertion of economic control over ex-colonies by advanced countries, replacing colonial authority after independence.

**New Town**    Planned urban centre, sometimes being an entirely new town, e.g. Milton Keynes, or a major expansion to an existing minor urban centre, e.g Cwmbran, Wales. A feature of post-World War II planning, they were designed to relieve congestion in dominant cities (e.g. Milton Keynes and other growth centres around London), or to act as a growth centre for regional development (e.g. Cwmbran and Newtown in Wales).

**Periphery**   Areas located near the margins of a country or region. They are generally poorly linked to core areas and are less developed regions with problems, e.g. West of Ireland, Mezzogiorno.

**Primate city**   A country's largest city with a population several times as great as the second largest city. It is most expressive of the national culture, and is usually the capital city as well.

**Rank-size rule**   An empirical rule whereby the population of any town can be estimated by dividing the population of the largest city in a country by the rank of the settlement under consideration.

**Rehabilitation**   Modification of old buildings to make them suitable for modern uses while preserving the outside appearance, e.g. old warehouses converted to offices or apartments.

**Renovation**   Frequently the destruction of old buildings to accommodate modern development, e.g. removal of high-density housing zones in the *inner city* and their replacement with high-rise office blocks, car parks and new roads. Without careful planning it can destroy the character and culture of the areas affected.

**Re-urbanisation**   Urban renewal; rehabilitation of city areas which have fallen into decline (urban decay).

**Rural**   Areas characterised by low population densities, primary industries and small settlements.

**Ruralisation**   An increase in the proportion of people classified as rural.

**Shanty town**   An area of spontaneous settlement, consisting of poor quality housing, often not recognised by the city authorities.

**Site**   The land on which a settlement is located. This refers mainly to its local physical setting, e.g. bridging point, deep-water port.

**Situation**   The locational attribute of a place relative to other non-local places, e.g. its position relative to international trade routes or proximity to coalfields.

**Slum**   An area of low quality housing, recognised by city authorities.

**Suburb**   An area of large-scale housing estates, usually located within or around the margins of urban centres; an important element in the continuous outward spread of the built-up environment of urban centres.

**Sustainable development**   'Development that meets the needs of the present without compromising the ability of future generations to meet their own needs' (Brundtland Commission, 1987, 43). This classic definition emphasises inter-generational equity and also assumes the possibility of development that can be accompanied by environmental stability or even environmental improvement.

**Tertiary sector**   The sector of the economy concerned with neither extracting primary products nor processing them; tertiary activities involve a range of services such as retailing, administration, teaching, health care and finance.

**Urban**   An area with specific urban characteristics such as a large population, high percentage employed in manufacturing and services, large built-up area, specific administrative functions, and defined as urban by the government.

**Urban Development Corporation**   A body set up by the British government to secure the regeneration of designated land within urban areas.

**Urban growth**   An increase in the absolute number of people living in an urban area.

**Urban sprawl**   An increase in the area covered by urban activities.

**Urbanisation**   Process whereby the proportion of a country's population classified as urban increases.

# Index